R. L. Woodberry
May 1988
Orinda, California

D1572433

The Gilgit Game

THE GILGIT GAME

The Explorers of the Western Himalayas
1865–95

JOHN KEAY

Archon Books

HAMDEN, CONNECTICUT.

In Memory of
TERENCE SCOTT
late of Chitral and Peshawar

Contents

Illustrations

ACKNOWLEDGEMENTS
   Nos. 1, 2, 3, 4, 6, 14 and 20 are reproduced by courtesy of the Royal
Geographical Society; Nos. 5, 11 and 16 are from *The Making of a
Frontier* by A. Durand, London 1899; Nos. 7, 8, 24, 25, 26 and 27 by
courtesy of Brigadier F. R. L. Goadby; No. 9. from *Memoir of W. W.
MacNair* by J. E. Howard, n.d., Nos. 10, 12 and 21 by courtesy of the
Director of the India Office Library and Records; No. 13 by courtesy of
Colonel Gerald Morgan; No. 15 from *The Asiatic Quarterly Review*,
vol. 2, n.s., 1892; No. 17 from *The Eastern and Western Review*, 1895;
No. 18 by courtesy of Dame Eileen Younghusband; Nos. 19, 22 and 23
by courtesy of the National Army Museum.
   The engravings in the text are taken from *Jummoo and Kashmir
Territories* by Frederick Drew, London 1875; the engraving on the title
page is from *Travels in Ladakh* by H. D. Torrens, London, 1862.

Acknowledgements

I should like to thank, first, Colonel Gerald Morgan and Dr. G. J. Alder. During the years that I have been working on the explorers of the Western Himalayas their suggestions, comments and encouragement have been invaluable; and not once has either of them made the obvious inference that I was poaching with impunity on their own chosen fields. More recently I have met with the same unselfish assistance from Dr. Schuyler Jones of the Pitt Rivers Museum, Oxford, and Mr. Graham Clarke of Lincoln College, Oxford.

My research has greatly benefited from the efficiency of the London Library, the India Office Library and Records, the Royal Geographical Society's Library and Archives (and particularly the cataloguing work of Mrs. C. Kelly), the National Library of Scotland, and the Library and Archives of the London School of Oriental and African Studies. For the patience and latitude shown by all in the face of erratic borrowings and irregular requests I am most grateful. I would also like to thank Dame Eileen Younghusband D.B.E. for allowing me to consult her father's papers, the Hon. Edward Biddulph for letting me see the journals of John Biddulph, and Brigadier F. R. L. Goadby for some helpful comments and some excellent photographs.

Janet Adam-Smith, Simon Ricketts and John Murray have kindly read through the text and made many useful comments. So, whilst typing two full drafts, has my wife, Julia; without her help, the project could never have been completed; without her encouragement and involvement it would never have been started.

Finally there are many friends in India who contributed to the mountain travels for which a book like this is the perfect excuse. Unfortunately I can't remember the names of the helpful officials and intrepid jeep drivers met in Hunza and Gilgit in 1967; but Christina Noble was then, as always, a perfect travelling companion. Geoffrey Raspin and the late Ferrier Mackay-James paved my way to Chitral where I was helped and accommodated by some of the many grandsons of Aman-ul-Mulk, notably the late Hisam-ul-Mulk, Burhan-un-din and, in Peshawar, Colonel Khushwaqt-ul-Mulk; happily I can report that their kindness utterly belied the supposed treachery of their ancestor. Also in Peshawar I received much help and encouragement from the late Terence Scott who loved the mountains dearly and to whom this book is dedicated.

Glossary
of Principal Dard chiefs

GHAZAN KHAN	Mir of Hunza, murdered by Safdar Ali in 1886.
SAFDAR ALI	Mir of Hunza 1886–91, son and murderer of Ghazan Khan.
AMAN-UL-MULK	Mehtar of Chitral, died 1892.
AFZUL-UL-MULK	Briefly Mehtar of Chitral in 1892, son of Aman-ul-Mulk, murdered by Sher Afzul's troops.
SHER AFZUL	Briefly Mehtar of Chitral in 1892, brother of Aman-ul-Mulk.
NIZAM-UL-MULK	Mehtar of Chitral 1892–5, son of Aman-ul-Mulk, murdered by Amir-ul-Mulk.
AMIR-UL-MULK	Briefly Mehtar of Chitral in 1895, son of Aman-ul-Mulk.
SHUJA-UL-MULK	Mehtar of Chitral from March 1895, son of Aman-ul-Mulk.
MULK AMAN	Ruler of Yasin until 1870, nephew of Aman-ul-Mulk.
MIR WALI	Ruler of Yasin in 1870, nephew and son-in-law of Aman-ul-Mulk and brother of Mulk Aman. Murdered by Pahlwan.
PAHLWAN BAHADUR	Ruler of Yasin 1870–76, nephew of Aman-ul-Mulk and half brother of Mulk Aman. Murdered by Mulk Aman.
JAFR KHAN	Ruler of Nagar until 1891.
UZR KHAN	Son and heir presumptive of Jafr Khan, deported in 1892.

INTRODUCTION

Flashpoint of Asia

Gilgit is a small township in the heart of the Western Himalayas. Remote in the extreme—two hundred miles from the southern fringe of the mountains in the Punjab and a similar distance from Sinkiang on their northern flanks—the place is today the administrative centre of Pakistan's sparsely populated Northern Areas. A dusty little bazaar does a roaring trade in Chinese cottons and hardware, 'fallen' from the backs of passing jeeps. The orchards are justly renowned for their apricots, grapes and apples, and there is even an embryonic tourist industry; a couple of rest houses and a projected luxury hotel cater for the adventurous visitor come to eye the mountains.

But all this is by the way. The point of Gilgit, now as always, is strategic. High above the snowline, somewhere midst the peaks and glaciers that wall in the Gilgit valley, the long and jealously guarded frontiers of India, China, Russia, Afghanistan and Pakistan meet. It is the hub, the crow's-nest, the fulcrum of Asia.

A little over a century ago none of these frontiers came anywhere near one another. Gilgit itself was a far-flung, disaster-prone and run-down outpost of the Maharajas of Kashmir. Beyond it, and on all sides save for a vulnerable supply line back to Kashmir, there stretched virgin territory. South to the Punjab of British India, west to Badakshan in Afghanistan, north to Tashkent in Russia and east to Sinkiang in China, this rectangular sea of mountains stretched for hundreds of all but impenetrable miles. The Gilgit Game is simply the story of how and by whom such a wilderness was explored and appropriated.

It was called a game in recognition of the process being a crucial episode in the Great Game, the century-long rivalry between Russia and British India for control of Central Asia. The latter phrase had been coined back in the 1830s but came into common usage about 1870. With the popular discovery of cricket, football

1

and tennis, suddenly everything became a game; the word was bandied about as loosely as, more recently, 'scene'. But it was also in the 1870s that the Great Game, after a mid-century lull, returned as a political feature to obsess the minds and dictate the policies of those who ruled Asia. In spite of some impossible terrain, in spite too of some of the improbable characters involved, here was one of the most desperate and portentous confrontations that the late nineteenth century had to resolve.

The Great Game has often been compared with the Cold War of the 1950s and 1960s. In both cases war as an instrument of policy was used sparingly and the global explosion that threatened never materialised. A safer outlet for imperial aggression was found in trying to secure a favourable alignment of minor powers and thus outmanœuvre the opposition. In the Great Game, China (although itself an empire), Afghanistan and Persia all provided ideal ground for such jockeying. So too, in the early days, did the khanates of Central Asia and, subsequently, the mountain states of the Western Himalayas. In retrospect the imperial rivalry looks fairly genteel and, indeed, there were those who at the time defended even Russian encroachments on the ground of Europe's civilising mission. Nevertheless, it is no exaggeration to say that, for most, the Tsarist threat in the late nineteenth century was as real and alarming as the Communist menace in the mid-twentieth.

Again like the Cold War, the Great Game was played, or fought, over a vast area and at many different levels. Any clash of British and Russian interests east of the Balkans had a bearing on the Game. The action had a way of shifting unpredictably from a concourse of statesmen in Europe to a sudden shunting of troops in the Hindu Kush; or from the activities of a lone Kiplingesque secret agent to some frantic excitement among the small-scale maps at military headquarters.

What was true of the Great Game also went for its Gilgit sector; the process of geographical and political penetration only makes sense when seen in the broadest possible context. Yet Gilgit was surely the wildest arena in which the Game was played. Diplomatic activity had to wait on the deliberations of military strategists and these in turn waited on the process of exploration. Because of the political vacuum in the area, the movements of explorers and agents could themselves constitute a valid claim to territory, and their chance friendships and difficulties could have the most far-reaching repercussions; it would be in the mountains around Gilgit that the two imperial frontiers came closest to collision. All of which, though occasionally leading to absurdities, makes the Gilgit Game vastly more exciting and romantic than most of the Great Game. From Rudyard Kipling to John Masters fiction writers have found their best material in the Gilgit story.

* * *

In *When Men and Mountains Meet* I wrote about the men who explored the Western Himalayas before 1875. They were the pioneers, and by this date the geographical outlines of what lay between India and Central Asia were established. It was now known, for instance, that the range that divided the rivers flowing south into the plains of India from those flowing west, north and east into Central Asia was a combination of the Hindu Kush and the Karakorams. In an inverted V these two systems locked together somewhere to the north of Gilgit. Their high passes could be reached only along the Chitral river up the left hand side of the V or along the Gilgit river on the right; and of these two the latter, via its several tributaries, afforded the best access to the apex. Hence the importance of Gilgit was already appreciated; of the eight or nine passes by which Central Asia could be reached direct from India, six in fact lay within a week's march from the little township. In the 1890s visitors would be so impressed with this discovery that, filled with the railway mania of the day, they would predict for Gilgit one of the world's great junctions. Here the line from India to Samarkand and Moscow would link up with the branch to Sinkiang, Mongolia and Peking.

It was also clear, though the railway enthusiasts would seem to have overlooked it, that in the Western Himalayas the greatest knot of mountains in the world had been uncovered. K2 to the east of Gilgit had just been measured and found second only to Mount Everest; there was a fair chance that a superior to both might yet be lurking somewhere to the north-west. Between Ladakh and Sinkiang the breadth of the Western Himalayas had been repeatedly crossed and all the main mountain systems had now been identi- fied; to the south of Gilgit and parallel to the Karakorams lay the

Great Himalaya and the Pir Panjal; north of the Karakoram–Hindu Kush watershed lay the Kun Lun on one side and, due north from Gilgit, an area known as the Pamirs. This last was still very mysterious and it was far from clear whether it was really a mountain range or a vast elevated plateau. There was also confusion about just where one range ended and the next began. The threads, in other words, had been identified but the knot had yet to be unravelled. Much the same went for the rivers. The Indus and its tributaries which drained the mountains to the south were now fairly well known. Further north, though, there was still controversy over the source of the Oxus and uncertainty over the mountain reaches of the Yarkand river.

All these points could, and would, have been cleared up by 1870 if, for the past thirty years, explorers had not been rigorously excluded from Gilgit and the lands beyond. There were two reasons for this. In the first place, the tribes of the Hindu Kush around Gilgit enjoyed a reputation for unrivalled ferocity, xenophobia and treachery. Under Kashmir's rule Gilgit itself might prove safe enough for the traveller, but the valleys that radiated from it were a law unto themselves. Due north on the road to the Pamirs there was the independent kingdom of Hunza, practically inaccessible and the perfect refuge for a people addicted to caravan raiding. Yasin, at about ten o'clock from Gilgit, was less politically stable and less defensible but had nevertheless been responsible for some of the worst raids on Gilgit. At eight o'clock lay the long valley of Chitral which had close dynastic ties with Afghanistan and was deeply involved in the slave trade. And south from Gilgit lay Chilas and the Indus valley peoples who made up for their lack of numbers with a well-deserved reputation for fanatical Mohammedanism.

For convenience as much as anything, these peoples would soon all be lumped together under the title of Dards. Compared to the pliant Buddhist Ladakhis who assisted travellers across the Himalayas to the east of Kashmir, the proud Islamic Dards would evince a jealous attachment to their independence and a deep suspicion of snooping travellers. Aided by the character of their mountain defiles, and to some extent armed by the powers who sought their loyalty, they would play a part out of all proportion to their numbers. While imperial diplomats contorted themselves

in an effort to avoid the dreaded Armageddon, the Dards seemed
positively spoiling for a fight. It was the fate of empires apparently
waiting on the word of some illiterate chieftain, or hanging on the
outcome of a battle fought by rock climbers, which gave to the
Game its air of baffling unreality.

The other factor which deterred explorers was the attitude of the
Kashmir authorities. Then as now, Kashmir was a political
anomaly. Properly speaking it was just the beautiful valley of
that name around Srinagar, the capital; but with the disintegra-
tion of the Sikh empire in the 1840s all the mountain lands
administered by the Sikhs were detached and designated as the new
state of Kashmir under their *de facto* ruler, Gulab Singh. By the
treaty of Amritsar in 1846 he was recognised by the British as
Maharaja in return for his settling the war indemnity levied on the
defeated Sikhs. But the treaty left to further negotiation the actual
boundaries of the state as well as the exact nature of its relationship
with British India. This was a situation that could be exploited by
both parties; and while the Government of India at first concentrated on trying to reduce the Maharaja to the impotent status of
other princely rulers within British India, the Maharaja and his
successors did their utmost, particularly in the Gilgit region, to
extend their territory. Freelance explorers who might publicise or
censure this activity, or surveyors who might attempt to lay down
a precise boundary, were therefore forbidden access.

On the other hand, as the new state of Kashmir was more firmly
incorporated into British India, it became clear that the frontiers
of the state could not be simply left to the energies of the Maharaja.
In the north and north-west they were, after all, the frontiers of
India itself, and in the event of attack the Indian government
would be expected to defend them. As the Russian threat developed
in the 1870s the question of finding a defensible Kashmir frontier
and a reliable system of guarding it became crucial. And, just as for
thirty years the jealousy of the Maharajas had kept out freelance
explorers, so for the next twenty years the strategic sensitivity of
the Indian government would have the same effect.

To those interested purely in the promotion of geographical
knowledge it was a tragedy. The core of the Western Himalayas,
the most challenging terrain in the world and the most inviting
void in Asia, was being reserved solely for political agents and

soldiers. Throughout the period the Royal Geographical Society in London pleaded with the government to release more information about its findings in the region; it was unsuccessful. But, conversely, one should not be surprised if some of the privileged agents and soldiers who did get to Gilgit look suspiciously like freelance explorers doing political work simply for the travel opportunities it afforded.

To the extent that the Gilgit Game takes the story of the exploration of the Western Himalayas forward in time and north-west to the extremities of the mountain complex it is a sequel to *When Men and Mountains Meet*. But with the spirit of geographical enquiry playing such a small part, it is true to say that the motivation for the Gilgit Game was entirely different. The story contains only one traveller who claimed to be a conventional explorer and his credentials are open to question. Likewise missionary and commercial incentives play no part. The object was not the usual one of finding a way through the mountains and opening it up, but of finding all possible ways through and closing them. The discovery of independent tribes and unclaimed valleys was cause for anxiety rather than celebration. A vacuum was a threat, defence was the priority, and demarcation the ultimate aim.

Compared to the earlier period of exploration, naturalists and geologists are also conspicuous by their absence. But one scientific discipline, ethnology, played an important part. Having committed itself to the idea of appropriating and defending such a remote frontier as the Hindu Kush, the Indian government was faced with the problem of how to control the tribes that lay within it. Their diversity proved as much a stumbling block as their ferocity. The study of the tribes, fascinating enough in itself, was expected to provide pointers as to how their loyalty could most readily be secured.

It did up to a point; but such recommendations were usually ignored in favour of some supposed essential of imperial strategy. And as a result, just as the Great Game often seemed to have something to do with skirmishes with the Pathans on the north-west frontier, so the Gilgit Game had a way of deteriorating from the lofty ideals of Anglo-Russian rivalry into frantic and embarrassing fracas with the mountain peoples. On what became known as India's northern, as opposed to north-western frontier, actual hostilities lasted for only four years and were never as bloody as those round the Khyber. But, because of the appalling terrain, because of the remoteness from the nearest British bases, and because of the anomalous position of Kashmir, they were both more bizarre and more critical.

PART ONE

Veni

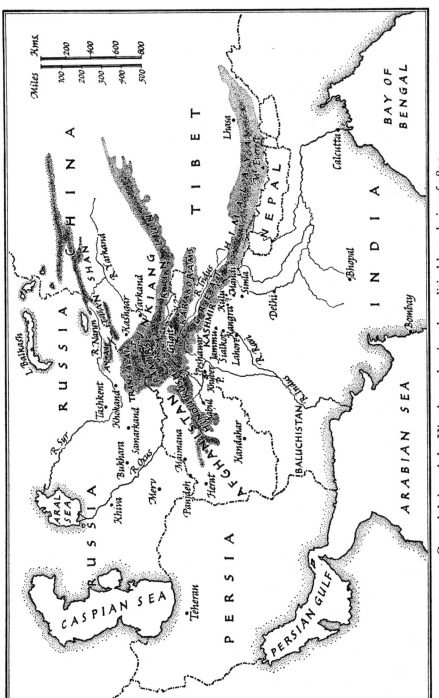

Central Asia and the Himalayas showing the political boundaries of 1895

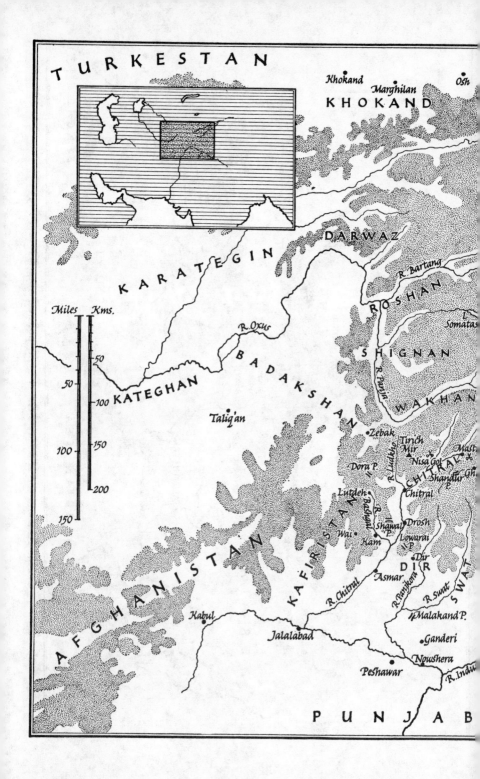

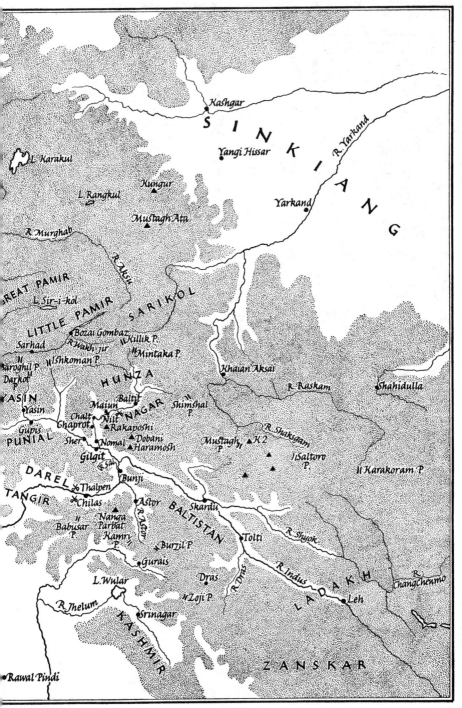

The Western Himalayas

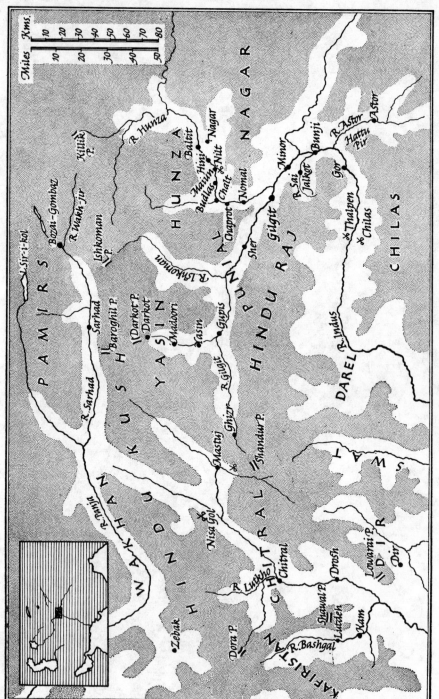

Dardistan and the Hindu Kush

1. Beyond the Indus

The maps mark a surveyor's trig. point above the village of Gor in the mountains of northern Pakistan. To reach it, you climb the side of the wild Sai valley, edge gingerly up a long serrated ridge of rocks and finally scramble the last few hundred feet over jagged boulders. The ascent promises nothing in particular; it could as well be that of any other spur or pass in the Western Himalayas. The altitude at the top is about 16,000 feet, enough to induce a headache, breathlessness and perhaps a slight nausea—but nothing worse; this jaunt is one for the ambitious trekker rather than the mountaineer. You flop down amidst the boulders, panting, thankful and expectant; the wind blows cold and strong. Then, cautiously, like one sampling a long cherished delicacy, you sweep the horizon.

Physical and overwhelming comes the response, a prickling of the scalp, a shudder of disbelief. But they were right; the two phlegmatic British officers who, a hundred years ago, first set eyes on this view did not exaggerate. No-one, not even the most apathetic, they wrote, could fail to be moved. Here, quite simply, is 'the most awful and the most magnificent sight to be met with in the Himalayas'.

You are standing on the extremity of a range known as the Hindu Raj which effectively blocks any view to the west of its grander parent, the Hindu Kush. But there is compensation. Eastward a chaotic sea of rugged ranges extends to the horizon. For over a hundred miles the eye roves anxiously across their grey, snow-flecked ridges. Somewhere in those deep folds should lie the villages of Baltistan and somewhere through that forbidding maze should flow the mighty Indus. But from above Gor you see just the mountains; the only relief is a hazy white where they touch the horizon. Yet even this is no soft and friendly cloud. You might just make out the black of bare windswept rock or the snow-smoke streaming off above it. It is in fact the heart of the Karakorams. K2, the second highest mountain in the world, is somewhere in that puff of white.

Turning to the left, the north, the ice bound heights draw closer. Thirty miles off, Haramosh and Dobani, the giants that guard the entrance to the Gilgit valley, are easily identified. Behind them rears the whittled point of Rakaposhi which dominates the Hunza valley and the road to the distant Pamirs. On each of these peaks you can follow the glaciers up till they finger out in ice choked gullies below the summit, or down till they tear deep into the straggling band of forest. Again, it is hard to believe that somewhere between you and Dobani there lies a green and smiling valley. Down there the orchards are laden with fruit and the streams stocked with trout. In Gilgit's bazaar the shopkeepers are sunning themselves in their open shop fronts while a clerk picks his teeth as he waits at the post office. The improbability of their situation is forgotten. It will take the distant drone of the plane from Rawal Pindi, as it weaves through the mountains and banks steeply to swing from the Indus valley into that of Gilgit, to remind them.

Before starting back down to the drowsy world of Gilgit, there is more to be seen from the cliffs above Gor; the greatest prospect of all remains. Turn back from the peaks of the Karakorams and face due south. Here lies the true horror of the Himalayas. This time there is no deep and distant perspective; the horizontal is unrepresented. You are staring at a wall; it rears from the abyss at your feet to a height for which the neck must crane back. Such is Nanga Parbat, 'the Naked Mountain'; its navel now confronts you. More a many-peaked massif than a single mountain, Nanga Parbat marks the western extremity of the Great Himalaya; it is a buttress worthy of its role. (As the plane to Gilgit works its way round it, the passenger sees nothing but snow, rocks and ice for a good ten minutes.) Beautiful is not an appropriate adjective. It is too formless; there is no slender fang like that of Rakaposhi or the Matterhorn and none of the grandiose harmony of Kanchenjunga or Mount Fuji. An uncut stone, it impresses by reason of its dimensions, not its shape.

Edge now a little nearer to the extremity of your vantage point. This mountain needs putting into some sort of proportion; it seems much too near. But move carefully; a steady hand and nerves of steel are called for. And when you are ready to look over, lie down. For between you and Nanga Parbat there is nothing.

The cliffs above Gor are sheer for three-quarters of a vertical mile from where you lie. Below that they continue down for another mile and a half of broken precipice and crag. It is probably the most frightening declivity in the world—and one rivalled only by that which faces you. Nanga Parbat too rises straight out of this trough. The top of the mountain is 26,500 feet above sea level, the bottom of the trough 3,500. At a range of ten to fifteen miles you are seeing in one uninterrupted sweep the greatest slope on the crust of the earth, 23,000 feet of elevation. That's four and a half miles from the bare black rock along the topmost ridges, down through the fields of snow and ice, down the precipices and over-hangs, down the long winding glaciers, down through the forest and scrub, and down the steep and broken slopes of gravel to the cliffs at the bottom.

What happens at the foot of these cliffs is hidden; but anyone who has driven the road from Chilas to Gilgit knows only too well. The heights above are horrifying, but the gorge of the Indus is worse. Down there one forgets about the Himalayas. It's more like the bottom of the Grand Canyon, a suffocating, rock-bound desert. Nothing grows there, no-one lives there. The rocks sizzle in temperatures around the 120 degrees mark, gravel trickles down the slopes with a dry rattle, and will o' the wisps fling sand into every parched nook and sun-cracked cranny. Through this waste land, its stern and alien ruler, the greeny-grey Indus, slides silently along. For some six hundred miles, across the Tibetan plateau, through the open valleys of Ladakh and into the tightening gorges of Baltistan, it has flowed north-west heading for the heart of Asia. But just a few miles to the north its further progress is blocked by the steep bluffs of Dobani. It careens straight into the mountain and, sinking ever deeper into its gorge, seeks for a way round, or even under, this massive obstruction. The way is barred; the buckled torrent subsides into a sulking flood, turns south and, cutting straight across the line of the Himalayas, curls down the desert canyon below.

Between the encounter with Dobani and its next collision, with Nanga Parbat, the river receives three considerable tributaries, the Gilgit and the Sai from the west and then the Astor from the east. For a moment the mountains stand back. The river, quieter but still sucking at any rock that stands in its way, emerges slightly from its gorge. Dreary lunar deserts though they are, one can speak of shores rather than cliffs. Here is the one place on its long course through the mountains that the Indus can be crossed. From above Gor you can see a stretch of the track which throughout the nineteenth century was the lifeline between Gilgit and Kashmir. Zig-zagging down the 6,000 waterless feet of the Hattu Pir spur it crosses the Astor river by the Shaitan Nare, the Devil's bridge, in those days a precarious affair of rotten rope and frayed twigs. Thence it winds up through the rocks to the settlement of Bunji and the Indus bridge.

* * *

A hundred years ago there was no bridge, just a ferry, and Bunji consisted of just a fort and a few mud huts. Outside one of these huts on a hot September's day in 1866 there paused a Dr. G. W. Leitner. He was not quite the first European to visit this remote corner of the then Kashmir state. In the late 1830s the explorer Godfrey Thomas Vigne had reached the Hattu Pir above the Astor river and had brought back from there the first eye-witness account of the Indus at Bunji. In 1847 two British officers had actually crossed the Indus and got some miles past Gilgit before being turned back; sadly their journey was never chronicled. By contrast there was also the oft told but seldom credited story of Alexander Gardiner who claimed to have passed clean through all the unknown lands beyond the river.* Surveyors working on the Survey of Kashmir had just completed their mapping of the whole country to the east of the Indus and sportsmen were already decimating the stocks of ibex and markhor in the mountains on that side. But few of these bothered to go down to Bunji itself; so far as Europeans were concerned it was a dead end. Whether or not the Indus ought to be the frontier of Kashmir was a debatable point. But, for a certainty, such authority as the Maharaja of Kashmir wielded in the lands beyond was of so tenuous a character that he was in no position to guarantee the safety of any traveller there.

All this country west of the Indus and as far as distant Afghanistan was usually lumped together under the title of Yaghistan,

* For Vigne, Gardiner and the Survey of Kashmir, see my *When Men and Mountains Meet*, London, 1977.

meaning the land of the ungovernable, of the savages. The Kashmir government's experience of it more than bore this out. In twenty-five years of trying to assert some influence there, its troops had been ambushed and besieged by each and all of the various Hindu Kush tribes. For most of the 1850s they had been forced right back across the Indus and now, in 1866, they were just reasserting their shattered rule in the Gilgit valley after another bloody uprising. Naturally the Yaghis were credited with an awesome ferocity. In Hunza captured soldiers of the Maharaja of Kashmir were used as human fireworks and in Yasin the natives were said to pluck out their hearts and eat them raw. Other tribes were supposed to be devil worshippers who offered human sacrifices. Any caravan that ventured into their valleys was immediately plundered and the only trade that could be said to flourish was the slave trade. In fact, in the absence of coin, mankind was the common currency; a hunting dog cost one male slave and a sturdy pony two females, preferably fair and fourteen.

Such at least was the reputation of the Yaghis as put about by the Kashmir troops. However, to a man like Dr. Leitner, Yaghistan had its attractions. He was not a medical doctor but an academic ('M.A., Ph.D., LL.D., D.O.L., etc.' modestly followed his name on all his gold-blocked notebooks). Particularly he was interested in ethnology, the study of races, and in how the language of a people was a reflection of its way of life. In this respect the Hindu Kush peoples sounded most promising. Discarding the term 'Yaghi' as pejorative and too political, Leitner identified them as Dards, supposed descendents of the Daradas of Sanskrit literature and the Daradae of classical geographers. This derivation was conjectural but it neatly gave to the Yaghis a distinct racial identity; it was a term of convenience yet it could be justified by what was then known of them. For example, it was clear that these Dards were neither Indian, nor Tibetan, nor of the Turkish stock of Central Asia. The miscellany of languages which they spoke, though far from being a homogeneous group, appeared totally different from any known tongue. And likewise, though most of the tribes had adopted Mohammedanism, they retained some distinctly non-Islamic cults. (The few who had rejected Islam, the Kafirs in the far west of the region, represented a still greater ethnological puzzle.) Blue eyes, fair skins and blonde or reddish hair were said to be commonplace amongst all the Dards. Vigne had been told that the people of Hunza and Nagar were so fair skinned as to be transparent; as they drank you could see the water passing down their throats. For centuries they had been shut away in their inaccessible valleys, immune from the great tides of history in Central Asia and northern India. With features that were nothing if not European, was it possible that here were the long lost descendants of the Greeks who had crossed Asia with Alexander the Great? Or, since even in Alexander's day there were reports of a similar people, were they perhaps remnants of the original Aryan race from which all the Indo-European peoples were descended? And was there perhaps substance in the myths that placed the garden of Eden somewhere in the valleys of the Hindu Kush?

Leitner must have peered across the eddying waters of the Indus at Bunji with considerable interest. In the bare hills beyond he could see the Sai valley and, high above it, that spur which ends on the cliffs above Gor. He could also make out the track that wound west up the valley towards Gilgit. Shadeless, barren and brown, it was not inviting. Nor was Leitner, at this stage, bent on following it; the idea was in the back of his mind but he had been forcibly warned of the dangers of doing so. Besides, he was more intrigued by what was going on around him. From one of Bunji's mud huts came voices. They were speaking what sounded like Chilasi, the language he had come so far to study. And like the prospector who finds a nugget in his first pan, he immediately staked out his claim; the Chilasis owned the mud hut so Leitner moved in. He unpacked and emerged, notebook at the ready.

Chilas itself is on the Indus below Bunji and below Gor. Its inhabitants had, in common with their neighbours along the river, an unusual form of government; they were republicans. Indeed each village was a self-governing entity with its own council of state to which even women might be elected. In Leitner's view this put the smallest of these republics, a village of seven houses, at a rather more advanced stage of development than the India Office in London. This peculiarity was one of the things he wanted to investigate; but there was also a rumour, which much interested the savants of the day, that Chilas might be the Kailas where dwelt the gods of Hindu mythology. Yet a third point for investigation, and in Leitner's view the most important one, was the Chilasi language. This and much else about Chilas had come to light as a result of a reprisal raid down the Indus by the Kashmir troops in 1851. Thenceforth Chilas had been nominally tributary to Kashmir sending each year a hundred goats and two ounces of gold dust. The men who accompanied this tribute in 1866—combining in a subtle way the functions of ambassadors, hostages and goatherds—had already been interviewed by Leitner in Srinagar, the Kashmir capital. There he had learnt enough to recognise their language; but, finding the Kashmir authorities reluctant to let him pursue his enquiries, he had followed the scent westward to the Indus.

Unfortunately the Kashmir governor at Bunji also had his doubts about this unexpected visitor who sat all day with his Chilasi landlord, pointing at things and scribbling in his notebook. It looked highly suspicious, considering the very questionable loyalty of the Chilasis. Accordingly Leitner was persuaded to move to a small mosque in the Bunji fort; he would have a bit more room there and, of course, he could still see his Chilasi friend. Next morning, instead of his friend, he awoke to find a guard of soldiers surrounding the building and turning away all comers. It would have tried the patience of a saint. Leitner's investigations had only just got beyond the stage where whenever he pointed at something he was told the Chilasi for finger; the work was scarcely begun and it was too bad to be baulked yet again. In a towering rage he stamped away from the fort and, like a petulant child, made the first gesture of defiance he could think of. 'I marched to the bank of the Indus, took the only boat . . . and crossed the frontier to the other side.'

Thus begins the first recorded narrative of a visit to Gilgit. It was an unconventional way to start an exploratory journey, but any other approach would almost certainly have failed. Had Leitner planned the journey in advance he would have organised porters, stores and probably a guard, all of which would have put the governor on the alert. Had he just warned his servants a few hours in advance the news would almost certainly have leaked out. As it was his move took everyone, including himself, by surprise. Faced with a *sahib* in no mood to be trifled with, and failing any orders to the contrary, the boatmen rowed him across. Within twenty minutes he landed in Yaghistan. His caravan consisted of his two servants, his guard amounted to a brace of pistols and his provisions were three jars of Bovril hastily stuffed into his pockets. If the scientific world later turned up their noses at this little foray into *terra incognita* it was hardly surprising.

But there were plenty of other reasons for raised eyebrows over the carryings on of Dr. G. W. Leitner. His career, his achievements and his personality were all, to say the least, improbable. They have the makings of a fascinating biography; yet what biographer would willingly tackle the span of countries and activities that they embrace? And, still more of a problem, how to get the measure of the man? Was he a 'self-seeking humbug' as many liked to think, or did he in fact deserve the extravagant, if prompted, praise of his admirers? There is such a wide divergence between the importance he himself attached to his every move and the derision it invariably met with in official circles, that a balanced appraisal becomes very difficult. Was he a great ethnologist and a pioneer in education, or just a glib linguist and a quack schoolmaster? Were his numerous crusades on behalf of the Dard peoples prompted by a sincere solicitude, or were they just ammunition for the inveterate sniper and sustenance to the glutton for publicity? And did he really matter? Twenty-five years after he crossed the Indus at Bunji the Viceroy of India would telegraph to London to find out who on earth Leitner was, because one of his publications was revealing classified information 'with the scarcely veiled intention of helping a possible enemy'. Lord Curzon, then a member of the India Council, replied that he knew both Leitner and the publication. 'The latter', he wrote, 'carries little weight, the former none. It would be a mistake to take any notice of him.' Yet people did take notice and this correspondence rather proved the point.

So who was Gottlieb Wilhelm Leitner? By the time he found himself on the wrong side of the upper Indus he had already crammed into his twenty-six years a remarkable career. Born in Budapest of German parents he was educated in Malta and Turkey and by the age of fifteen could speak fluent German, French, English, Arabic and Greek. With the outbreak of the Crimean War he had decided to put this knowledge to some use and was duly appointed to a first-class interpretership with the British forces, a position which apparently carried the rank of colonel. Leitner remained inordinately proud of this achievement for the rest of his

1 Dr G. W. Leitner and his Dards

2 George Hayward in 1870 with trophies of his first visit to Yasin

life, not because he was fifteen at the time—he never mentions
this—but because he had served with the British army in the
Crimea and ranked as a colonel. He was surely the youngest
veteran of them all.

After the war he returned to his studies in Turkey. He was now
a teacher and launched the first of many educational experiments
by refusing to converse with his students and colleagues in any
language other than ancient Greek. He passionately believed in
breathing some life into the dull business of conjugation and
declension; learning languages was not just a useful discipline but
the only way of getting some insight into the lifestyle and thinking
of those who had spoken them. Thus, as the Government of
India was soon to discover, if you asked Leitner to investigate a
language, you ended up with a gazetteer of the historical, geographical and cultural environment of those who spoke it, not to
mention their appearance, beliefs, diet and diseases.

In 1858 Leitner proceeded to England and enrolled at King's
College, London as a postgraduate. He was soon appointed a
lecturer in Arabic, Turkish and Greek and then, as dean and
professor, headed the new Oriental Section of the college. As with
'The London Society of German Savants', one of his first attempts
to provide a platform for his ideas, he claims to have actually
founded this department. About this time he also studied law at
the Middle Temple and was called to the bar. The string of
initials after his name was growing.

In 1864 he answered an advertisement for the appointment of
Principal at a big new government-run college in Lahore, the
capital of the Punjab province of British India. If the oriental
section of King's College was all that he made it out to be, it is odd
that he should have wanted to leave for the East so soon. But, still
more surprising, considering that he was only twenty-three and
not even a British subject, was the success of his application to
Lahore. The position was a highly responsible one demanding
administrative capabilities as well as academic qualifications.
Moreover, the newly acquired province of Punjab was the show-
piece of British India and a forcing house for young administrators.
Go-ahead and outward looking, its government believed in letting
a young man have his head. Compared with the slowly grinding
cogs of the Calcutta bureaucracy, Lahore whirred with energy and

GG—C

experiment. It was just the sort of atmosphere that the educational-ist in Leitner longed for. He took up his new responsibilities in late 1864.

For the next twenty years India was his home. It is worth anticipating his career during this period since, from the moment he arrived in Lahore, it cast him in a mould that was already set by the time he broke bounds across the Indus. Leitner found fault with most things and the Lahore Government College, indeed the whole educational set-up in India, was no exception. The college was designed to turn out intelligent English-speaking clerks who would be able to fill the lower echelons of the administration. To Leitner this was anathema; it was not an education, just a training. What of Sanscrit and Arabic, the classical languages of Hindu and Muslim? These too must be taught and the pupils given some pride in their cultural heritage. For this, what Lahore needed was not a college but a university. Raising educational standards at the College would be a step in the right direction but a University should be the product of something little short of a cultural renaissance. With an energy that the Punjab authorities could only admire he set about mobilising public opinion. Books and periodicals poured from his office. There were Arabic grammars, a history of Mohammedanism, treatises on education, an Urdu translation of *Macbeth*, a daily newspaper, two weeklies, critical journals in Sanskrit and Arabic, and an endless stream of appeals for funds. He aimed particularly at the rich and the culturally influential within Indian society and they seem to have responded nobly. His evening 'entertainments' were a real effort to bring British and Indian society together and, though too arrogant to win friends anywhere, he was genuinely sympathetic to native opinion and respectful of Indian culture.

By 1870 the Lahore College had sixty undergraduates, and in 1872 the Punjab University College was founded. It was not quite a fully fledged University but would soon become so and Leitner, as well as being Principal of his college, became Registrar of the University. This, however, was as far as he got in the academic world in India. His ideas were right and his achievements con-siderable; but he was not admired. Amongst the men who ruled India in the mid-Victorian period, conceit and moral superiority were common enough vices to pass without comment. Leitner's egotism, though, was on a totally different level. It was not an unconscious racial presumption but a personal and belligerent bragging. Some could forgive it. After all he was a mid-European intellectual; you couldn't expect the sangfroid on which the British prided themselves. Most, though, could not. 'Leitnerian outbursts' sent shivers of horror down the good straight spines of the patriarchs of the Punjab. The man was insufferable. Exhibiting his command of languages simply to impress (he now spoke twenty odd), posing as the only European who really understood the native mind, meddling in matters, like the administration of the railways, which were none of his concern, and all with the same ungracious, garrulous, publicity-seeking impertinence, he fully merited the undying hostility of all who had dealings with him. In reality it was never quite as bad as that. Leitner's one saving grace was his predictability. Once you knew what to expect you ceased to be outraged. Subtlety or cunning did not enter into his make-up, and it was not enmity that he aroused but ridicule.

It was a case of first impressions proving right in the end. Anyone who had run the gamut of unease, distaste and horror eventually came back to their first recollection of the man. Then it would have been his absurdity that registered. He stood five feet eight inches tall and, in spite of a torso that he describes as 'vigorous', weighed over fourteen stone. His eyes were small, blue and very intense, the lids narrowed with self-importance. To conserve moisture for the next outburst the mouth too was compressed. Once he warmed to his subject he spoke with a strong guttural accent. The tone grew increasingly menacing. He would switch languages for no apparent reason and, gesticulating wildly, work up to some devastating crescendo of indignation. And all the while strutting about like a bantam.

In 1865, for his first summer vacation, Leitner had gone to Kashmir. Like most Europeans he was much taken with the cool mountain climate and the grand proportions of this most famous of Himalayan valleys. In Srinagar, the capital, he got his first taste of the racial diversity of the region and this made even more of an impression. Today the Indo-Pakistan ceasefire line has severed all contact between the Kashmir valley and the Dard tribes of the Gilgit region. But there still live, in and around the bazaars of Srinagar, communities of short, slit-eyed men from Tibet and

Ladakh, tall gangling Gujars from the lower slopes of the Pir Panjal, and wizened Yarkandi refugees from across the Karakorams and Kun Lun in Sinkiang. Along with the deputations from Chilas, Gilgit and Hunza these excited the Doctor's curiosity, and in the following year he devoted his vacation to a ten-week tour of the Western Himalayas. The journey would be his making as a traveller and would provide the inspiration for his assault on Gilgit.

If Leitner was such a misfit in British India, imagine how he measured up to the ideal of the explorer. In the mid 1860s it was the African travellers who led the field; Baker had just returned from his epic journey up the Nile, Burton was still contesting the significance of Speke's discovery of Lake Victoria, and Livingstone was setting off into the interior for the last time. Glamorous and controversial, these men had won for exploration a wide and appreciative audience. People now knew what to expect of an expedition, the long columns of porters with loads on their heads, the menace of the jungle and the distant drums, the wild beasts, the lethal fevers and the naked savages. And they knew how the explorer should react as he grappled with these horrors. Against the barbarous and unchristian, the Victorian virtues should shine out in unsullied glory; deliberation, patience, fortitude and clearsightedness must triumph in the end. An excitable German, with three jars of Bovril and a penchant for outrageous tirades, would be up against it.

2. Friend of the Dards

'At 7 a.m. on the first of May 1866 I started from Lahore on a tour through Kangra, Mandi, Lahul, Zanskar, Ladakh and Kashmir with Mr. Henry Cowie, the brother of Mr. David Cowie, then Advocate-General of Bengal.'

Thus begins the narrative of Dr. Leitner's first journey which would have as its sequel the visit to Gilgit. In spite of the precise itinerary the rest of the first paragraph makes it clear that this is to be no simple holiday hike. The previous winter had been exceptionally severe, the paths were blocked by landslides, the bridges washed away, the snow still deep. So many were the dangers and hazards encountered that Leitner reserved them for a separate book; alas it never materialised. Sufficient to say, therefore, that he and his companion succeeded in reaching Leh, the Ladakh capital, a whole month earlier than any previous traveller coming by the same route. And that, in˙ the process, they managed to see 'a good deal that had been missed by previous travellers', to make some important archaeological discoveries, to strike up friendly relations with 'the excellent Middle and South Tibetans', and to open the way for future contact between British India and the forbidden city of Lhasa.

In a word, Leitner is off. His travelogue is much like the tirades his colleagues in Lahore so dreaded; credibility is strained, modesty discarded. The reader who knows his man may simply conclude that the two travellers, though they followed a route known to Europeans for half a century, managed to negotiate it a little earlier in the year than usual.

From Ladakh they headed west for Kashmir and further tribulations. Anyone who cried 'wolf' as often as Leitner was asking for trouble. Yet they were now on comparatively safe ground. The route from Ladakh to Kashmir was even better known than that up from Mandi. It was June; conditions were improving, native caravans were on the move and the passes were much lower. They

23

passed Kargil where the ex-ruler, on the orders of the Maharaja of Kashmir, was 'confined in a cage in which he could neither stand, sit, nor lie down'. Then came the bridge over the Dras river. This was a notorious structure of planks, without railings, spanning a gorge about twenty-five feet deep at the bottom of which frothed a big and boisterous river. It was a place where the laden beast obviously needed to be led and where the rider automatically dismounted. Young Cowie, however, thought otherwise. According to Leitner:

> In spite of a warning, my companion insisted on crossing it on his pony, which fell into the river with its rider. I was not so fortunate as on a previous occasion [when, presumably, he had rescued his friend]; and although at one time within a yard of me, Mr. H. Cowie was swept away into the middle of the torrent, whence he was hurled into a waterfall and disappeared.

Men were dispatched downstream to try and recover the body while Leitner pressed on for the Zoji La, the pass by which the traveller from the highlands of Ladakh finally descends into the Kashmir valley. Like all the passes that debouch into Kashmir from the north, the Zoji attracts a heavier snowfall than its height, 11,500 feet, would seem to justify. It remains unpredictable well into the summer with freak blizzards, and snow bridges that become increasingly fragile. The young doctor was depressed by Cowie's death and admits that he was less careful than usual. But that hardly exonerates him from losing one man through exposure and two men and two mules through falls.

Returned to Lahore, Leitner let it be known that his colleagues were lucky to see him back alive. Not only that, but he had amassed a considerable collection of 'ethnological material' (inscriptions, utensils, clothing, etc.) which he generously displayed at one of his soirées; the fortunate few who were able to attend were also favoured with his rendering of a number of Ladakhi refrains. Somehow the idea got about that he really had done something remarkable, and his zeal and dedication caught the attention, in particular, of two of the Punjab's most respected administrators, Sir Donald MacLeod and Sir George Campbell. The latter, as a doyen of the Bengal Asiatic Society, recommended that he be sent back into the mountains to continue his researches, while the former, as Lieutenant-Governor of the Punjab, made the invitation official. Leitner feigned reluctance but, once assured of the government's 'deep interest', he agreed; by the beginning of August he was back in Srinagar.

His brief was to study the language and customs of Chilas and to ascertain if it had any connection with Mt. Kailas. Leitner chose to interpret this as an open invitation to investigate all the Yaghi, or Dard, peoples. He was also warned that on no account should he cross the Indus. In doing so he was certainly contravening the wording of his instructions, though perhaps not the spirit in which they were conceived. The Punjab administration was intensely interested in the lands that lay to the north and west of Kashmir. It had no sympathy with the then Viceroy's policy of discouraging all trans-frontier exploration, and it attached great importance to the commercial and political possibilities of contact with the peoples of the mountains and beyond. Moreover Leitner did at first try to keep his sights fixed on the Chilasis. If, in the end, he was forced to take his enquiries elsewhere, it was not he who was to blame but the man whom he conceived to be his arch-enemy, Ranbir Singh, Maharaja of Kashmir.

His suspicions were aroused as soon as he returned to Srinagar. One of the men who had been sent in search of Cowie's body had duly reported to his *munshi* (secretary). The men had followed the Dras river down to the Indus and eventually located the *sahib*'s body at Tolti in Baltistan, a country now under Kashmir rule. However, the Maharaja of Kashmir denied all knowledge of the recovery of the body and, when Leitner asked to see the man who had brought the news, it was found that he had disappeared. Next an ex-ruler of Baltistan, from whom further news of Cowie was expected, was suddenly arrested. It could all have been coincidence; but Leitner knew better. Where Cowie's battered corpse had finally washed ashore might not seem a matter for deep concern; but to Leitner everything that concerned him was invested with profound significance. And this being the case it was natural enough to suspect others of dark designs to frustrate him.

Two weeks later, on the way to Bunji, he again met a man who claimed that the body lay buried at Tolti. Time was precious now but he recognised the call of duty; the restless spirit of his one-time companion was crying out for a Christian burial. He turned about and headed for Skardu, the capital of Baltistan. To keep ahead of the postal runners, whom he imagined to be converging on Skardu with news of his approach, he marched round the clock across the dreary Deosai plateau. At dead of night he descended on the little town. The Governor's *munshi* was located, dragged from his bed and ordered to produce the body forthwith. He couldn't, he said, because it wasn't there; it was buried four marches away, at Tolti.

The fort at Skardu

Perseverance had been rewarded and a triumphant Leitner dispatched his men to recover the remains.

I sent off a dozen men with instructions to take the whole block of earth in which the body was buried and to bring it to me. The men were under the charge of Mr. Cowie's bearer, Kerem Beg, who was profoundly attached to his late master and had followed me partly in the hope of recovering his body. When it was brought in we two washed away the earth with our own hands, found the skeleton, a portion of his shawl, but no vestige of his rings, watch, etc. etc. Most singular events then happened which I must not now, if ever, relate. Suffice it to say that we found and copied an entry in the Governor's official diary in which he duly reported to the Maharaja the recovery of the body, on the 22nd June 1866, of the Englishman who was drowned at Dras, whilst on 17th August following that potentate had denied to me the reception of any news on the subject. I then put the limbs into a light coffin, after wrapping them in linen, shawl wool and certain gums. An attempt was made to carry the body away, which I defeated, and against the repetition of which I guarded by keeping it under my camp bed during the remainder of my travels.

So far as is known Leitner never did reveal the nature of those 'singular events' but, really, the business is mysterious enough without his tantalising touches. Why on earth, one wonders, should the Maharaja of Kashmir have cared one way or the other about Cowie's corpse? His death had been a palpable accident and there were no secrets about Baltistan that needed to be kept from the likes of Leitner; the place was regularly visited by British sportsmen and had been thoroughly mapped by the Kashmir Survey. If it was just a question of the Maharaja hoping to rid himself of this troublesome German, then he might just as well have had the body brought to Srinagar.

That the Maharaja did, dearly, want to get rid of him was self-evident to Leitner. His enquiries were being intentionally frustrated, his servants tampered with, his supplies cut off and his very life endangered. Even if Ranbir Singh had a clear conscience about the Cowie affair, he had much to hide as regards the Yaghis or Dards. For Leitner maintained not only that the Kashmir troops had committed as many atrocities across the Indus as their enemies, but also that their presence there was in direct contravention of Kashmir's treaty arrangements with the British.

When, in 1846, Ranbir Singh's father had been created first Maharaja of Kashmir by the British, little was known of the mountain state and only a handful of Europeans had ever visited it. The Treaty of Amritsar described its extent as 'all the hilly or mountainous country, with its dependencies, to the eastward of the River Indus and the westward of the River Ravi'. Against the evidence of a map this proved meaningless and, with Kashmir's frontier being in effect the frontier of British India, two attempts had been made to define it more clearly. These established that Gilgit, though west of the Indus, did acknowledge Kashmir's rule; in 1848 the British actually urged the Maharaja to strengthen his hold on the place.

On the other hand Leitner was right in thinking that the position was suspiciously vague and that the Maharaja was taking advantage of it. Many of his contemporaries could never forgive Lord Hardinge, the Governor-General in 1846, for having failed to annex such a paradise as Kashmir; they would make a point of discrediting the Maharaja whenever opportunity offered in the hopes that the government would eventually see fit to dispossess him and take over the whole state. Leitner, however, was not impressed by the idea of Kashmir becoming 'a little England in the heart of Asia'. In fact he was in favour of all the mountain lands remaining under local rulers. His quarrel was simply with the Maharaja, 'that potentate', whose territorial encroachments, illegal and heavy handed, were threatening the independent way of life of all the Dard peoples. In 1860 Lieutenant Montgomerie, the officer in charge of the Kashmir Survey, had watched Ranbir Singh receive deputations from the Dard peoples of Chitral, Chilas, Yasin, Hunza and Nagar; it was clear to him that they were all rendering tribute and therefore might be considered as under the orders of the Maharaja. Now, Gilgit may have been tacitly acknowledged as a dependency of Kashmir, but these places certainly had not. Moreover, as Leitner continually points out, it was not simply a question of unsolicited offers of allegiance. The campaigns against Chilas in 1851, Yasin in 1860 and 1863 and Hunza in 1865 showed that the Maharaja was actively employed in coercing the trans-frontier peoples; and this was clearly contrary to the Treaty of Amritsar and to the principles on which relations with the princely states of India were founded.

It was therefore understandable that the Maharaja resented Leitner's quizzing of the Chilasis. He had no wish for the nature of his relations with any of the Dard peoples to be closely investigated or publicised. Knowing Leitner, it is also understandable how this chance of unmasking an impostor was far too good to miss. Overflowing with self-righteous indignation he tore into his task with zeal. In the process he completely overlooked the possibility that, regardless of the treaty, the government in Calcutta might be as happy as the Maharaja to see the western frontier of Kashmir left open for the time being.

*   *   *

From Skardu Leitner had made good progress to Astor, where he left Cowie's body in safe hands, and down to Bunji. Now, having taken the irrevocable step of crossing the Indus, he continued to set a breakneck pace for Gilgit. As a trespasser on the wrong side of the river, there was again a chance of his being overtaken by letters that would tell the local Kashmir officers to turn him back. Sure enough, a courier with just such instructions for the Governor of Gilgit fort, caught up with him on the first day. Leitner reports that at the time he was changing his clothes in a small stone hut beside the road. The courier approached, hurled his package through the open door and turned back; the hut was evidently a staging post. Needless to say, that missive went no further.

Though no doubt fastidious in his habits, it may seem odd that the traveller should pause to change his clothes in the middle of his first day out—if only because, given his lack of baggage, one has a right to an explanation of where the outfit came from. This is not forthcoming. Nor was the occasion one for just a simple change of breeches and shirt. Leitner had decided that the situation called for disguise; a rather tubby Mohammedan *mullah* in the turban and gown of Bukhara re-emerged into the blazing sun. What with the brace of pistols, the clattering jars of Bovril and a cork bed, 'light as a feather' strapped to his back, it must be doubtful whether the transformation was convincing.

I went on through burnt out villages and along paths here and there disfigured by hanging skeletons of people said to have been insurgents against the Maharaja's authority, but declared by the natives to be peaceful peasants hanged to support false reports of victories. . . . I crossed the bridge [over the Sai] at Jalkot where the head of the chief formed a *tête de pont* and ascended the Niludar ridge. . . . On the other side we saw the Gilgit river and the Plain of Minor.

This is the half way stage on the grim road from Bunji to Gilgit fort. Leitner and his two servants had made fourteen miles in the heat of the day over rock and sand. They were exhausted and in a cave beside the Gilgit river they hove to for the night; at last the cork bed justified its presence. But not for long. Shots rang out, the doctor tumbled out of bed, and a visitation from a man with 'a yellow moustache and cat-like eyes' was successfully repulsed. This assailant, he noted, looked just like a Russian he had met in the Crimea. It was interesting that such fair hair could belong to a Dard but also rather galling to be attacked by one of those he had come to save. Later he was much relieved to learn that the man was in the service of the Kashmiris.

Another attempt on the traveller's life, which was made next morning, also looked like the work of this renegade. Striding out in his full Bukharan canonicals Leitner 'trod on a stone trap, the effect of which is to loosen the mountainside and to hurl one into the abyss below'; the stratagem, he explains, was one often adopted by the Dards against the invading Kashmir troops. 'I was saved by accidentally falling backwards.' To him it was, of course, inconceivable that this little landslip could have been a natural phenomenon; Leitner's suspicious mind left precious little to providence. The bare lower slopes and cliffs along all the rivers in the Gilgit region are notoriously unstable. When the snows above melt they dissolve into thick avalanches of mud that spew out onto the valley floor and form the lofty fans of alluvium which are such a distinctive feature of the region. In drier weather the frost or the sun takes over, cracking and crumbling the mud and rocks and keeping up a constant fusillade of stones on the paths below. Leitner was right to cite the ingenuity of the Dards in exploiting this phenomenon; but a lot more people have been killed by natural landslips than by 'stone traps'.

Commandeering some stray ponies Leitner's party pressed on up the Gilgit river and reached the fort by early afternoon on the second day. They were not expected. The fort had just weathered another long siege and now the Kashmir garrison lay licking their wounds—literally if Leitner is to be believed. The place stank to high heaven. The sick and disabled were scarcely distinguishable from the half buried dead, and disease was rampant. Leitner was so appalled that he forgot he was supposed to be an itinerant *mullah* and, in the imperious tones of a *sahib*, demanded to see the commandant. Asked who he was, he drew himself up to his full five feet eight and said he was a European and he wanted the place cleaned up immediately. The commandant, 'rubbing his eyes from [the effects of] an opium siesta', thought it odd that he had had no instructions about receiving a *feringhi*. But, yes, he would make the place presentable and, pending news from Bunji, the visitor was welcome to stay.

Leitner spent that night in the fort but the next day moved out; the local population was proving elusive enough without his becoming identified with their dreaded oppressors. The township, indeed the whole valley, was deserted. Installed in a spacious ruin well away from the fort, he pondered the question of how to make contact with the Dards. In the recent disturbances the tribes, emboldened by the failure of a Kashmiri attack on Hunza, had poured down on the Gilgit valley and for a time only the fort had held out. But it was better provisioned than usual and when a relieving force arrived from across the Indus, the Dard confederacy had broken up, the besiegers taking to the mountains. By the time Leitner arrived on the scene the Kashmir forces had departed on a punitive raid into the hills south of Gilgit. The wounded had been left in the fort with just a token garrison since the surrounding villages had all been deserted; the only Dards were a few snipers waiting their chance on the rocky cliffs above the valley.

Leitner's solution of how to entice them down was simple and characteristic, a Gilgit soirée. Borrowing a drum from the fort he set about composing, in the few Gilgiti words he knew, a suitable proclamation. Next day, all day, one of his servants marched up and down the valley beating his drum and shouting to the deserted ruins and silent hills the glad tidings; *Doctor-Sahib* was giving a party, all Dards welcome. Amazingly, it worked. The Kashmir governor had sufficient respect for a *feringhi* not to interfere and, as darkness fell, a trickle of wild looking men with long hair curling from under their turbans descended from the heights. When the smell of roasting sheep reached their more cautious companions they too followed; that night a hundred and fifty ragged warriors enjoyed the traveller's hospitality. They gorged themselves on mutton and apricots and, when the moment seemed right, Leitner suggested a song. The musicians, usually a fife, clarinet and drums, struck up, the doctor sat back the better to appreciate his first experience of Dard culture and, obligingly, the men rose singly and in set groups to sing the sad songs and to dance the slow rhythmic dances of the Hindu Kush.

The scene was later immortalised in a drawing in the *Illustrated London News*. There sits Leitner on the verandah of his ruin,

smiling benignly and clapping his hands to the music. Before him
the dancers, ringed by their crosslegged companions, are caught in
the middle of an eightsome reel. It looks a little too vigorous. The
artist has sought to convey some idea of movement by emphasising
the swirl of the dancers' baggy clothes; cuffs, kummerbunds and
shawls trail about them as if they were whirling dervishes. But,
this apart, it rings fairly true, even to the gaunt shape of the distant
fort and the ghostly mountains behind. Some such scene may still
be met with in the valleys of Hunza, Yasin, Chitral or Gilgit. On a
moonlit night the thin strains of the flute carry far and wide in the
silent mountain air. The flare of a blazing torch glints in the wide
eyes of the frenzied drummer while the dancers, thin young boys
and gnarled old warriors, move trancelike in a slow and measured
shuffle. They seem as aloof from the music and the clapping of the
onlookers as the peaks sailing above them.

The experience is not easily forgotten. Few mountain people
blend with their surroundings as perfectly as the Dards of the high
Hindu Kush. The Balti of the Karakorams or the Inca of the
Andes seems somehow to have been defeated by his mountains,
misshapen and impoverished by the rigours of climate and terrain. But not so the man of Hunza or Chitral. He shares something of the romance of his scenery; he has kept his dignity. When
he dances he rolls his eyes and stares defiantly up at the heights.
Like the Highland shepherd on his heathered hills or the Arab
Bedouin adrift in the desert, he seems to belong.

It would be nice to think that Leitner felt something of all this.
His scholarly interests precluded a quiet enjoyment of the scene
and he was, anyway, rather unnerved by the danger of his situation; he characterises his stay in Gilgit by describing himself as
scribbling with a pencil in one hand while clutching a revolver in
the other. Yet this night with the Dards near Gilgit was one of the
highlights of his eventful life and a watershed in his career. Thirty
years later he was still telling his audiences in London of how he
braved the rigours of the Western Himalayas, the hostility of the
Kashmir authorities and the supposed savagery of the Dards, to
be the first to bring back an authentic account of their languages
and customs. Added to which he does seem to have been captivated
by more than just the sociological peculiarities of this people. He
was touched by the trust they placed in him when accepting his

invitation on that September night in 1866. And for years to come he would crusade remorselessly for what he believed to be in the best interests of the Hindu Kush tribes. It would be churlish to discredit these efforts simply because of the infuriating conceit with which he promoted them.

Next morning he left Gilgit. 'Fearing that another attempt on my life might be successful, I rapidly moved back to Bunji, so as to give no fixed locality or time for an assassination.' He had been there just over thirty-six hours. Later his numerous detractors would make much of the absurdity of his setting himself up as an authority on the area after less than two days' residence. It is true that for the rest of his life he wrote and lectured continuously about the Dards. He claimed to have discovered them (which was not true), to have invented the name Dardistan (true, though the word Dard had been around for a long time) and to have been the first to study their languages (also true). To be fair to Leitner he did not claim to know everything about the geography of the country but only everything about its people. This was something that did not necessitate a long stay. For, though he never again visited Dardistan, he would be surrounded by Dards for the next twenty years.

Two of the men who would share his home in Lahore now accompanied him back across the Indus. They headed for Astor, where Cowie's coffin lay waiting, and then for Srinagar. Leitner was due back in Lahore by October 20, and it was now the end of September; there was precious little time for the usual intrigue-filled diversions. Nevertheless, he packed in more incident than most travellers meet with in a year of wandering. At Astor he got into deep trouble when he discovered a cache of Dard prisoners, girls from Yasin 'as fair as any Englishwoman', who were awaiting distribution amongst the Maharaja's favourites. At Gurais he survived another attempt on his life and taught the culprits 'a lesson they will never forget'; and then, on the next day's march, rescued 'by a timely dash' a teacher from Amritsar who had been press-ganged by agents of the Maharaja. In Srinagar he was baulked in an attempt to have matters out with 'that potentate', but he contrived a blazing row with the local British representative over the disposal of Cowie's body. The latter wanted to bury the gruesome little box while the Doctor, still keeping it wedged under his bed, refused; he must take it to Lahore and surrender it to Cowie's family. And so he did. With just four days for the final two hundred miles, he 'rode or walked day and night, carrying Cowie's body myself, when I could not immediately obtain coolies, and finally arrived at His Honour, the Lieutenant-Governor's house in the evening of the appointed day when I was received with great kindness in spite of my dilapidated appearance and the presence of a small party in evening dress'.

His two Gilgiti followers were soon housed in the compound of his bungalow and, taking three months leave, Leitner set about eliciting from them the secrets of their unknown tongue. Later the government procured for him two Kafirs and a Chilasi and in 1872, while inspecting schools on the frontier, he acquired representatives of the Indus valley tribes. By then the compound of his bungalow had become a standing joke amongst the British in Lahore; it was like an ethnic zoo. But it was an open zoo and many came without his prompting. There were visiting *mullahs* from Central Asia and Turkey, Baltis and Ladakhis from the Karakorams and, from beyond the mountains, natives of Yarkand and Badakshan. While his contemporaries posed for the newly invented camera with one foot on a slaughtered tiger, Leitner proudly lined up his performing Dards as if they were the school football team and sat himself in the middle. On home leave he invariably took along his prize acquisition to parade on the London scene; in 1868 it was a Yarkandi, in 1873 a Kafir and in 1887 a native of Hunza— each was the first of his race to be seen in Europe. At the same time he kept up a busy correspondence with some of the ruling families of Dardistan. The Raja of Nagar's son he had met in Gilgit in 1866 and he was still writing to him in the 1890s. A future ruler of Chitral sent him letters written on birch bark and rolled in the hollow of a twig. The Indian post office handled them reverently and the contents added substantially to the doctor's much prized collection of Dard fairy-tales.

Thus it was, by correspondence and painstaking examination of every Dard that came his way, that Leitner pieced together his dossiers on Dardistan. Unfortunately this piecemeal compilation is painfully evident in the results. A pencil-written note would first be rushed out as a pamphlet or newspaper article. It would then be included in his next published work, all of which, snowball

3   A not untypical piece of road in the Hindu Kush

4 The Gilgit valley photographed in 1895

5 The Agency Bungalow, Gilgit

style, would then be lumped into his next compilation, and so on.
The enquiry into the Chilasi language, which had prompted the
1866 journey, blossomed in due course into *The Languages and
Races of Dardistan*, published in 1877. Here the linguistic material
is swamped by introductions, footnotes, appendices and digres-
sions in the text itself. Four lists of contents covering some fifteen
quarto pages still fail to keep up with the mass of accretions at the
end. *The Times* would later describe his books as like the *Talmud*,
so full of diverse material are they. To Leitner's way of thinking
the suggestion that he was just parading his knowledge was, of
course, malicious nonsense. The Druses of the Lebanon, to whom
he devoted a chapter, might not, on the face of it, seem to have
much relevance to the Dards of the Hindu Kush. The doctor,
however, suspected there were similarities between their brand of
Mohammedanism and that of the men of Hunza; and anything
that bore on the life of a people was relevant to their language.

In so far as all this tended to discourage the reader, whether
linguist, ethnologist or explorer, it was a tragedy. For tucked
away in sub-section i of Section 22 of Part II of Volume I, one
might find a really practical gem like the 'Traveller's Vade Mecum
in Astor, Gilgit, Chilas and Guraiz'. Leitner berated the government for letting subsequent travellers visit Dardistan without the
inestimable benefit of his scholarship; all it had to do was give him
more time off to edit his material. And, sure enough, there in the
Travellers' Vade Mecum lie several handy phrases which, if understood by the next visitor to the region, might have put a very
different complexion on its exploration. 'We kill all infidels', 'Beat
him now, kill him afterwards', are prominent amongst the Conventional Forms of Dard Greeting.

In 1886, twenty years after the visit to Gilgit and ten after the
appearance of the *Languages and Races*, Leitner was summoned to
Simla, summer capital of British India; the government, it
transpired, wished him to undertake another linguistic enquiry.
Vindication at last, thought Leitner. The enquiry was to be into
the languages of Hunza and Nagar. Might this not lead to works
on Chitrali, the Kafir tongues, Badakshi, Yarkandi etcetera?
Visions of groaning shelves on all the languages of Central Asia
swam before him. He attacked the new task with relish. Given his
known antipathy to the Kashmir government and his increasingly

critical attitude towards British policy, Leitner was perhaps an odd choice for the job. And there would soon be reason to regret the appointment. But in 1886 it does seem that he was not alone in regarding himself as the leading authority on the region; he was not yet dismissed by the government as a 'self-seeking humbug' whose work was 'egotistic and worthless'.

By this time Dardistan was beginning to loom very large in the anxious minds of those who directed British India's external relations. There was no question of Leitner being allowed access to Hunza; he had to be content with a visit to Srinagar. But there as usual he found Dard hostages-cum-emissaries and with their help he corrected his vocabularies and ethnographical dialogues. Then, on the grounds of ill-health, he retired to England to complete the work, taking with him a man from Hunza. After three years and a thousand pounds of government money, the *Hunza-Nagar Handbook* appeared. It is not the handiest of handbooks. Flat it makes an ample chair seat, and opened out might do as a short bed; strapped to the back would certainly be the best way to carry it. The government raised no objections to its format, and neither they nor anyone else was in a position to judge the accuracy of its grammar. But there was disappointment when by 1892 it had sold only one copy. This was heightened when in 1893 there appeared, most unexpectedly, a second and much expanded edition. Here the snowball effect of Leitner's literary output is taken to absurdity. The appendices are so numerous that they have had to be printed as a separate volume; there are no less than six introductions and rather more than three quarters of the material consists of reprints of his previous works. But the mystifying point about this new volume was that it was published not by the Government of India but by something calling itself 'The Oriental University Institute, Woking' (motto: 'Ex Oriente Lux, Ex Occidente Lex'). And it was being sold at two guineas a copy. Urgent enquiries soon revealed that about a hundred copies of the official edition were indeed missing. They had been removed by the author who apparently regarded them as an 'honorarium'. The identity of the new publisher was not hard to guess.

With the appearance of the Oriental University Institute, Leitner's career enters its final phase. Since the 1870s he had been petitioning for extensions to his home leave and, after his spell of duty in Srinagar in 1886, he relinquished his post in Lahore and retired finally to England. He even became a British citizen. Woking, then a small village with a good railway connection to London, was a far cry from the Hindu Kush; but he seems to have decided that from there he stood a better chance of influencing the fate of Dardistan than he did in India. Nowadays the place epitomises suburbia and one can't help suspecting that that grandiloquent institute may have actually operated from some dingy terraced house where the doctor would try out his latest polemic on his crusty Victorian landlady over the toast and marmalade. The scene would certainly fit with Curzon's verdict on the Institute's erratic periodical, *The Asiatic Quarterly Review*, which was 'a struggling journal' and indeed his verdict on its author, who carried even less weight than his publication.

But Leitner's career is ever full of surprises. The Oriental University Institute of Woking was not a terraced house but a massive neo-Elizabethan palace well suited to be one of the first red brick universities. It had been built to house the Royal Dramatic College, 'an asylum for decaying actors and actresses' of which Dickens had been a patron. Later the main hall would be found ideal for building aircraft in for the 1914–18 war. Leitner bought the place in 1884 and immediately stamped it with his own inimitable style. It was supposed to become the centre of oriental learning in Britain; and for a time it did. The suites of rooms, where the failing stars had passed their final days, were thrown open free of charge to visiting Hindu and Mohammedan scholars. It was affiliated to the Punjab University and its inmates could even take their degrees there. In the main hall was displayed the doctor's collection of ethnographical material, coins, sculptures and manuscripts illustrating India's past, as well as all his mementoes of Ladakh and Dardistan. As a publishing house it produced a plethora of critical journals in Sanscrit and Arabic plus *The Asiatic Quarterly Review* through whose pages Leitner kept up a steady bombardment of official policy as it was deemed to threaten his beloved Dards.

To cater for his students' religious needs there was also 'the Shah Jehan mosque'. Again unworthy suspicions are aroused. A mosque in Woking? More probably just a room in the Institute set aside for Mohammedan prayer. And again one is wrong. The Shah

Jehan mosque, complete with cupolas and minarets, was built in
1889 with money donated by the ruler of Bhopal. It was the first
mosque in western Europe and it still stands today. The blue glaze
on the main dome has succumbed to the weather and the mosaic
courtyard with its reservoir, (about which the doctor was so
particular that he had the architect wishing the thing had been
built 'in Jericho or some place distant enough not to have troubled
us'), has become overgrown. But there it is, the Imam still calls the
faithful to prayer and it is still the headquarters of the British
Muslim Society.

Leitner died of pneumonia in 1899 aged 58. *The Times*, in an
obituary which gave no hint of his controversial character,
generously conceded his achievements. 'As a linguist he had
probably no living rival'. His was 'the first serious attempt to
breathe life into the dry bones of the educational system of the
[Indian] government' and he was truly 'both originator and
founder of the Punjab University'. The Lahore newspaper which
he had started had by then become the *Civil and Military Gazette*
with which Kipling was closely associated. And the Punjab
University and the Lahore Government College are still, today,
going strong. By contrast his crusades for the Dard peoples and his
work in England, indeed even his name in England, have now
long since been forgotten. The Oriental University Institute
collapsed with his death. His books are hard to come by and he is
seldom mentioned in accounts of Dardistan and the Hindu Kush.
He was a failure as an explorer and had little effect on the course of
events in the region.

Yet, behind the cacophony of sounds to which the Gilgit Game
will be played, the whispered debate of the strategists, the fanfares
for the explorers and the bugles of the advancing troops, there is
always this one strident voice of protest. Immoderate, eccentric
and sadly ineffectual, it is at least persistent. No move will be made
without Leitner taking up his pen, and his writings thus form a
unique commentary on the whole story.

They make a lot more sense today than they did a hundred years
ago. The young German scholar who blundered into Gilgit in 1866
passionately believed that there he had discovered a pocket of
humanity which had been miraculously preserved in something
approaching a state of nature. He saw it in the peculiar customs

and language structure of the whole region and particularly in the Burishaski tongue of Hunza. This he believed to be 'the cradle of human thought as expressed in language'. A single consonant sound appeared to represent an idea or association of ideas, from which he concluded that he was getting to the very root of human speech, the point at which the customs and environment of the people corresponded exactly to these primitive sounds. If the Dards were really the original Indo-Aryans it followed that a study of their language and lifestyle might reveal much about how half the world still thought and spoke. For at least as long as it took to exhaust this line of enquiry it was vital that the whole area be left as undisturbed as possible.

He steered clear of the notion of the noble savage. The Dards were far from noble and not uncivilised. But he was still tempted to romanticise. Dardistan was 'a paradise', a place where men still believed in fairies and it was the ruler's job to invoke the rain. The Gilgiti for syphilis was *farangi rok*, the foreigner's disease; it, and cholera, were unknown until the arrival of Kashmiris and Europeans. Suddenly one senses familiar ground. It is the story of the Polynesians or the American Indians all over again. Leitner today is immediately recognisable as the conservationist, pleading for the preservation of a primitive and helpless people. Writing in the early 1890s he was prepared to concede defeat.

Industrial handicrafts, historical superstitions and reminiscences, national feasts, which existed in 1866, exist no longer. . . . The fairies and the prophetesses of Dardistan are silent, the Tham of Hunza no longer brings down the rain, the family axes are broken, the genealogists have been destroyed and the sacred drum is no longer heard. . . . I do not palliate the old Hunza practice of lending one's wife to a guest or of kidnapping good looking strangers in order to improve the race . . . but I do find a reproach on European and Indian morality in the fact that not a single Hunza woman showed herself to the British or Kashmir invaders. . . . It shall not be said that the races which I, so disastrously for them, discovered and named, shall suffer from any misrepresentations so far as I can help it, however much the political passions of the moment may deprive my statements of the weight that has hitherto attached to them in this speciality.

Vae victis et victoribus—for history now marches rapidly towards the common disaster. *Finis Dardarum.*

With such apocalyptic stuff the doctor inveighed against the rape of Dardistan. Nowadays he might just have scared off a development corporation. But in the late nineteenth century, a lone and immoderate polemicist defying an imperial destiny, he stood not a chance.

3. Desirous of Active Employment

From 3.30 till 4.30, weather permitting, Fellows of the Royal Geographical Society in London may still take tea on the Society's lawns. In the hallowed stone-flagged hall a grandfather clock chimes the hour; the french windows stand open. But there comes no more the stampede of thirsty explorers; instead just an uncertain shuffle punctuated by the tap of a cane. Out of the map room, past the Greenland canoe of Gino Watkins and a chunk of the tree that marked Livingstone's grave, lurches an elderly academic. A giant bust of Speke, some faded globes and a showcase of relics from some Antarctic endeavour are passed unnoticed as the professor wheels left for the fruitcake and the sunshine.

In its modern role as an august association devoted to the advance of geography the R.G.S. is, of course, a highly energetic and influential body. Yet its headquarters still retain the flavour of the last century and of an age when the explorers, not the academics, made the the running. The Society is justly proud of this past; the archives and photographic collections are being carefully catalogued and prints of most of the Society's medallists have recently been rehung in a position of prominence. Here surely is one of the finest portrait galleries of explorers. From 1839 onwards two gold medals were awarded each year and, in the nineteenth century, they invariably went to travellers. Many of the names are familiar enough; Burton, Livingstone, Baker, Sturt, Scott, Shackleton, Fawcett and Fuchs. But many are now forgotten, and none more so than the considerable number of Asian explorers. Take one of the medallists for 1870, George J. Whitaker Hayward. His frame is next to that of Samuel Baker of the Nile and it faces H. M. Stanley's. In the whole gallery there is no photograph quite so striking as Hayward's. Instead of a head and shoulders studio portrait, here we have a full-length portrayal of the romantic explorer dressed in local costume and armed to the teeth. It stands out a mile and yet, until recently, not even the Society seemed aware of its existence. This neglect is all the more

41

remarkable when one realises that of all the medal-winning travellers in Central Asia, Hayward alone was actually sponsored by the R.G.S.

Elsewhere in the world it was not unusual for the Society to mount its own expeditions or to make substantial grants towards private ventures. Indeed it still does. But Asia was usually the exception—and an exception which the tragic and compromising fate of the Hayward expedition would seem to justify. Not that the Fellows were uninterested. Medals were showered on the pioneers of the Western Himalayas, and it was in this corner of the globe, according to the President's address in 1870, that all the main geographical advances were being made. In fact their only regret was that they could not take a more initiatory role in this exciting field. The trouble was that the Society was supposed to be purely scientific and emphatically non-political, whereas in the *terra incognita* of Asia no such thing as a purely scientific non-political expedition was possible. Here what might be regarded, geographically speaking, as an inviting slice of virgin territory was, politically speaking, no more virgin than a treacherous jezebel.

Dr. Leitner's visit to Gilgit in 1866 had drawn attention to the debatable status of Dardistan and to the highly volatile situation existing on this remote frontier of British India. That was only part of the story. Of infinitely more moment was the power struggle that was brewing over the mountains and deserts beyond and which was bringing face to face the two mightiest empires in Asia. It was this dimension that gave to the squabbles of the Kashmiris and Dards a significance out of all proportion to the size and resources of the narrow valleys and ice-bound heights of the western Himalayas. For Dardistan and the Pamirs, with Afghanistan on one side and Sinkiang on the other, was all that now separated the much coveted British-Indian empire from the steadily advancing might of Russia. It will be necessary to follow this deepening crisis closely but for the present it is sufficient to note that since the 1840s there had been ample reason for the R.G.S. to steer well clear of sponsoring expeditions to such a critical no-man's land.

Why then did they bother with Hayward? In 1868 this unknown young man waited on Sir Henry Rawlinson, vice-president of the Society, and declared himself 'desirous of active employment' on any exploratory expedition that Sir Henry might care to suggest. Within days rather than weeks he was directed towards this very region, furnished with surveying instruments, voted the sum of £300 and packed off on the first possible sailing to India. Such at least was the explanation subsequently given, though a more unlikely sequence of events it is hard to imagine. Amidst all the other mysteries that would surround Hayward's brief career as an explorer and that would bedevil every attempt to unravel the circumstances of his death, this question of why the R.G.S. adopted him in the first place is easily ignored.

Hayward's career had been as obscure as most things about him. He first appears in 1859 as an ensign commissioned in the 89th Regiment of Foot which was based in central India. There is no record of his birth in England but, since the Regiment was one of those recruited in Ireland, it seems likely that he was born there, probably about 1840. In 1863 he purchased his promotion to Lieutenant and in 1864 transferred to a Scottish Regiment, the Cameron Highlanders. The following year he terminated this short and undistinguished military record by selling his commission. The business of buying and selling commissions was about to be abolished but as yet was quite normal. Only one clear inference can be drawn from this episode; regimental life in India did not suit him. Swapping regiments and then selling out altogether were radical steps for one not obviously blessed with influential connections or a private income. Later the only aspect of military life that he recalled with pleasure was the opportunity it had afforded for sporting forays into the mountains. It could well be that the endless drill of the parade ground and the petty business of lobbying for recognition proved the despair of an independent and impulsive would-be explorer. Equally it may have been that the chronic debts, that every red-blooded young officer seemed to run up, got out of hand. Perhaps both, and then one thing more. If officers like Hayward overspent, gambled and drank it was hardly surprising. In the hill stations of British India, where alone they could hope to enjoy a normal social life, the crinoline was still in fashion and the music of the moment was the Viennese waltz. Wagner, still unperformed in England let alone India, would have been more up Hayward's street. There was an intensity about this gaunt young man, a pent-up deluge of determination and a disregard for consequences, which is irreconcilable with the shallow tenor of social life in mid-Victorian India.

Between 1865 and 1868 Hayward's movements are uncertain. Some, if not all, of this time was spent stalking the enormous wild goats, the ibex and the markhor of the Western Himalayas, for by the time he returned to England he knew Kashmir and Baltistan well. The fact that he chose to approach Rawlinson is evidence enough that the idea of returning to this part of the world was his as much as anyone's. Rawlinson, a distinguished soldier, traveller and scholar, a member of the council which advised the Secretary of State for India, and soon to be President of the R.G.S., had made Central Asia and the Himalayas his speciality. No-one in England was more conscious of the threat posed to British India by Russia's advances and no-one did more as a publicist and statesman to draw attention to this deepening crisis. In the councils of state he urged the adoption of a 'forward' policy which by trade, treaties and subsidies would bring countries like Afghanistan, Dardistan and Sinkiang within the framework of India's outer defences. At the same time, in the R.G.S., he monitored every step in the exploration of the region, badgered the Government of India to adopt a more adventurous attitude towards explorers and did all he could to wheedle from it such geographical information as its native agents in the region might obtain. It was hardly surprising if occasionally he sullied the Society's non-political stance by lapsing into the rhetoric of Whitehall. But equally, he more than anyone saw plainly that in Asia there could be no firm line between geographical discovery and political interference. Hayward's instructions emphasised the purely scientific and independent character of his expedition; in fact his being a private individual with no official connections was one of his chief recommendations. But again, geographical discoveries in such a crucial region must have a bearing on military strategy and thus on political thinking. Hayward, knowingly, was being used not just to advance science but to bring pressure to bear on the Government of India.

One other point worked in his favour; Hayward himself seemed just right and so did the timing. Since 1864 the Viceroy in India had been Sir John Lawrence whose external policy was generally characterised as 'masterly inactivity'. Now, with only six months till the end of his five-year term, this policy of non-interference in the affairs of India's neighbours was coming under strong attack. Russia's continuing advance into the Central Asian states of Khokand and Bukhara made a British policy of inactivity look anything but masterly. Reluctantly Lawrence was adopting a more friendly approach to Afghanistan and, with Disraeli in power at home (the Conservatives invariably took Anglo-Russian relations more seriously), there was good reason to expect that the man chosen to succeed Lawrence would be someone more disposed to listen to the 'forward' talk of Rawlinson. Hayward could expect to incur official disapproval and discouragement but, given this new drift of policy, there was a fair chance that if he picked his path carefully he would not be expressly forbidden to cross the British frontier.

According to the R.G.S. his destination was the Pamirs and, more specifically, the source of the Oxus. Thirty years earlier the only European since Marco Polo to have seen this remote and forbidding mountain system thought that he had solved the problem of the Oxus. Lieutenant John Wood, an endearing and improbable explorer—he was actually a naval lieutenant—had made a winter foray up the river to Lake Sir-i-Kol on the Great Pamir; the R.G.S. had awarded him a gold medal for the feat in 1841. But there was now reason to doubt whether Sir-i-Kol, or Lake Victoria as it had been renamed, was in fact the main source of the river. Native travellers had reported other and bigger lakes on what they called the Bam-i-Dunya, or Roof of the World, and other and longer tributaries winding down its open windswept valleys. Hayward, having evidently steeped himself in the travels of Burton and Speke, made much of what he christened 'the lake region of the Pamir' and was soon convinced that Lake Karakul would prove to be the real source of the Oxus and the true Victoria of Asia. This was reputedly a vast sheet of water that it took twelve days to walk round, altogether a more worthy parent than Wood's tarn, which was only nine feet deep and a mile or two across.

The Oxus was one of the great rivers of classical geography and the mystery of its source 'in high Pamere' was as old and evocative as that of the Nile. The attempt to solve it lent respectability to Hayward's venture as well as providing a focal point. But, needless to say, that was not all. The river, or its watershed to the north or south, might soon become the Anglo-Russian frontier. If a war, so terrible as to be unthinkable, was to be averted by territorial delineation, then Rawlinson for one wanted to know a good bit more about the terrain and its peoples. For instance, the idea of an Anglo-Russian agreement about the northern boundary of Afghanistan was already under active consideration. This boundary would constitute in practice a line between the accepted British and Russian spheres of influence. The problem was to define it, particularly at its eastern extremity in the Pamirs. Here even the Afghans themselves were unsure of the extent of their subject territories. In 1869 Rawlinson would be asked to supply precisely this information. He did so to the best of his ability but the agreement based on it would result in a quarter of a century's wrangling and intrigue and would give rise to at least one major war scare. All of which might have been obviated if Hayward had supplied the goods.

Not that he didn't try. Between July 1868 and July 1870 he would make four attempts to reach the Pamirs. His first idea was to follow the track from Peshawar through Dir, Chitral and Wakhan. The earlier pioneers of Central Asian travel, William Moorcroft and Alexander Burnes, had both sent native agents to investigate this route, and Colonel Gardiner, the American adventurer whom Hayward had already met in Srinagar, had himself travelled much of it. He firmly believed that it was the shortest and easiest route between India and Sinkiang. Hayward agreed and, surprisingly considering how little was known about it, they would eventually be proved right. However, the terrain was not everything and the reason that this line of approach had yet to be explored by a European had nothing to do with the height of the passes or the availability of supplies. It was shut, and would remain shut for another quarter of a century, because of its inhabitants. When the Lieutenant-Governor of the Punjab heard of Hayward's scheme to follow this route even he, who had encouraged Leitner's efforts to shed some light on Dardistan, declared it 'absolute madness'. The more favoured route to Sinkiang, that through Ladakh, passed largely across uninhabited tracts where carriage and directions were in the hands of the Ladakhis, a peaceable and smiling race of Tibetan origin. But, on the Chitral route, from Peshawar to Dir the traveller would be at the mercy first of some of the most warlike of the Pathans and then of the fanatically Islamic and anti-British Akhund of Swat. According to the Kashmir troops, the Chitralis, next in line, were quite the most treacherous and slavery-minded of all the Dards and, once out of their clutches and over the Hindu Kush, he would still have to contend with the Wakhis and the Kirghiz; the former Wood had found downright obstructionist and the latter, on whom all travel across the wastes of the Pamirs would depend, were said to owe allegiance to Khokand where the Russians were making massive inroads. Hayward's idea, also no doubt copied from Gardiner, was to travel disguised as a Pathan mercenary; he was tall and bony enough and had picked up a smattering of Pushtu in his army days. But with his breech-loading rifles, his sextants and drawing materials, he would have been pushed to convince anyone, let alone real Pathans, that he was not a snooping European. Luckily he was persuaded to give up the idea.

Discretion, in Hayward's book, was rarely the better part of valour, but in the choice of route he was also forced to bow to circumstances. What Lord Salisbury would call 'the Englishman's right to get his throat cut where and when he likes' was not gener- ally acknowledged; had he persisted with the Chitral route he would certainly have been officially forbidden it. However, honour was partly satisfied by his discovery in the Punjab Govern- ment's records of a forgotten native account of the whole of this route; he forwarded it to Rawlinson for publication in the Society's journal. He was also pleased to report that, though his original plan had had to be abandoned, prospects of reaching the Pamirs were now better than ever. He had evolved a second plan. He would take 'the easier line' across the Western Himalayas, by way of Kashmir, Ladakh and Yarkand in Sinkiang and endeavour to return by way of Chitral. Early in September 1868 he duly set off from Kashmir to cross the Western Himalayas.

No European had yet reached Yarkand and returned to tell the tale. The 'easier line' which Hayward now followed was easier only in so far as the government were less inclined to stop him. Three of the world's highest mountain systems had to be crossed, the Great Himalaya, the Karakorams and the Kun Lun. There were five passes of over 18,000 feet, four hundred miles of uninhabited glacier and tundra, and at the end a very fair chance of being sent packing straight back to India. Moreover the precise route that Hayward selected was one which even native travellers did not use. On the other hand he did have a companion of sorts. Robert Shaw, an English tea planter, was also making an attempt to reach Yarkand and it was probably news of this venture that reconciled Hayward to the change of plan. If Shaw, who had been studying the situation and laying his plans for the past eighteen months, reckoned the journey was now feasible, then Hayward could do no better than hitch his modest caravan to Shaw's and, once across the mountain barrier, strike out on his own for the Pamirs.

* * *

The R.G.S. usually met once every two weeks from November till July with a long autumn recess. In 1868, 1869 and 1870 all three of the November inaugural meetings were taken up with developments in Central Asia. Rawlinson himself delivered a powerful paper on 'The Trade Routes between India and Turkestan' in 1868. He took the opportunity to apprise the Fellows of how the Society's Council had decided to support Hayward's venture and of how, although his plans had had to be changed, Hayward was now well on his way. Then Rawlinson was off on to forbidden ground, the trade routes being as good an excuse for launching into political matters as commerce was for pursuing expansionist policies. In a flurry of rhetorical questions he dismissed the Government of India's reluctance to countenance exploration; there was as yet no possibility of a Russian invasion of India; the government might therefore explore and trade in the lands that intervened between the two frontiers without fear of complications; India had as much right to do so as Russia and, by implication, he warned that if she failed to do so, Russia would swallow up these lands as surely as she had swallowed all the rest.

The meeting went on late into the night. Flushed by a sense of the great issues at stake Fellow after Fellow rose to add the weight of his authority or the benefit of his experience to this stirring talk. The Great Game was in play. Before roaring fires in big country house grates, or from leather armchairs in the corner of club smoking rooms, the same talk would go on into the small hours for another twenty-five years. If there wasn't a four for bridge there was always the Great Game. Hayward, slogging his way across the Karakorams, became the merest pawn; the masterminds were here by their firesides sipping their brandies. To send them amicably to bed was the only real test of diplomacy. At the R.G.S. the Chairman cleared the hall with a staggering piece of eyewash. Misapprehension, he believed, was all that kept nations apart; with men like Rawlinson so devoted to dispelling it, all would be well. The sheepskin of non-aggression, it seemed, could be draped over the most 'forward' of policies.

Nothing more was heard of Hayward or Shaw during the 1868–9 session and, when the Society went into recess in July, there were high hopes that the former might already be on the Pamirs. It was known that Shaw, at least, had been well received in Yarkand, and the fact that neither traveller had returned before the passes were closed by the snows of winter was a good sign. Compared to Dr. Livingstone, who had been missing since 1866, there was certainly no cause for alarm.

On November 8, 1869 the Society reassembled. It was another crowded meeting; even a native of Yarkand in flowing *choga* and turban, who was proudly presented to the Fellows by Dr. Leitner, failed to distract them from a rapt hearing of the President's address. The news on all counts was gratifying. Letters had arrived from Livingstone; a young man with the unlikely name of Ney Elias had just explored the changing course of the Yellow River in China; and Hayward, having returned safely from Sinkiang to British India, was about to try yet a third approach to the Pamirs. As the President put it, it seemed that all the objects which most exercised the Society's thoughts in the previous session were 'in the way of being satisfactorily carried out'.

Unfortunately he was wrong; this euphoria would be shortlived. Livingstone was soon lost again and would remain so until the famous meeting with Stanley. Elias' journey along the Yellow River would soon be eclipsed by his marathon across Asia and his travels in the Pamirs; it would be he who eventually realised Hayward's dreams. And as for Hayward himself, his new plan would soon be regarded as a decisive and fatal step.

A month later, in January 1870, Hayward's paper on the journey to Yarkand and Kashgar was read to the Society. He and Shaw, who read his own paper on the journey a few weeks later, were anxious to go down as the men who had opened up this new corner of Central Asia. Having staked everything on such a hazardous venture they could hardly be expected to underplay the significance of their discoveries. They thus went out of their way to emphasise the prosperity of the country, the ease of the routes they had followed to get there and the commercial encouragement afforded at the other end. Sinkiang, or Eastern Turkestan as it was then called, had recently broken away from the Chinese empire; both men suggested that under the firm rule of Yakub Beg it would continue as a stable and independent Muslim state of crucial importance in the power struggle between Russia and British India. The fact that they had both been held prisoner during the whole of their stay, that they had at times despaired of ever returning alive, that they had seen virtually nothing of the country and that they had suffered the most appalling hardships on the journey, was glossed over. In this respect Hayward was slightly less guilty than Shaw, but the gist of his paper was enough to send the Fellows into eulogies of congratulation. It was 'a communication of the very highest order of merit', beyond the President's wildest expectations and deserved 'the highest honour we can bestow on him'.

Hayward's geographical work during this journey had been largely confined to excursions amongst the Karakorams and Kun Lun; the production of a compass in Sinkiang would have been asking for trouble and, as for continuing on to the Pamirs, this had proved quite out of the question; when he had tried to break out of captivity in Yarkand the whole city had been ringed by troops before he reached the gate. However, that was not the point. The Fellows of the R.G.S. were now told that the Pamirs had been only one of his objectives and that the cities of Eastern Turkestan had been the other; Hayward, though he had failed on one count, had therefore succeeded brilliantly on the other, and sure enough he was awarded the Society's highest honour, the Founder's Gold Medal. His work on the hydrography of the Kun Lun was also valuable and he had displayed extraordinary stamina and determination; but this award was equally in recognition of the political and commercial importance that attached to the journey. Rawlinson, accepting the award on his behalf, was at last willing to declare himself; Eastern Turkestan and the Pamirs were of interest, he had told Hayward, 'not only geographically but commercially and politically'. The way was now open for British trade and diplomacy to compete with that of Russia in at least one of the vital areas that separated the two empires; in fact the first official British mission to Yarkand was already fitting out.

Rawlinson was also delighted that his protégé, far from being satisfied with his success—or, as Hayward saw it, discouraged by his failure—was already blazing yet another trail with the idea of 'bagging the Bam-i-Dunya' (i.e. the Roof of the World, the Pamirs). The new undertaking was 'still more hazardous' than the last but Hayward was now a giant among explorers. 'If any Englishman can reach the Pamir steppe,* and settle the geography of that mysterious region, the primeval paradise of the Aryan nations, Mr. Hayward is the man.' He had shown the necessary 'tact, temper and diplomatic skill [and now] that same indomitable will, the same fertility of expedient, the same disregard of dangers and hardships, the same iron constitution and bodily activity . . . will stand him in good stead in his present and still more hazardous undertaking'.

Many would soon be questioning Hayward's tact, temper and diplomatic skill, but of his bulldozing determination and iron physique there can be no doubt. Anything less and he would not now have been contemplating a further approach to the Pamirs which would, in effect, combine all the mountain rigours of the road to Yarkand with the lawlessness of the Chitral route. In a letter to the Society dated Srinagar, November 17, 1869, he outlined his plan.

I am leaving here for Gilgit tomorrow in the hope of being able to penetrate the Pamir steppe and the sources of the Oxus from that frontier. . . . The officials here maintain the risk to be great and give a very bad character to the tribes inhabiting the head of the Gilgit and Yasin valleys. Although not so fanatical as the Mohammedans further west they are sufficiently untrustworthy to render success very doubtful and it is quite possible that I may be a second time foiled in my attempt to penetrate to the Pamir. The danger is certainly great. . . . whether I shall be

---

* The Pamirs were still erroneously described as a steppe or plateau. See chapter 9.

able to cross the passes at the head of Gilgit before the spring
of next year is doubtful.

For Hayward, who was usually incapable of recognising danger, let
alone dwelling on it, this was an ominous letter. A hastily added
postscript gave even greater cause for alarm. In the letter he had
only praise for the co-operation and advice of the Kashmir authorities. Now, presumably in the space of a few hours, matters had
changed; he begins to sound much like Leitner. 'The Kashmir
government is trying to dissuade me from going via Gilgit not
wishing an Englishman to see the exact state of that frontier . . .
and I feel certain that every obstacle will be thrown in the way of
proceeding beyond the Gilgit frontier.' Dards from Hunza had
recently been mutilated and killed by Kashmir troops; reprisals
seemed certain. It was as if the situation was being stirred up
simply to bar his progress, and in such a climate it was impossible
to say how an Englishman would be received in Dardistan. 'However I shall make the attempt; and if not allowed to go, or to enter
from Gilgit, it will be a satisfaction to have tried one's best . . . I
believe I shall eventually succeed in the object of my labours but
it may take months, nay, years, to do so'.

This letter was read at a meeting of the Society in January 1870.
In the ensuing months there came more letters from Hayward
and from the Government of India, which gave further cause for
alarm. But the Council of the Society kept them quiet and nothing
more was made public, even to the Fellows. Hayward seemed bent
on compromising the supposedly scientific character of his expedition, and the council, though most unwilling to wash their hands of
him—they had actually just voted him another £300—deemed it
wise to minimise their involvement. When in July the Society
went into recess, all hopes once again rested on their indefatigable
explorer pulling something out of the fire by the time they
assembled in November.

In the event they didn't have to wait that long. First to hear the
news would have been Rawlinson in his capacity as a member of
the India Council. On September 9 the Secretary of State for
India got a telegram from Lord Mayo, the new Viceroy. There
were rumours in Kashmir that an Englishman had been murdered
in Dardistan; if true, it must be Hayward. By the end of the month

the news was confirmed and already Mayo sensed that this was no simple case of misadventure; there were some 'very queer stories afloat' that needed careful sifting. On October 3 the news was made public in a telegram published in *The Times*. The matter was 'yet very dark' but the foul deed had taken place somewhere beyond Yasin and the motive was said to have been robbery. Further reports during October and early November suggested that Mir Wali, the ruler of Yasin, was behind 'this saddest event', but when the Fellows of the Society reassembled the air was still thick with conjecture; they wanted to know the full circumstances. Nowhere was an Englishman's life supposed to be more sacred than in India. So how could such a thing have happened? What was the government doing about it and what of the persistent rumours that its feudatory, the Maharaja of Kashmir, was somehow involved? What had Hayward been up to during the full year that had elapsed since last they had been given any news of him and was it true that the Society was in some way compromised by the whole affair? It would be wrong to call it an angry meeting; the Fellows hadn't enough to go on. But they were distinctly uneasy and they looked to the President and to Rawlinson for a full explanation.

Meetings of the Royal Geographical Society in the 1860s and 1870s were major scientific and social occasions. An equivalent today would have to combine the tension of a vital press conference with the decorum of a royal premiere. Before the meeting, up to a hundred of the senior Fellows dined together and entertained the principal speaker and guests; the Prince of Wales, the King of the Belgians, the King of Sweden and the Emperor of Brazil all figured on the guest list during this period. Meanwhile the conference hall filled to capacity and beyond; police had to move in and prevent the crowd from rushing those places set aside for the Council of the Society. The Fellows wore evening dress and, in the absence of lantern slides, were provided with programmes which included relevant maps. Facing the terraces of stiff white shirt fronts, bristling whiskers and waving papers, was a long table at which sat the main dignitaries. A lectern for the speaker was on one side and on the other, under the steely eye of the steward and only just inside the door, was another lower table for the gentlemen of the press.

On November 15, 1870, it was Sir Roderick Murchison, the

President, who opened proceedings. He confirmed the tragedy and gave just the bare facts. Hayward had indeed been murdered, the motive was said to be robbery and the instigator Mir Wali, chief of Yasin. It was an appalling loss to geography but he was thankful that the deceased had known of his having been awarded the gold medal; in fact the award had been made so promptly, while Hayward was still in the field, because the Council had realised that he might easily lose his life.

Rawlinson was more forthcoming. He recalled that the last time he had addressed the Fellows about Hayward had been when he received the medal on the latter's behalf. Hayward was then setting out, 'a young man in the full vigour of manhood, proud of his past honours, full of high hopes for the future, starting on the daring enterprise to explore the Pamir steppe, resolved to achieve success and with every prospect of success before him'. This last statement didn't quite square with what Murchison had just said about the Council rushing to confer the medal because they half expected Hayward to come to grief. But this is carping; Rawlinson was in full flight. 'Now all is changed. Mr. Hayward lies cold in death; not on the battlefield, not in Christian or hallowed soil, but under a heap of stones on a bleak hillside near the crests of the Indian Caucasus,* the victim of a barbarous, cold-blooded murder.' It was hard to speak coolly on the subject. Hayward may have been indifferent to his personal safety; it was one of his qualifications as an explorer and, if it was a fault, it was one for which he had paid dearly. But what of his murderer? Rawlinson quoted one of the Calcutta papers with profound approval.

We have more to hear yet of this Mir Wali—Scoundrel!—more to hear yet of how poor Mr. Hayward died. The latter is certain enough gone to the great silence, and gone with his foot to the last on the path of duty. Such a death breeds heroes but such a murder should bring down penalties on the head of the murderer. We hope the Government will now do its duty as Mr. Hayward did his.

* 'The Indian Caucasus' was a general term applied to the whole mountain complex of the Himalayas including the Great Himalaya, Pir Panjal, Hindu Kush, Karakorams and Kun Lun.

More would indeed be heard of how poor Mr. Hayward died. Rawlinson set the ball rolling by giving a review of all the existing evidence. There were also the letters from Hayward written during the last year which were now made public. A few weeks later there came the report of a British subject, sent to investigate the murder, which afforded the Society opportunity for another long discussion of the affair. Later still at least two other accounts of the murder, supposedly based on eye-witness reports, came to light. And finally there was a long official correspondence dealing with both the motives for the crime and the attempts to bring the supposed murderer to justice.

Using all these it is possible to piece together a reasonably accurate account of events leading up to the crime and of its aftermath. It is hard to do so without hindsight making the whole tragedy appear inevitable but for once this involves no distortion of the facts. If ever a crime appeared all but inevitable it was the murder of George Hayward. Before he set off on his last journey he himself knew it and, in spite of those 'high hopes of success', Rawlinson knew it. Danger threatened from every conceivable quarter. The question was who, in the end, would actually be responsible for the crime and how it would be arranged. Oddly it is precisely these two points that have never been satisfactorily settled.

4. At Eight or Nine in the Morning

"It is just before dawn in the valley of Darkot. Not far from a grove of pollard willows stands a single tent. In this tent sits a solitary weary man; by his side on the table at which he is writing lie a rifle and a pistol loaded. He has been warned by one whose word he cannot doubt that Mir Wali is seeking his life that night, and he knows that from those dark trees men are eagerly watching for a moment of unwariness on his part to rush forward across that patch of light-illumined ground and seize him. All night he has been writing to keep himself from sleep, which he knows would be fatal; but as the first rays of dawn appear over the eternal snows, exhausted nature gives way and his eyes close and his head sinks—only for a moment, but in that moment his ever watchful and crafty enemies rush forward, and before he can seize his weapons and defend himself he is a prisoner and dragged forth to death."

'Ye have robbed', said he, 'ye have slaughtered and made an end.
  Take your ill-got plunder, and bury the dead:
What will ye more of your guest and sometime friend?'
  'Blood for our blood', they said.

"He makes one request—it is to be allowed to ascend a low mound and take one last glance at the earth and sky he will never look upon again. His prayer is granted; he is unbound and, in the words of our informant, as he stands up there, 'tall against the morning sky, with the rising sun lighting up his fair hair as a glory, he is beautiful to look upon'. He glances at the sky, at those lofty, snow-clad peaks and mighty glaciers reaching down into the very valley itself with its straggling hamlets half hidden among the willow groves, whence rises the smoke of newly kindled fires, he hears the noise of happy children, and then with a firm step he comes down, back to his savage foes and calmly says: 'I am ready'."

56

And now it was dawn. He rose strong on his feet,
    And strode to his ruined camp below the wood;
He drank the breath of the morning cool and sweet;
    His murderers round him stood.

"He is instantly cut down by one of Mir Wali's men, and as he
falls he receives the death stroke from the sword of his treacherous friend, whose honoured guest he had so lately been."

Light on the Laspur hills was broadening fast,
    The blood-red snow-peaks chilled to a dazzling white:
He turned, and saw the golden circle at last,
    Cut by the Eastern height.

'O glorious Life, Who dwellest in earth and sun,
    I have lived, I praise and adore thee.'
                          A sword swept.
Over the pass the voices one by one
    Faded, and the hill slept.

The verses above come from Sir Henry Newbolt's *He Fell
Among Thieves*; they are inserted into the actual account of
Hayward's death, on which the poem was based. This account
was collected from one who claimed to be a witness of the
event by Col. R. G. Woodthorpe in 1885.* With the suggestion
of an almost divine transfiguration it represents the apotheosis of
the Hayward legend, if not of the man himself. Such Victorian
romanticising invites the historian's contempt and there is no
doubt that Woodthorpe, or his informant, indulged in as much
poetic license as Newbolt. It is, for instance, quite certain that
Mir Wali, 'the treacherous friend whose honoured guest he had so
lately been', did not deliver the death blow; he was not even
present.

On the other hand there is interesting corroboration in earlier
reports of many of the circumstances as here given. By all accounts
Hayward knew in advance that trouble was brewing, he sat up
through the night with a loaded pistol in one hand and a rifle
across the table. It was only when he finally nodded off that he

* It was published in *The Gilgit Mission 1885–6* by W. S. A. Lockhart
and R. G. Woodthorpe, London, 1889.

was overpowered. To judge from an account gathered by Dr. Joshua Duke, who was in Gilgit five years before Woodthorpe, there was also substance in the story of his climbing the hill for a last look at the mountains. 'He went up, knelt down, faced the rising sun and prayed'. Then he returned, resigned and serene, to his execution. Duke was told that his murderers were so impressed by his cool behaviour that, if only he had spent a little longer over his prayers, they would probably have taken fright.

The long vigil and the prayer on the hill are moving enough, but to anyone who has seen the sun rise on a mountain wilderness, more impressive by far is the notion of a brutal and bloody murder being perpetrated in that bright, disarming light. Hayward knew about killing. His taste for exploration had developed from a love of hunting. Bagging the Marco Polo sheep of the Pamirs was as important to him as bagging the Pamirs themselves. In fact his place of execution was within sight of *nullahs* (side valleys) up which he had earlier stalked. He knew how, tired and hungry at the end of the day, the sportsman was inclined to let fly at anything that moved, caring little if he frightened other unseen game. And he knew that at dawn, for the first shot of the day, it was a very different matter. Then the hunter stalks with infinite patience, checks his rifle, carefully selects his shot and aims with cold precision. Killing by the light of the rising sun is a clinical business; it is the hour for the hangman's rope. Even a Dard at such a time would need good reason to sever a stranger's head.

Amidst all the uncertainties about Hayward's death one thing is clear; it was as deliberately planned as it was ruthlessly executed. The desolate site surrounded by trees was well chosen; the success of the attack was the reward of vigilance and co-ordination; and the slaughter of Hayward's servants was surely an effort to remove all who might shed light on what lay behind the crime. As he knelt to pray, Hayward himself probably had little idea about how the attack had been engineered. But as to who might be responsible he had no doubts. Before leaving Srinagar he had made it perfectly plain that, if anything did happen to him, the man to arraign was the Maharaja of Kashmir; so far as is known nothing had subsequently occurred to make him change his mind.

For what lay behind this accusation we must retrace the events of the last year of his life. It was in November 1869 that he had written from Srinagar that letter about an imminent departure for Gilgit. Having added the ominous postscript about the attitude of the Kashmir government, he had set off. The passes over the Hindu Kush beyond Gilgit were an unknown quantity, but he had only to study conditions on the Great Himalaya passes on the Kashmir side of Gilgit to realise that the season was much too far advanced. The Kamri pass is normally closed by November 15th and sure enough this was the case in 1869; in Gilgit the long isolated winter had already begun. Hayward thought otherwise. No man in the days before mountaineering ever took more chances with the Himalayas. On the journey to Yarkand he had slept with neither tent nor fire in fifty degrees of frost. He had been saved from starvation by eating, raw, his only yak, and over the worst terrain in the world he had still managed thirty miles a day.

What horrors this winter trek to Gilgit may have held he never revealed. But the journey which usually took ten to twenty days now lasted two months. He described a massive arc, crossing the Great Himalaya by the Zoji La, following the course taken by Cowie's bloated corpse down the Dras river to the Indus, and then hugging the base of Dobani along the Indus to its junction with the Gilgit river. The total distance would be about three hundred miles and the last quarter, scrambling over spurs of the Karakorams above the cliffs on the right side of the river, had never before been attempted by a European.

In Gilgit he was expected. The Kashmir garrison had been warned of his plans and duly did their best to frustrate them. To reach Yasin or Hunza meant crossing not simply a frontier but a line of battle. The Gilgit authorities had no more wish to help him befriend their foes than the Dards had to welcome a man travelling under Kashmir's auspices. 'And in this has lain the great difficulty', wrote Hayward, 'to go through either hostile camp as it were, and still keep friends with both.'

Leitner had emphasised the distinctive languages and racial origins of the Dards; these were reasons enough for their detestation of the Kashmiri newcomers. Hayward, rightly, explained this hatred on religious grounds. The Kashmir troops were known as Dogras, that is members of the martial Rajput caste to which the Maharaja himself belonged. In practice many of the Gilgit garrison were Sikhs; but, whether Sikhs or Dogras, they were

Hindus and so was their Maharaja. The Dards, on the other hand, were Muslims to a man. To them the notion of living at peace with 'the cow-worshippers' in Gilgit was anathema. Every war was something of a *jehad*, every fallen Dard became a martyr and every defeat meant defilement. When a Dogra force pushed its way into a Dard valley no holds were barred. On both sides perfidy and atrocities were the order of the day.

For a whole month Hayward patiently tried to negotiate with the Dard chiefs. Presents and reassuring letters were laboriously smuggled into the neighbouring valleys. They were received with silent suspicion or answered with evasive excuses. The only concrete fact to emerge was confirmation that the Hindu Kush passes between Dardistan and the Oxus were, anyway, closed. They would, it was said, remain so at least until June. Hayward as usual was undismayed. Gilgit had seemed impossible yet he had made it. He had found a way through the Great Himalaya and would do the same with the Hindu Kush if given a chance.

At last, in mid-February, there came an encouraging answer; it was from Mir Wali, the ruler of Yasin. This man was one of three brothers each of whom at one time ruled Yasin. The oldest, Mulk Aman, had already been dispossessed by Mir Wali and had now thrown in his lot with the Kashmiris; the youngest, Pahlwan, at the time governor of the northern part of Chitral, would soon succeed Mir Wali. Their father had been generally acknowledged as the most bloodthirsty of all the Dard chiefs and had twice driven the Kashmir Dogras out of Gilgit. But it was Aman-ul-Mulk, the chief of Chitral and uncle of the three brothers (and also the father-in-law of Mir Wali), who now exercised the strongest influence in the area and largely dictated the turbulent careers of the three brothers.

A prodigious memory and a taste for algebra are needed to sort out the complex equations by which the ruling families of Dardistan were related; even a three-dimensional family tree would scarcely do them justice. But, in a land where dynasties rarely lasted longer than a reign and where succession was as much a matter of might as right, it will be helpful to bear in mind the three brothers who each coveted Yasin and, behind them, the cunning genius and pre-eminent authority of Aman-ul-Mulk, ruler of Chitral. All of them were to become deeply involved in the Hayward tragedy.

Though well primed on the treacherous character of all these chiefs, Hayward left Kashmir territory confident of a good reception from Mir Wali. All along he had felt that if only he could make the acquaintance of one of the Dard chiefs he would be able to allay all suspicions. In the event it seemed that, if anything, he had been too cautious. 'The courtesy and bearing of the chief was quite beyond what I expected to meet with in Yaghistan.' He found not just a co-operative raja but a real friend. Together they stalked the markhor and ibex, tested the various passes leading out of the valley, and discussed the routes beyond. The passes were all closed, so choked with snow that even Hayward had to accept the fact. But he was not discouraged. For one thing it appeared that all existing maps had the relative positions of the Chitral, Yasin and Oxus valleys wrong; the passes leading north from Yasin debouched on the Oxus itself and there was no need, as he had imagined, to trespass into Chitral and the perilous clutches of Aman-ul-Mulk; nor, on the other hand, into the Sarikol region which had just been subdued by his old adversary, Yakub Beg of Kashgar. Furthermore, Mir Wali seemed happy to assist his progress. He agreed to help with porters and supplies, and offered an armed guard to see the traveller safely across the mountains and over the Oxus. Hayward was delighted and fearing to overstay his welcome or in any way to prejudice these excellent arrangements, he returned to Gilgit to await the warmer weather.

'And did Hayward', it would soon be asked, 'give nothing in return for this attention from such a known avaricious man as Mir Wali?' He certainly gave a few presents, but of far more substance was an undertaking he made to represent Mir Wali's grievances against the Kashmir Dogras to the Government of India. Hayward, like Leitner, knew of the terms of the Treaty of Amritsar; he, too, interpreted it as outlawing the Maharaja's claims to Gilgit or anywhere else west of the Indus. On the other hand, through their father, the Yasin brothers had themselves a claim to Gilgit and it was this that Hayward agreed to urge on Lord Mayo's attention. It was a foolish move, but he had the sense to warn Mir Wali that he was not a government agent and that there was little chance of success.

He was right. Lord Mayo had no intention of antagonising the

Maharaja of Kashmir when the only gain would be the doubtful
gratitude of some remote and faithless Dards and the encouragement of a meddlesome explorer. Hayward, however, had two other
tricks up his sleeve, and to reveal them personally to the Viceroy
he now took another lunatic risk; he tackled the direct route from
Gilgit to Kashmir some six weeks before it was normally open. At
Astor he waited for the weather to clear and then took a headlong
rush at the Great Himalaya. Horses and baggage had been left in
Gilgit. For three dazzling days and tentless nights he waded through
fifty miles of waist deep snow. And again he survived; the weather
held and by late April, suffering from nothing worse than
temporary snow-blindness, he caught up with the Viceroy in the
Punjab.

Both the revelations he had to make concerned the behaviour of
the Kashmir forces in Dardistan. The first was the evidence he
had seen with his own eyes of a massacre of genocide proportions
perpetrated by the Dogras on the Dards of Yasin. It had happened
seven years before but it was conclusive proof that the punitive
raids of its feudatory exceeded in both severity and territorial reach
anything that could reasonably be countenanced by the British
Indian Government. His second point was that he himself had
almost been the pretext for yet another Dogra attack on Yasin.
On the trumped-up excuse that he had been robbed by the Yasinis,
Dogra reinforcements had been summoned to Gilgit and were
about to march on Yasin when he made his unexpected return. Had
he not turned up in the nick of time the Dogras would have
advanced, Mir Wali would have held him responsible and the
Pamir expedition, not to mention its leader, would have been
doomed. Which in Hayward's view, had been the purpose of
the whole exercise.

Mayo listened without enthusiasm; but three days later when
he met the Maharaja at Sialkot he had Hayward's written report in
his pocket. Right up till the last minute he seems to have been in
two minds about taking the Maharaja to task. But he didn't.
A man of great charm and with all Rawlinson could wish for in
the way of 'forward' thinking, Mayo, like Rawlinson, was firmly
wedded to the idea of winning Kashmir's co-operation for the
extension of British influence in Sinkiang; he too was concerned
more with the great issues of Anglo-Russian rivalry than with the

squabbles of Dard and Dogra. Moreover to have levelled Hayward's accusations would have been prejudicial not only to his own negotiations but also to Hayward himself; if the Maharaja guessed their source Hayward's game would be up. Nothing therefore was said beyond a friendly warning to the Maharaja not to lean too hard on his neighbours.

And there the matter should have ended; except that a week later, on May 9, *The Pioneer* newspaper unexpectedly came out with two and a half columns of packed print on the Yasin atrocities; Hayward's name was at the bottom. It was explosive stuff. In 1863 on the promise of a safe conduct, the beleaguered Yasinis, according to Hayward, had laid down their arms. The Dogras then corralled the women and children into the fort.

They threw the little ones in the air and cut them in two as they fell. It is said the pregnant women, after being killed, were ripped open and their unborn babes hacked to pieces. Some forty wounded women who were not yet dead were dragged to one spot, and were there burnt by the Dogra sepoys. With the exception of a few wounded men and women who ultimately recovered, every man, woman and child within the fort, and, in all, 1200 to 1400 of these unhappy villagers, were massacred by the foulest treachery and cruelty. After plundering the place Yasin was burnt and all the cattle carried off, together with some 2,000 women and men . . . most of the women are still in the zenanas of the Dogra leaders and sepoys. I have visited Madoori, the scene of the massacre, and words would be inadequate to describe the touching sight to be witnessed on this now solitary and desolate hill side. After the lapse of seven years since the tragedy, I have myself counted 147 still entire skulls, nearly all those of women and children. The ground is literally white with bleached human bones and the remains of not less than 400 human beings are now lying on this hill. The Yasin villagers returned to bury their dead after the Dogras retired, and the skulls and bones now found at Madoori are presumably only those of villagers whose whole families perished in the massacre. . . . I have written all this in the hope that the Indian public may be made aware of what our feudatory the Maharaja of Kashmir has perpetrated across the Indus. Apart from the infringement of any treaty, and putting all political motives aside, I trust that every Englishman and Englishwoman in India will join in demanding justice upon the murderers of innocent women and children. . . . The English public must not think that these innocent women were 'niggers' as they might choose to term them. They were descended from the ancestors of the true Aryan stock and had eyes and tresses of the same hue as those of their own wives and children.

The letter went on to argue that the only way to prevent a repeat of the tragedy was to insist on the withdrawal of the Dogras to their legal frontier, the Indus. Mir Wali, 'its rightful owner', should then be installed in Gilgit and a fully fledged British resident stationed in Kashmir as a further check on the Maharaja. Russian agents, it claimed, were already being welcomed in Srinagar, and Kashmiri agents, travelling by way of Gilgit and Dardistan, were intriguing in Central Asia. On the grounds of imperial defence, as well as of humanitarianism, the Maharaja's wings must be ruthlessly clipped.

Although written whilst he was in Dardistan, Hayward seems to have brought this letter back to India himself. Presumably it was therefore after his meeting with Mayo, and probably after the Sialkot conference, that he released it to the press. Publish and be damned, he must have thought; it was the blind impulse of a man who cared nothing for the consequences. Two days later, unrepentant, he was still standing firmly by it. In fact it was almost two weeks before he began to have second thoughts. 'Most unfortunate', he then told Rawlinson, was the publication of the letter; it was 'likely to interfere very much with the objects I have in view'—a classic understatement—whilst the resentment aroused amongst the Maharaja's officials was 'very great and it cannot be doubted that they will in every way *secretly* [his italics] strive to do me harm'. He also claimed that the editor of *The Pioneer* had run the story in opposition to his instructions. Certainly he had asked that his name be kept out of it, but there is no evidence of his trying to stop publication. On the contrary, the day before it appeared he was writing to a friend that he wanted not just the Indian press but the British public at home to know all about it.

And no doubt public opinion was incensed over the report. But

so too was Lord Mayo at the man who had so sneakily under-
mined his whole policy of soothing Kashmir. Publication of the
letter he described as 'a simply wicked thing'. He had tried before
to dissuade Hayward from returning to Dardistan; now he
telegraphed to London to get the Royal Geographical Society to
forbid it. He argued that Hayward's life was in real danger as a
result of his indiscretion and, though his death would not greatly
upset the Viceroy, the fact that, by it, the Maharaja was likely to
be further compromised, would.

This put Rawlinson in a difficult position. Hayward was his
protégé and the Pamir expedition was as important as ever; Sir
Roderick Murchison had just brought all his influence to bear
to get the Tsar to give Hayward a safe conduct through Russia
should he decide to return that way. But Rawlinson also agreed
with Mayo; the friendship of Kashmir was crucial to British interests. He must have been furious that Hayward had presumed
to discredit this vital British feudatory. The idea of forcing the
government's hand had completely misfired; if the goodwill of
the Dards, or any other frontier people, could only be won at the
price of Kashmir, it was definitely not worth it.

But how could he stop Hayward? The man was not an agent of
the Society; the journey, he now conceded, had been undertaken
on Hayward's initiative and at his own risk. There were no
strings attached to the grants he had received and, if the Society
should attempt to recall him, he was quite at liberty to disregard
it. Which was precisely the point Hayward now made. He
offered to sever all connection with the Society but made it quite
plain that he would continue as planned. Rawlinson, powerless to
interfere, therefore let the matter rest. On June 10 Mayo fired off
his final warning at Hayward—'If you still resolve on prosecuting
your journey it must be clearly understood that you do so on your
own responsibility'—and a few days later Hayward set off from
Srinagar for the last time.

He still clung to the belief that, once out of Kashmir territory
and back with Mir Wali in Yasin, all would be well. But, better
than any of those who warned of the dangers, he himself must
have realised that his position was desperate. While the Kashmir
authorities fumed over the *Pioneer* article, he had actually been in
Srinagar at their mercy. Well-wishers advised him to return to

British administered territory fast. His camp was full of alarming rumours, his servants refused to accompany him because they feared foul play and Hayward himself was convinced that attempts were being made to poison him. A prostitute was apparently hired to administer the fatal dose, 'but somehow that fell through'. Outwardly the Kashmir authorities were friendly enough. In moments of optimism he interpreted this as evidence that his disclosures had put them on the spot and that, for fear of the obvious conclusions being drawn, they would not now move against him. At other times he was close to despair. Of course they would not openly or obviously waylay him. No native court enjoyed a higher reputation for intrigue and cunning; if he was to die, the one thing that was certain was that the Kashmir authorities would not appear to be responsible. In fact this outward friendliness was far more suspicious than their earlier prevarication.

Such being the case he must still have been uneasy when he reached Gilgit without mishap. But when he was allowed to proceed to Yasin and duly crossed the frontier he must have scarcely dared to acknowledge his good fortune. Sadly no records of this journey survive, but when he wrote his last note from Gilgit on July 5 there was nothing untoward to report. He seems to have left there about the 9th, reached Yasin about the 13th and Darkot at the head of the valley on the 17th. Early on the morning of the 18th, the day he expected to cross the watershed into the Oxus valley and the Pamirs, he was murdered. So too were his four servants and his *munshi*.

If bravery is obstinate, reckless, selfish and, for all that, still somehow admirable, then there died that morning a very brave man. Hayward knew the risk he was taking and he faced it with relish. But in a sense he had no choice. To have abandoned the enterprise would have been to accept that his exploring days were over; after the *Pioneer* episode no one was going to let him loose on the unknown again. It must also be suggested that to Hayward danger was attractive. He courted death as the one supreme situation left against which to test his mettle. Earlier he had written in bitter jest of 'my insane desire to try the effect of cold steel across my throat' and of the likelihood that he would 'finally be sold into slavery by the Moolk-i-Aman or Khan of Chitral'. Now, there was precious little of jest in such prognostications. The driving urge to bag the Bam-i-Dunya had become suicidal. He was beyond recall before he died.

* * *

News of the murder reached Gilgit in early August and India by the end of the month. While the government tried unsuccessfully to suppress it, secret agents of varying degrees of competence were infiltrated all along the frontier. At listening posts from Peshawar to Ladakh, Commissioners collected every available report and forwarded them to the Lieutenant-Governor of the Punjab who in turn reported to the Foreign Secretary. Thus, for nearly a year, the news continued to trickle in. But if the government really expected the facts to emerge purely by the accumulation of evidence they were disappointed. Never, surely, can a crime of this sort have been the subject of so many conflicting reports. By spring 1871 almost every man of any influence in the Western Himalayas had been implicated; the official correspondence ran to several hundred sheets; allegations and counter-allegations were doing far more harm than the original crime; the suspects were clearly beyond the reach of justice; and the truth was more obscure than ever. Not surprisingly the government opted to close the case; they accepted an explanation which, if not exactly convincing, was at least politically convenient.

The news came by two main channels and these roughly corresponded with the two most likely explanations. One was Kashmir where the Maharaja's officials reported direct to the Lieutenant-Governor of the Punjab; the other was Chitral where Aman-ul-Mulk corresponded with the British Commissioner in Peshawar. At first these two sources showed remarkable unanimity. Mir Wali had ordered the murder off his own bat and his own men had actually committed it. Aman-ul-Mulk of Chitral had promptly disowned him and had despatched Pahlwan, nicknamed 'The Wrestler', the youngest of the three Yasin brothers, to take over the country. Mir Wali had fled to Badakshan. According to information supplied to Pahlwan by the Yasinis, the immediate cause of the trouble had been an argument between Hayward and Mir Wali about the supply of porters.

Even given that in Dardistan life was cheap, this last statement sounded peculiarly unconvincing—especially in view of the supposed friendship between the two men. But in all the subsequent reports, it was confirmed that there had been a quarrel; the question was whether or not it was pre-arranged.

The most thorough investigation was undoubtedly that conducted on the Maharaja's instructions by Frederick Drew, a geologist who was employed by the Maharaja to assess Kashmir's mineral deposits. He subsequently became Governor of Ladakh and later still returned to England to be a master at Eton College. It would have been better if he could have been a wholly independent investigator but his impartiality was well attested and he was at least an Englishman. He had even come to know Hayward personally. All this recommended him to the Maharaja; surely information from such a man would be sufficient for the Government of India. Drew also happened to be in Baltistan during that September of 1870 and could therefore make Gilgit at short notice. He arrived there about the end of the month.

By October 11 the first instalment of his report was ready. Based on evidence given by the Wazir, or Chief Minister, of Yasin it adduced four reasons for Mir Wali's change of heart; Hayward's failure to get the British to acknowledge his claim to Gilgit, Hayward's refusal to proceed first to Chitral as requested, the unreasonable demand for porters, and the fact that this time Hayward's presents were destined not for him but for the chiefs beyond Yasin. Hayward was said to have publicly slighted Mir Wali and then in a heated exchange to have called him 'by a hard name that he was likely to resent'. All in all there was cause enough for an unscrupulous brigand like the suspect to rob and murder. Drew had the poorest possible opinion of the Dards; the safety of a stranger in their hands would be more unaccountable than the murder of one. Mir Wali's friendship during the first visit could only be ascribed to his expectations of what Hayward might achieve in India and of what further presents he might bring back. Disappointed on both counts he reverted to character. Drew was among those who had warned Hayward not to proceed, and he was now inclined to take the line that Hayward had brought the whole thing on himself. The fellow had been amiable enough and quite frighteningly determined; but he was too hot-blooded and domineering for an explorer among such treacherous people.

He should have been sent to Australia or Africa, thought Drew, where 'a knowledge of human nature and a skill in dealing with various races of men' were not so vital.

Rather surprisingly, considering he was a servant of the Maharaja, Drew discountenanced the idea that Aman-ul-Mulk of Chitral, whom the Maharaja habitually regarded as the instigator of any Dard hostility, had anything to do with the crime. Rumours that Mir Wali sought the Chitrali's advice about Hayward had been rife for some time. It was said that Mir Wali was wholly under the influence of his uncle-cum-father-in-law and that the latter had demanded that Hayward be sent to Chitral. When Hayward refused to comply, Mir Wali was ordered to murder him. These rumours were greatly strengthened when it emerged that Mir Wali, after fleeing to Badakshan, had been permitted to recross the Hindu Kush and was now living in Chitral on the best terms with Aman-ul-Mulk. Was the whole business of Pahlwan's pursuit of the murderer and takeover of Yasin just an elaborate piece of window-dressing? It certainly looked that way when Aman-ul-Mulk first refused to surrender his guest and then, a year later, actually helped him to regain, briefly, the throne of Yasin. Drew, of course, was writing his report long before all these developments, but investigating the bare rumours at close quarters he failed to see how Mir Wali could possibly have consulted with his uncle over a hundred miles away during the few days which elapsed between his meeting with Hayward and the murder. Equally he knew that at the time, Aman-ul-Mulk had been trying to curry favour with the British authorities. This would explain the Chitrali's anxiety to see Hayward whom he regarded as a government agent. But murdering him made no sense at all.

One other observation of Drew's is worth of note. In Gilgit he learnt to his surprise that not only had Mir Wali fled but also the eldest of the Yasin brothers, Mulk Aman (not to be confused with Aman-ul-Mulk of Chitral). Mulk Aman had gone over to the Dogras some months before when he had been ousted from Yasin by Mir Wali. He had been living in Gilgit as a pensioner of the Maharaja awaiting the moment when his claim to Yasin might be put to advantage. Hayward had met him on his first visit—'an unscrupulous villain who had already murdered an uncle, a brother and the whole of that brother's family'—and so too had

Drew who reckoned him a determined fighter. That he too had now disappeared from Gilgit did not strike Drew as particularly sinister; he could see no connection between this and the Hayward business, and simply reported it as a matter of course.

Others, however, saw this piece of information in a very different light. So far the evidence examined has been mainly that presented by the Kashmir government. Against it must now be set the mounting pile of reports which, though from a variety of sources and often contradictory in substance, all evinced a profound distrust of Kashmir's role in the affair. Aman-ul-Mulk of Chitral provided some of the earliest reports of the crime, and in the second of these, which reached Peshawar as early as September 1st, he claimed that Mir Wali had acted on the instructions of Mulk Aman. Not much credence was given to this at the time—it was known that the uncle had no love for this particular nephew and that the two brothers, Mir Wali and Mulk Aman, were sworn enemies. Sir Henry Durand, the Lieutenant-Governor of the Punjab, merely asked the Maharaja to keep Mulk Aman under house arrest as a routine procedure.

It was assumed that this had been done and Durand was thus very surprised to discover, two months later, that Mulk Aman had in fact escaped. The news leaked out in a conversation with one of the Maharaja's officials. Almost immediately Drew's report holding Mir Wali solely responsible was given to Durand. The Kashmir government had been sitting on this for some weeks and now clearly felt it should be released to counteract any suspicions aroused by the escape of Mulk Aman. Luckily Durand was personally inclined towards the Maharaja's point of view. He had earlier in the year reassured the Kashmir authorities that no-one took much notice of Hayward's wild talk or placed much confidence in the *Pioneer*; never believe anything in India, went the popular adage, until you see it contradicted in the *Pioneer*. (Durand recommended the London *Times* and duly took the Maharaja's order for it.) He was thus inclined to accept Drew's report *in toto* and, though it was now clear that Mulk Aman had escaped at least a month before he got to hear of it, he also accepted the Maharaja's explanation of the affair.

There the matter rested and, with no indication of why or how Mulk Aman could have got involved in Hayward's doings, it might reasonably have been ignored, one of the many red herrings spawned in this extraordinary episode. But two weeks later, in mid-November, there came, from a totally unexpected quarter, further developments.

Following the visit of Hayward and Shaw to Sinkiang in 1868-9 a diplomatic mission had set out for Yarkand in 1870. It was led by Douglas Forsyth, a Punjab civil servant, and again included the ubiquitous Shaw. In all of its many guises as a trade commission, diplomatic feeler and scientific expedition the mission was a dismal failure. Brought to near disaster by the covert hostility of the Kashmiris and the unfathomed duplicity of the Yarkandis, the mission doggedly retraced its footsteps across the Kun Lun and Karakorams in the autumn. On October 2 Forsyth was nearing the end of the long leg across the dreary Aksai Chin plateau when he was met by a postal runner from Ladakh. Avidly he read the first news from India in months and from Mayo's private secretary learnt of the death of Hayward. Next day his party straggled down into the Changchenmo valley where a Kashmiri escort waited to conduct them into Leh. The escort confirmed the news of Hayward's murder and, in a private conversation between one of its officials and a Kashmiri member of the mission, dark deeds were hinted at. Late that night when the camp was asleep these two men crouched down over the dying embers of the fire. In whispered tones made doubly eerie by the empty silence of the bleak and inhospitable valley, one revealed to the other the blackest secret of the hour and next morning this confidence was duly betrayed to Forsyth.

The gist of the story was that the Maharaja of Kashmir had, as Hayward had always feared, been the instigator of his murder. Incensed by the *Pioneer* article, jealous of what he took to be British dealings with the Dards and anxious about the consequences if Hayward's journey was successful, it was he who had resolved to get rid of him. Instructions had been sent to his wily governor in Gilgit to arrange things in such a way that the Dogras would never be suspected. The governor had then enlisted Mulk Aman and for a fee of 10,000 rupees the latter had organised the murder. When the order subsequently came for Mulk Aman's arrest, the governor had duly warned him to flee and had escorted him into exile before reporting back that he had escaped. Drew's inquiry was instituted simply to assuage British curiosity; a trusted Kashmiri agent had been sent to Gilgit at the same time expressly to see that Drew never got near the truth.

Forsyth forwarded this account to the Punjab. Like almost every other traveller in the Western Himalayas he had the poorest opinion of the Kashmir authorities and held them responsible for all but annihilating his own expedition, a prejudice that was duly noted by Durand. But it was also clear that there was no possible way in which this story could have been fabricated by anyone on the mission. Facts like the escape of Mulk Aman, now backdated still further and thus confirming the suspicion that it had been wilfully concealed, could only have come from someone in the Kashmir government's confidence. It could still be a fabrication and Durand clearly thought so. He couldn't believe the Maharaja capable of 'so atrocious and cold-blooded a scheme of revenge'; the man was renowned, on the one hand for 'humanity and tenderness' and on the other for 'an acumen' which would have found the whole scheme far too risky.

However R. H. Davies, who succeeded Durand as Lieutenant-Governor of the Punjab when the latter died on January 31, was nothing like so sure. With spring and the opening of some of the mountain passes, there came news from Chitral that Aman-ul-Mulk now also believed the Maharaja responsible; he had it on the word of the Mir of Badakshan to whom Mir Wali had first fled. Davies made allowance for the inveterate hatred between Chitral and Kashmir but pointed out that there could be no possible collusion in the accusations levelled by Forsyth in Ladakh and those now coming from Chitral and Badakshan. While the Maharaja's credibility was in question from one end of the Himalayas to the other, little store could be set by his efforts to resolve the mystery.

By now, April 1871, it was eight months since the murder. All the main witnesses had been discredited, the scent had gone cold and there must have been few who could still follow the labyrinthine trails of evidence. To make quite sure that even they would bow out in confusion there now stepped onto the scene Dr. Dardistan himself, Gottlieb Leitner. With a truly mind-blowing deposition he virtually rung the curtain down on the whole affair. The same Yarkandi who had sat beside him at the R.G.S. when Rawlinson first rose to sing the praises of George Hayward had been supposed to accompany the Forsyth mission to Yarkand. However, he reached Leh too late and the British Joint Commissioner there had redirected him towards Yasin, probably with the idea of keeping an eye on Hayward and checking his story about the Dogra atrocities. Nine months later the Yarkandi re-emerged from the mountains and duly reported himself to Leitner's cosmopolitan compound in Lahore. Leitner had never met Hayward but he had commented favourably on the latter's attempts to make something of the Dard languages and he was of course in sympathy with the *Pioneer* article; he would reprint it in full in his next book. Already he was of the opinion that the Maharaja must be behind Hayward's murder; but the report of his Yarkandi was altogether more intriguing.

This man, on evidence given by Mir Wali's *munshi*, claimed that Aman-ul-Mulk, Mulk Aman, Mir Wali, Pahlwan, the Maharaja, the Governor of Gilgit, the Wazir of Yasin and, a new persona, the Wazir of Chitral, were all involved. Some had actually instigated the Darkot murder, others merely helped to conceal it, but since those not directly involved in the crime had organised another murder scenario just a few marches ahead, it made little difference who did what. The actual sequence of events is too tortuous to follow, but there was enough already established detail to suggest that here again was more than just wild invention. On the other hand was it possible that all the suspects, most of whom were sworn enemies, could possibly have acted together to conceal the facts? And could Hayward have marched blindly into not one murder plot but two? It stretched credibility beyond breaking point.

Holding up their hands in horror, the British authorities seem finally to have abandoned the case. Investigations came to be directed more towards discovering the whereabouts of Mir Wali. For four years he continued to flit back and forth across the Hindu Kush until run to earth by one of Pahlwan's henchmen. In a scene worthy of vintage Hollywood the two men met on a rocky precipice, locked in mortal combat and finally hurtled over the edge. Mulk Aman fared rather better. Finding sanctuary in Tangir, south of Gilgit, he continued to exercise a sinister influence in Dardistan and was still there fifteen years later, accused of attempting to snuff out another British initiative in the region.

It would be absurd at this remove to attempt a verdict on the
Hayward murder. The most one can do is to present all sides of
the case, particularly since no such objectivity was shown at the
time. The British had a vested interest in retaining the goodwill
of the Maharaja. It was therefore the Kashmiri version of events
and particularly the Drew report which were officially adopted.
Mir Wali was held to be the sole culprit and the motive robbery;
it was conveniently ignored that to rob a man it is not necessary
to kill him, even less to kill all his servants, or that the repercussions of such a murder would far outweigh the acquisition of
a few guns, stores and knick-knacks. Allegations against the
Maharaja were of course investigated, but under a blanket of
strict secrecy; anyone giving public utterance to them was severely
reprimanded. Anti-Kashmir prejudice was running high at the
time. Hayward's revelations about the Dogra atrocities had been
bad enough, but if the idea that the Maharaja was responsible for
his murder had gained any ground, the popular outcry for his removal and the annexation of his state might have been overwhelming. Witness Rawlinson's adamant denials to the R.G.S.
when Hayward's death was first confirmed. Murchison, the
President, had risen waving a piece of paper in the air. 'You have
entirely exonerated the Maharaja of Kashmir; but there are
persons, and I hold a letter in my hand from one, who still have
their doubts about it.' This was before Drew's report had been
made public and Rawlinson had only the flimsiest evidence to go
on. But he was positive; there was no foundation whatever for
inferring Kashmir complicity and no possible connection between
Hayward's indiscretion over the 'exaggerated' *Pioneer* article and
his murder.

One final question needs to be answered. Why was a British
officer not sent to investigate? It was said that the Maharaja had
himself suggested this and had only sent Drew when the offer was
refused. The reason given at the time was that it was too dangerous
an undertaking and that the co-operation necessary to make the
thing a success could not be counted on. But if, like Drew, the
man never ventured beyond Gilgit, there was surely no risk. And,
as to the lack of cooperation, a British officer would surely have
stood a better chance of getting at the truth from the Dards than
did Drew, an employee of the Maharaja. It is hard to resist the

conclusion that the government did not want an independent British-led enquiry. Perhaps they feared that in the process more Dogra misdealings on the frontier would be uncovered. Perhaps they knew that, for all his apparent willingness to co-operate, the Maharaja would deeply resent any such intervention. Or perhaps there was a real fear that such an enquiry might reveal a Kashmir involvement too embarrassing to contemplate.

There was yet one last journey for George Hayward. His

Hayward's grave as drawn by Drew

battered remains had somehow to be recovered and given a Christian burial. Pahlwan strongly opposed the idea of anyone visiting Darkot, but eventually a lone Dogra, deputed by Drew, was allowed to visit the scene of the crime. From one of several artificial piles of stones he noticed a pair of hands protruding. They were bound together, the palms turned upwards. 'I recognised them as those of the sahib not by the colour, for that was changed [it surely must have been; this was three weeks after the murder], but by their form. Clearing the stones away I saw by the hair and beard that this was indeed the sahib's body.' The extreme dryness of the Hindu Kush climate had kept it partially intact. Along with a few personal effects—pony, tent, books, the legs of

a table, a watch and sword—the corpse was carried down to
Gilgit. Drew himself read the burial service and, over the newly
dug earth in the corner of someone's orchard, a final salute was
fired by a party of Dogra soldiers.

Hayward must have turned uneasily in the sandy soil. Here was
irony run riot. To be buried by a servant of the government he
mistrusted above all others, to be saluted by its soldiers, and then
to be given a headstone* by its ruler was bad enough. But if
Rawlinson had had his way, worse would have followed. Exactly
two years after the murder, a Mrs. Fanny Fison addressed the
Government of India about getting some compensation for the
murder. She was an aunt of Hayward's, but her concern was for
his impoverished sister and family who lived in New Zealand.
Rawlinson conceded that they had no real claim on the government but he thought it a travesty that the murder was still un-
avenged; he suggested that the Kashmir government impose a
£500 fine on the Yasinis. If this was not paid—a fairly safe pre-
diction—it should be used as the pretext for a joint Anglo-
Kashmir subjugation of all the Dard peoples. What Hayward
would have regarded as a far worse crime than his own murder
was actually being urged in his name. Luckily nothing came of the
suggestion. The Hayward family received no compensation and the
Dards were left to carry on their fight for political survival.

Besides recovering Hayward's body, the Dogra soldier also
managed to get the first eye-witness account of the actual murder.
It came from the village headman and has no more claim to
authenticity than the later reports; the Dogra in question was soon
promoted by the Maharaja and the headman would certainly
have suppressed anything prejudicial to his local standing. Yet,
in its simple details and stark narrative, and in the headman's
anxiety to stick to his own field of observation without offering

---

*The epitaph read:
Sacred to the memory of Lieut. G. W. Hayward, Medallist of the Royal
Geographical Society of London, who was cruelly murdered at Darkot,
July 18th, 1870, on his journey to explore the Pamir steppe. This
monument is erected to a gallant officer and accomplished traveller
by His Highness the Maharaja of Kashmir at the instance of the Royal
Geographical Society of London.
The headstone was still standing in the 1960s but recent enquiries have
failed to discover its whereabouts.

any explanations or accusations, there is here a certain ring of truth.

That night the sahib did not eat any dinner, but only drank tea, and sat watching the whole night in his chair with guns and pistols before him and a pistol in his left hand while he wrote with the other. In the morning, after taking a cup of tea, he lay down for a hour or two's sleep. Shah Dil Iman, having sent a man to see, and found that he was sleeping, took his men by a round to the ground in the forest above where the tent was, and then himself coming asked the khansaman [cook] if he were asleep; on his being told that he was, Kukali entered the tent. One of the Pathan servants asked him what he was about, and took up a stick to stop him, but others coming round and keeping the Pathan back, Kukali went into the tent and caught the sahib by the throat, and, more at that moment coming in, put a noosed rope round his neck, and, with the same rope, tied his hands behind him. The servants were all overpowered and bound at the same time. Then they brought the sahib, thus bound, away from the village into the forest for a distance of a mile or mile and a half; and as they were going he tried to induce them to spare his life by promises, first of what was in his boxes—but that they jeeringly said was theirs already; then of a larger ransom to be obtained from the English country; and lastly, he said that he would write to the Bukshee [governor] at Gilgit for the money for them. This, however, they would not listen to. Then the sahib asked for his *munshi* to be brought, but he had been taken off in another direction, and could not quickly be found; then they took the ring off his finger, and then Shah Dil Iman drew his sword, on which the sahib repeated some words which seemed like a prayer, and Shah Dil Iman felled him with one blow. Then Kukali brought the sahib's own sword, and said he would like to try it; so he struck a blow with it on the sahib's body. It was eight or nine in the morning when the murder was committed.

PART TWO

Vidi

5. The Hunza Road

The explorers of the Western Himalayas include many unsung heroes. Although Hayward, and later Elias and Younghusband, enjoyed the recognition of the Royal Geographical Society, in the popular mind they never rivalled men like Stanley and Livingstone; they remained essentially explorer's explorers. As for the rest, they achieved not even that distinction. In an atmosphere as highly charged with political secrecy as the Gilgit Game, discretion came to be regarded as the would-be explorer's one vital attribute; not surprisingly many of the greatest pioneers thus remain the most obscure.

To make matters worse, this personal reticence is invariably coupled with a most abstemious approach to travel writing. Blow by blow accounts of the journey and graphic descriptions of the terrain are the exception rather than the rule. Where a personal journal exists, it often proves no more colourful than the official report. After all, if you may never write anything more entertaining than official reports, why bother? Younghusband, of course, would. To a commendable discretion he added a yen for popular recognition; somehow the world just had to share his excitement whenever the rising sun tipped the topmost peaks a flamingo pink. But the only way he could get away with this was by withholding so much about his actual movements that one sometimes knows neither where it is all happening nor why he is there.

More typical, both as an obscure explorer and a reluctant travel writer, is John Biddulph. By 1880 no man had seen as much of the Western Himalayas as Biddulph. Younghusband would scarcely equal his record and, in terms of the ground actually covered, he had outmarched even the indefatigable Hayward. In 1886 he had heard news of Leitner's and Cowie's fiasco at the Dras bridge while he was shooting wild yak on the uppermost Indus inside Tibet. In 1873 he had accompanied Forsyth on his second mission across the Karakorams to Sinkiang. From Kashgar he had followed the ancient caravan route to China further into the Takla Makan

desert than any predecessor since Marco Polo and the Jesuit, de
Goes. The following year he had made an excursion across the
Pamirs to Wakhan and inspected the northern face of the Hindu
Kush. And in Dardistan between 1876 and 1880 he would become
the first European to visit Hunza and the first into Chitral.

Altogether a remarkable record. But if one looks for his name in
the rolls of fame, one looks in vain. With the R.G.S. he made no
contact at all. Some of his journeys were certainly top secret, but
others could have easily been presented in such a way as not to give
offence; one at least was undertaken on his own initiative and purely
for the sport. The conclusion must be that here was a man who
cared little for the armchair geographers and their gold medals. A
certain irreverence is also detectable in his political work; and
again his praises remained unsung. He pinned his reputation on an
entirely new departure in British policy towards the Gilgit region;
he saw it through and he saw it fail. No knighthood, not even a
medal, came his way. And for the rest of his career he forswore all
interest in the mountains.

His only enduring contribution to the subject was a book, *The
Tribes of the Hindoo Koosh*. More organised than anything Leitner
wrote, it became the standard work. Earlier writers had dropped
tantalising hints about the strange Dards and their peculiar languages and customs. Here at last was a sober and authentic
account by a man who had apparently lived and travelled in the
Hindu Kush. It had to be a modest success and, with a bit of
imagination, could have been a sensation. As it is, the only remarkable thing is how anyone with Biddulph's experience could have
written such an austere account. Somewhere, surely, the traveller
must slip unconsciously into a bit of narrative or toy with an evocative description. If the pioneer on virgin soil in the most dramatic
terrain in the world takes no such liberties then who can? But no,
Biddulph sticks to facts, to vocabularies and genealogies. He is
writing a gazetteer, not a travelogue.

There is one brief but significant exception. Dealing with the
northern outlet from the Gilgit valley up the Hunza river, he
writes:

The river here flows between perpendicular rocks across the face
of which none but the most experienced cragsman can find a

6   The Hunza gorge

7   Near the crest of the Baroghil Pass

8   Approaching the Ishkoman Pass in Yasin

path. On the occasion of my visit to Hunza in 1876 I suddenly found myself confronted with a more difficult and dangerous piece of ground than I had ever traversed in a tolerably large experience of Himalayan sport.

The statement springs off the page. What can this piece of ground have been like, to stop such a one as Biddulph dead in his tracks and to interrupt the prosaic and impersonal rhythm of his scholarship?

For nearly half a mile it was necessary to scramble over rocky ledges, sometimes letting oneself down nearly to the water's edge, then ascending 300 or 400 feet above the stream, holding on by corners of rock, working along rocky shelves 3 or 4 inches wide, and round projecting knobs and corners where no four-footed animal less agile than a wild goat could find a path.

The book is almost bursting into narrative; another paragraph, in which there is a grandiloquent description of Rakaposhi, slips past before composure is regained and it can continue on its dogged path. In his confidential report to the government and in his personal diary Biddulph uses much the same words. Clearly it made a deeper impression than anything that Ladakh, the Karakorams or the Pamirs had to offer. But to anyone who has followed in his footsteps this will come as no surprise. Biddulph was just inaugurating a tradition among travellers that lasts to this day—that of straining every literary muscle in an effort to do justice to the Hunza road.

All the Hindu Kush valleys are far narrower at their mouths than higher up. The phenomenon was first remarked by Biddulph who marvelled how valleys that supported several thousand families were accessible only by the highest of passes at the top end and the narrowest of gorges at the bottom; it seemed to explain how the Dard tribes had individually remained so distinct. According to Leitner, the men of Hunza were the most distinctive of all and, seeing the gorge by which they maintain contact with the outside world, that would seem highly probable. If ever there was a crack in the mountains up which man was not supposed to travel, this surely is it. From Gilgit to Hunza is a distance of fifty-two miles.

GG—G

On a good day, travelling by jeep, it takes seven hours. Throughout, the track follows the course of the Hunza river. This river, charged with clearing the debris of glaciers, avalanches and landslides from the Karakorams on one side and the Hindu Kush on the other, is in spate for most of the year. An analysis of its liquid would probably reveal as much solid matter as water. Rocks the size of buses trundle along in the midst of the grey flood and, whenever the volume falls, a moraine is left to mark the floodline. There are no pools for fishermen, no falls for the photographer and no grassy banks for the picnicker, just this thundering discharge of mud and rock.

It is a revolting sight, though one glimpsed only rarely. For throughout the journey up to Hunza the track runs not beside but above and over the river. At fifty feet up one can feel the rush of icy air that accompanies the flood and one must shout to be heard. Five hundred feet up and one can still hear it roaring below like some insatiable monster. At this height the place is revealed for what it is, less a valley or gorge than some gigantic quarry. The lack of any kind of vegetation is less striking than the absence of yellow excavators; one feels a distinct need for a tin helmet. A trickle of pebbles slithers down onto the track ahead. A few stones follow, bounding playfully on their way down to the river. Then a chunk of rock, in fact a whole slice of mountain, is on the move; it looks to be falling in slow motion but within seconds the track is gone and the river below is gobbling up the last of the debris. No-one travels the Hunza road without seeing a trickle of stones and wondering what may follow. The track is obliterated, on average, once a week and several hundred men are employed, permanently and perilously, in reconstructing it.

Landslides are commonest on those stretches where the loose mountain is less than vertical. The rock precipices which make up the rest of the route are absolutely sheer. Sometimes the track manages to zig-zag up and over them. The actual rise in elevation between Gilgit and Hunza is about 5,000 feet, but the road climbs and falls more like 50,000. The hairpins are so frequent that one seems to be covering more ground vertically than horizontally; so tight are they that the jeep has to reverse several times to get round. (Alternatively the passengers may be called on to bounce the rear of the jeep round; there is less danger of going off the edge but, given the gradient, a very real possibility of the vehicle turning a somersault.)

Where the sheer rock can in no way be circumvented the famous parapets or galleries conduct the track straight across the cliff face. In places engineers have managed to blast a groove wide enough for a jeep, but there are still long sections where the driver must trust to the traditional arrangement of scaffolding and trestles. The river here is glimpsed not just over the side of the road but through it. Furze, perhaps spread with a bit of mud, is the surface; the foundations are timbers, old and worn tree trunks, resting on others embedded all too loosely in any handy crevice that the cliff face offers. That is all. No sign of concrete, no cantilevers and no suspension wires. The logs creak and bounce as a jeep approaches; pedestrians cling to the rock face as much to keep their balance as to allow it to pass. To peer down on the gurgling flood four hundred feet below takes the nerves of a steeplejack.

In a way the scale of the whole thing is the most daunting feature of all. For the last few miles the opposing wall of the gorge is hewn out of the pedestal on which stands Rakaposhi, that most photogenic of mountains. Twenty five thousand feet up and yet visible from the track, its snowswept ridges wall out the day. Then slowly it grows lighter. The cliffs become slopes and, high on a sun splashed ledge, vegetation reappears. The road climbs for the last time and there, like a table spread with unbelievable colour and plenty, is Hunza.

Such was the Hunza road in the 1960s. What it must have been like in the days of pedestrians only, one can scarcely imagine. Biddulph's immediate successors speak of single logs where now there are parapets and corkscrew staircases or flimsy wooden ladders where now there are hairpins. During the winter months when the river was at its lowest a horse could just be led along it; but even then there were places where it had to be lowered by ropes and steadied by men hanging onto its tail. Laden ponies were out of the question; the only carriage was by porters. In his official report Biddulph maintained that there might be something artificial about its horrors. It hadn't actually been sabotaged but he reckoned that the Hunza people, 'intrepid cragsmen', preferred to keep it dangerous. It was their best defence against the Dogras at Gilgit and they would probably resist any attempt to improve it.

He was quite right. Hacking away at the Hunza road 'to allow of a man passing over the worst places without using his hands' contributed to his own downfall and would eventually precipitate the first Anglo-Dard campaign.

*   *   *

In the aftermath of the Hayward tragedy there must have seemed scant prospect of another lone Englishman being allowed to scramble with guns and dogs up into the perilous kingdoms of the Hindu Kush. But, in fact, since 1870 one or two dedicated sportsmen had annually been given a grudging permission to cross the Indus at Bunji and stalk in the immediate vicinity of Gilgit. To all appearances John Biddulph, clawing his way along the Hunza road in 1876, looked just like another of these. His passion for sport was patently sincere. In Gilgit the harrowing business of having to shoot poor Vanguard, his rabid spaniel, had upset him more than the near death of his companion or the customary prevarication of Dards and Dogras. His personal diaries read much like gamebooks, and if it hadn't been for the shy ibex and inaccessible markhor he would surely never have set foot in the Western Himalayas.

But Biddulph was also a captain in a crack regiment of the Bengal cavalry and an A.D.C. to, and close personal friend of, Lord Northbrook, Mayo's successor as Viceroy. In Dardistan he was travelling on duty. Outside of the Indian foreign department only the Maharaja of Kashmir and his deputy in Gilgit knew the facts; and they were sworn to secrecy. But this innocent-looking hunting trip was actually a front for a highly confidential and crucial piece of espionage.

That there existed tracks over the Hindu Kush between the Dard valleys and the Oxus had been public knowledge for years. Chitral boasted close ties with Badakshan and Hunza with Sinkiang; in both cases they straddled the mountain spine. Native agents working for the Government of India had brought back eye-witness accounts of some of the passes, and Hayward had personally investigated the approaches of all those that led north from the Yasin valley. But in Hayward's day no special importance attached to these tracks. They might be all right for the slave dealers goading on their pathetic caravans of Kafir children and

Dard peasants by the least frequented routes that led to the
Bukhara slave-market, but they were scarcely viable as trade
routes, let alone as military roads. Too lawless for the former and
too difficult for the latter, they were also considered inaccessible
to the Russians; the Pamirs effectively walled them off to the
north.

Or so it had been thought in 1870. But by 1874 all this had
changed. In that year four British officers, Biddulph being one
of them, had crossed the southern Pamirs from Sinkiang to
Wakhan; ostensibly they were testing the ground for the return of
the second Forsyth mission to Kashgar. In the process they
investigated the extent of Afghan territorial claims in the region,
re-examined the supposed source of the Oxus and checked on
the significance of the Pamirs as a strategic barrier. In each case
they came up with devastating discoveries. First it was confirmed
that Rawlinson's line for the Afghan frontier on the Pamirs, which
the Russians had just accepted as a limit to their sphere of influence, was a nonsense. Without the expected benefit of Hayward's on-the-spot investigations, Rawlinson's red pencil had
followed the line of what was thought to be the Oxus. Now it
was discovered that all the Afghan dependencies in the region
sprawled along both sides of this river. Not only, therefore, was
the agreement worthless as a limitation but, in so far as the
Afghans would soon choose to assert their influence beyond the
river, extremely dangerous.

Perhaps by way of softening the blow the mission had reported
that the river Rawlinson thought to be the Oxus actually wasn't
anything of the sort. The true Oxus, they decided, flowed not
west from the Great Pamir but east from the Little Pamir. Otherwise known as the Aksu, Murghab or Bartang, this river pursued
its course hundreds of miles to the north of Rawlinson's Oxus and,
this being the case, made a literal interpretation of the 1873 agreement meaningless. Furthermore, besides getting the geography
of the Pamirs all wrong, people had also got the wrong idea about
their strategic importance. Colonel Gordon, leader of the party,
Trotter his surveyor and Biddulph his political advisor, all agreed
that strategically the Pamirs were no barrier at all. A column of
Russian artillery advancing from Khokand could reach Wakhan
and the north face of the Hindu Kush considerably quicker than

a British one sent up from the Punjab could reach the southern face in Yasin or Hunza—if it could get there at all. Gordon's party had lost twenty-one out of their thirty mules while crossing the Little Pamir, the wind had flayed their faces till the blood ran, and the geologist of the party would never recover from the effects of altitude and exposure. But it was April and the mountains were still in the grip of a winter exceptionally severe even by Pamir standards. With extraordinary detachment they insisted that for the other nine months of the year the Pamirs posed no obstacles. The passes were low and easy, the grazing was some of the richest in the world and the open valleys were well stocked with the herds and flocks of the nomadic Kirghiz. From Osh in Khokand to Sarhad in Wakhan only thirty miles of road needed attention.

Not only would a Russian force coming by this route have no difficulty in reaching the Hindu Kush; they would have no difficulty in crossing it either. For the last and most unexpected bombshell unearthed by the 1874 mission was the apparent ease of the Hindu Kush passes. An informant told Gordon that the Killik pass over to Hunza was 'remarkably easy' and 'open all the year round'. In Wakhan they heard tell of the Baroghil pass into Chitral and the Darkot to Yasin, the former gentle enough for field artillery of sorts to have crossed it in recent years. And the ruler of Wakhan appeared to have yet another route up his sleeve; 'Before you leave,' he told Gordon, 'I intend to tell you of a good road to India.' Gordon paid off all £45 of Wakhan's national debt, thus establishing a tradition of munificence that subsequent travellers would find hard to follow. His reward was to be told of the Ishkoman pass and the road thence to Gilgit, Chilas and on down the Indus.

Before leaving the area, John Biddulph had been sent to inspect the northern approaches to these passes. The most westerly was the Baroghil and he had tackled this first. Still, it was the wrong time of year. His horse had got stuck in a snowdrift and eventually, a mile short of the crest, so had he. The Darkot, Ishkoman and Killik passes proved still more unapproachable. But again he was not impressed. Compared to the terrible crests on what was then the only regular route across the Western Himalayas, that from Ladakh to Sinkiang, these Hindu Kush passes were child's play. The Baroghil was not much over 12,000 feet as against 17,000 and 18,000 in the Karakorams and Kun Lun. Nor could you really call it a pass; it was more like a 'break in the great mountain barrier', 'a gate' badly needing to be secured against the intruder. It was said that you could cross it without slowing from a gallop and that it was open for ten months of the year. It was a pity April happened to be one of those months when it was closed, but Biddulph was quite convinced that when it was open so too, wide open, was India.

The Government of India in the person of Lord Northbrook and his advisers had examined these various revelations in their political context. Beyond the Pamirs Russia's advance seemed at the time inexorable. In 1873 the khanate of Khiva, which for thirty years had resisted the bear's embrace, finally succumbed. Khokand and the Syr valley, nibbled away throughout the 1860s, were annexed in March 1876 and in that year Russian explorers, having already crossed the Alai ranges, first appeared on the Pamirs; a year later the Russian flag would be flown near the shores of Lake Karakul. Thanks to the Kirghiz who wintered in Khokand but in summer grazed their flocks on the Pamirs, they even inherited some sort of claim to the region. But the annexation of Khokand also had serious implications for Sinkiang. With control of the Syr valley also went access to the easiest of passes leading to Kashgar; Sinkiang was now theirs for the picking. The invasion of India direct from there through Ladakh and Kashmir could be discounted but, if a push were to be made across the Pamirs and Hindu Kush, the possession of Sinkiang, securing the flank of the advance and affording unlimited sources of supplies and carriage, had the most sinister implications.

In these circumstances any British move, however 'forward' or heavy-handed, seemed to be justified if the Hindu Kush passes could be made impregnable. But there was of course the other dimension, that of Dogra and Dard. And this, by contrast, called for extreme caution. There was nothing the Russians could do if British Indian troops were sent to hold the passes, but, in the light of what had happened when just one Englishman showed his face in Yasin, such a move was unthinkable. The murder of George Hayward had done more than any other single event to bring Dardistan to public attention. In 1874 and again now in 1876

Biddulph was commissioned to further probe the case. On the grounds of imperial prestige it was highly unsatisfactory that an Englishman's life should be forfeit within three marches of the then frontier and well within the desired one. If nothing else, the case had highlighted the impossible nature of the terrain and the volatile state of Dard–Kashmir relations. It suggested that the Maharaja had little say in the affairs of Yasin and was therefore in no position himself to undertake the defence of the Hindu Kush.

Yet this, the extension of Kashmir rule right up to the passes, and the establishment there of Dogra troops, was much the simplest answer to the problems of imperial defence as posed by all these strategic revelations. Biddulph's highly confidential assignment in 1876 was to assess the feasibility of such a scheme and to continue from the south his investigation of the passes themselves. He was thus the first official secret agent to set foot in Dardistan. Before anything much was known of the area, spies were taking precedence over such traditional pioneers as surveyors, scientists, missionaries or merchants; the region was already an official preserve. It was of necessity that Biddulph and many another political agent were shadowy, faceless figures, and it is no coincidence that we know so little of them. But if they suppressed the flamboyance of the popular explorer; if they eschewed the colourful detail and cultivated an excessively professional esprit, their status made their probings and wanderings doubly dangerous and doubly important. Clandestine reports afforded little scope for the publicity-conscious, but many a more famous traveller would willingly have traded the acclaim from an article in *Blackwoods* for the influence of a report from a roving political agent.

Hunza was not included in Biddulph's original itinerary. The principal objective of this was the Ishkoman pass, the one of which the Wakhan ruler had spoken so highly. It lay within Yasin territory and Biddulph had soon experienced the same sort of trouble that Hayward had had in trying to make contact with the Yasin chief; Pahlwan was engaged on traditional business, stalking brother Mulk Aman who was still holed up in the Hindu Raj. The invitation from the Mir of Hunza thus came as a welcome, if slightly suspect, distraction. Biddulph would ignore the question of whether already the Dards had guessed the true reason for his presence and would make a round trip, exploring up the Hunza valley to Wakhan and returning down the Ishkoman.

He had, however, taken elementary precautions. Enough was now known of the Dards for any invitation from that quarter to be treated with caution. If he was to visit Hunza, he replied, perhaps the Mir's son would like to take a short holiday in Gilgit, simultaneously; a pledge of friendship, he called it. Ghazan Khan, the Mir, could see no need for pledges between friends and asked Biddulph not to trouble himself with the matter. No trouble, replied Biddulph, but if the Mir's son were unable to get away perhaps his chief minister's son would benefit from a temporary change of scene. The negotiations dragged on through July and August. Biddulph was happy for them to take their course; Captain Grant, his ailing companion, had to be escorted back to Kashmir and there were plenty of markhor to be shot in the high forests above Gilgit. Since the idea of the visit had originated in Hunza it seemed reasonable to expect that the Mir would eventually agree. This he did and on August 13 1876 an eager Biddulph, with his escort of five sepoys and an N.C.O., headed north into the Hunza gorge.

In describing this lethal track no mention has yet been made of habitations. There were in fact half a dozen small villages dotted along the length of the gorge. Wherever a side tributary had worn back the retaining walls to create a cultivable slope, small box-like houses were stacked on a mound of steeply terraced fields no bigger than billiard tables; a fort of mud and timber crowned the position. Nomal, the first of any consequence, lay on the right hand side and though frequently attacked by Hunza forces was usually regarded as Gilgit, and therefore Dogra, territory.

Chaprot and its near neighbour Chalt, also on the right, were a very different matter. Here, after a treacherous stretch that included the worst half mile in Biddulph's 'tolerably wide experience of Himalayan travel', the track entered independent Dardistan and promptly divided. At Chalt a bridge of plaited twigs hung limply across the gorge and conducted a trail to Nagar. Hunza proper occupied only the right hand side of the river; the left was Nagar, its twin and deadly rival. And to both states the control of Chaprot and Chalt represented the difference between being besiegers and besieged. Until the previous year Hunza had been in the ascendancy but, when Biddulph passed through, the forts had just gone over to Nagar. This, as he rightly appreciated, created some interesting possibilities; Nagar, much the more peaceable of the two states, lived in dread of a counter-attack. Its only chance of maintaining its hold on the two forts lay in enlisting Kashmir support. A request to this effect had already been made and Biddulph was convinced that if the Kashmir Dogras could thus gain command of the two forts, both Nagar and Hunza would be brought to heel. At the mercy of strong garrisons commanding the approaches to both states, their co-operation in the defence of the Hindu Kush passes could be taken for granted. Or so, at least, he reasoned.

The next halt was Budlas on the new Hunza frontier. Here Biddulph dug in his heels. The Wazir's son, the hostage, was supposed to have reached Gilgit before he set off. He hadn't, nor had he been passed en route. When your only predecessor in independent Dardistan had been hacked to death, you couldn't be too careful. Biddulph refused to budge until the boy was produced, and even then moved on with the gravest misgivings. Next day these were partly dispelled. At Maiun a thin voice was heard calling from across the gorge; it was the people of Nagar sending greetings. Biddulph got out his field glasses and could just pick out a group of gesticulating figures on the walls of Nilt fort. He would have been less consoled had he known that the chasm through which the river here flows would soon figure in the military textbooks, and that the men sending their greeting swould one day take up the same positions in order to blaze away at his fellow officers. As it was, he returned the compliment; three of his men lined up along the edge of the precipice and in unison bellowed back. Then came Hini where the Mir's son, Safdar Ali, who would soon be portrayed as the worst villain on the Indian frontier, proffered a courteous welcome and escorted his guest into the incredible eyrie that is Hunza.

At over 8,000 feet above sea level, on a narrow ledge between the gloomy chasm of the river and the sheer backcloth of glacier scarred rock, Hunza is like some forbidden fairy-tale garden. Vines smother neat little houses, they wind their way up the loftiest poplars and cascade down from the topmost branches. The earth is strewn with mulberries and on every flat stone a carpet of yellow apricots lies drying in the dazzling sunlight. To Biddulph's mind the tiny fields were the best cultivated in the whole of the Western Himalayas. But fruit was the staple diet and during the summer months the people ate nothing else; to conserve fuel and precious cereals, cooking was then forbidden. In winter there was flour to be made from the apricot kernels, brandy to be distilled from the mulberries and a new vintage to be sampled from the grape pressings.

In later years, spurred on less by Biddulph's heavy prose than by the rich copy of the glossy magazines, Hunza came to epitomise the notion of an earthly paradise. The people were portrayed as peaceful and industrious, living the simple life amidst idyllic surroundings and in total isolation. There was prosperity without money, security without taxes, no police force and no crime. In a land where nervous tension, coronary thrombosis, obesity and lung cancer were also unknown, it was hardly surprising that centenarians were plentiful. Nor was the picture marred by the more brutish aspects of primitive life. There was a delicacy about Hunza. The menfolk were quick, intelligent and obliging, the girls unveiled, pretty and no less obliging. Each village had its band, every man was a dancer and the wine never ran out. Rakaposhi, towards which all houses seemed to be orientated, endowed the scene with an irresistible serenity. Life was as full as its gently swelling flanks and as satisfying as its honed summit.

What a contrast to the late nineteenth century's attitude to this 'robber kingdom'. Biddulph was impressed but he had no illusions. If the place had an air of prosperity it was thanks, not so much to the husbandry, as to the traditional amusements of waylaying rich caravans on the Leh–Yarkand road or of selling neighbours into slavery. The keen expression on a Hunza face was one of profound cunning, and that air of peaceful industry scarcely belied the fact that here was one of the most martial of all the Dard peoples. Ghazan Khan was a genial host, 'a short stout man of about forty-five with coarse but not unpleasant features and small twinkling eyes'. He betrayed a weakness for breech-loaders and scotch; his red cabbage complexion 'betokened intemperance'. He also had a somewhat exalted notion of his own importance; the isolated and almost impregnable character of Hunza led him to regard the throne of Baltit as being on a par with those of Peking

and St. Petersburg. Yet, as Biddulph soon appreciated, he was no
fool. Somehow he had already discovered that Biddulph was one
of the Englishmen who had been snooping round Wakhan two
years before. He had no illusions about this so-called sportsman
and intended to extract the maximum advantage from his visit.

The reason behind his invitation was soon apparent. Ghazan
Khan wanted the restitution of Chalt and Chaprot; Biddulph
might proceed to Wakhan only when this little matter had been
satisfactorily settled. With ill-disguised relish he commiserated
over the fate of Hayward and waited for Biddulph to act. The
similarity between his own circumstances and those of Hayward
was not lost on the Englishman, but still he had no intention of
obliging the Mir. When Ghazan Khan demanded the return of the
hostage being held in Gilgit, and when he sought to deprive his
visitor of his porters, Biddulph stood firm. He pledged his own
rifle (and no doubt a case of whisky) if he be allowed to proceed to
Wakhan, but he refused point blank to arrange the surrender of
Chaprot. Thus the matter stood for four critical days during which
he was virtually a prisoner. But his firmness paid off. Ghazan Khan
relented to the extent of allowing him to retreat, and Biddulph
scurried back to Gilgit territory. It was an ignominious start to his
dealings with the Dards; but, in the light of what happened when
the next Englishman reached Hunza, Biddulph seems to have
managed things exceptionally well. Faced with precisely the same
situation his successor, though accompanied by three other officers,
a large bodyguard and an army of followers, would capitulate within forty-eight hours.

The nature of Biddulph's recommendations for the future of
Ghazan Khan and his state were not hard to guess. 'With regard
to Hunza it is certainly advisable that Chaprot should be occupied
by the Maharaja's troops. . . . This would effectively secure Gilgit
from attack on that side. Hunza and Nagar should be openly
claimed as British territory on the strength of the tribute they pay to
the Maharaja and a frontier exploration of the north part of Kun-
joot (the upper part of Hunza) should be insisted on.' If Biddulph
had his way, Ghazan Khan was going to pay dearly for his presumption.

The 'tribute' referred to above was paid by all the Dard states
not just to Kashmir but to most of their other neighbours. By the

British and the Dogras it was seen as the ideal pretext for advancing
their rule, a convenient way of giving some semblance of legality
to what was, more truthfully, naked aggression. The tribute consisted usually of a few ounces of gold dust, a couple of hunting
dogs or a herd of sheep. Emissaries-cum-shepherds, like those
Leitner had met from Chilas, accompanied it and, if the Maharaja
was keen to foment trouble with the donors, these *vakils* could be
detained. But in return for this so-called tribute the Maharaja paid
out annual allowances of far greater value, 5,000 rupees in the case
of Hunza at this time. He and the British might please to call
them 'subsidies' or 'pensions' but to the Dards they were simply
protection money; it was the Kashmir government's only way of
buying off their neighbours' natural inclination to overrun Gilgit.
Usually there was no document setting out the precedence in these
arrangements and it was a gross distortion of the facts to read into
them any sort of acknowledgement of Kashmir sovereignty.

The excursion to Hunza was certainly the highlight of
Biddulph's 1876 travels, but his report was concerned far more
with the question of Yasin and the defence of the Hindu Kush
routes. The Ishkoman pass proved impossible. In recent years
glaciers had plunged right across its southern approaches interposing
two hundred foot walls of unscalable ice. New information had
it that Darkot was also extremely difficult and that the Baroghil,
though simple enough in itself, gave on to 'an easily defensible
gorge of first rate importance'. Reluctantly Biddulph conceded
that the alarm he had raised over the passes in 1874 might have
been premature. Their insignificance as defensive obstacles was
more than made up for by the fearful chasms that led down from
them; evidently the Hunza gorge was typical of the whole region.

On the other hand this was no ground for complacency. At the
key positions in these gorges a whole army could be kept at bay by
just a handful of defenders; equally the whole position could be
betrayed by just a handful of traitors. The point was that the defence must rest with men of unquestioned loyalty and in this respect
the Dards were useless. Pahlwan of Yasin had treated Biddulph
with effrontery tinged with outright hostility; at one point his
progress towards the Ishkoman had been barred by eighty armed
men. 'A dirty little man with a fierce spirit' was how a subsequent
visitor described Pahlwan, adding that he fully deserved the nick-

name of The Wrestler. Yet this was the man who controlled not only the Yasin and Ishkoman valleys but also the upper Chitral valley with that 'easily defensible gorge of first-rate importance'. He held the keys to India and the sooner they could be transferred to safer hands the better.

Biddulph proceeded to examine how best this could be achieved. Yasin could be held without difficulty by a small force of British troops, but he was realist enough to appreciate that such a scheme was unlikely to be sanctioned. To support and supply such a force three hundred miles from its nearest base, the whole-hearted co-operation of the Maharaja of Kashmir would be essential. This could not be relied on. On the contrary the Maharaja was almost certain to oppose the scheme. Particularly since the obvious alternative was to entrust to him and his Dogra troops the defence of the passes. The Dogras had already shown themselves more than willing to take Yasin. But could they hold it? Ill-armed, ill-provisioned and permanently under strength it was as much as they could do to hold on to Gilgit.

Biddulph, however, had a better opinion of the Kashmir troops than most of his contemporaries; he thought that, with two provisos, this latter scheme might just work. But the Maharaja must first be helped with arms, cash and advice on how to strengthen his position in Gilgit and he must, secondly, accept the presence there of a British agent. In this last, of course, lay the rub. The Maharaja was to be assured that such a man would in no way interfere with his own administration and would simply operate as an intelligence channel. This needless to say was not the whole truth. As the Maharaja surmised and as Biddulph officially recommended, such a man would also be expected to act as a political liaison with the Dards, to provide the Dogras with military advice and to check on their handling of the situation. In other words, in return for being given a free hand in Yasin, the Maharaja should be asked to accept the principle of a direct British interest in Dardistan.

This would constitute a complete reversal of previous British policy and, in retrospect, may be seen as the first step towards total political control of Dardistan by the Government of India. However Biddulph was not sticking his neck out quite so far as that suggests. The idea of a British agent in Gilgit had been around for three or four years and probably originated with Forsyth who, given his way, would have had political agents in every town in Asia. Northbrook almost certainly led Biddulph to believe that some such scheme as he now proposed would have a very fair chance of acceptance. He also seems to have left Biddulph in little doubt as to who was likely to get the Gilgit job. Before taking up what would surely be one of the loneliest posts in the British Empire, such a man deserved a few months of relaxation and society. Biddulph, his report completed, therefore sailed for England and six months' leave.

6. Nearly a Big Business

Given the intense parliamentary rivalry at Westminster during the 1870s and 1880s, British policy in India shows remarkable continuity. One of the most important Cabinet posts was that of Secretary of State for India and this, of course, changed hands with the fall of governments. Yet bi-partisanship on Indian affairs was the order of the day; Indian debates were seldom controversial and were notoriously ill-attended. The only major exception to this happy state of affairs was India's frontier and foreign policy. Here there was neither consensus nor continuity. Disraeli stood for the Empire and the Monarchy; by the former he meant India as surely as by the latter he meant Victoria. To him and to the Tories the security of India was paramount and the most serious threat to it, the Russian, was taken very seriously indeed. Gladstone and the Liberals, on the other hand, put reform before Empire and Bible before Queen. In foreign affairs, policies were evaluated according to whether they were just and whether the nation could afford them; to neither of these criteria did adventures in the Himalayas and Central Asia conform. As a result the policies and personalities of the Great Game tend to come and go with the swing of votes. The first Gilgit Agency was destined to flourish under the Tories but to wither under the Liberals.

In 1874 Disraeli had been returned to power with a massive majority; as a measure of the importance he attached to India, Lord Salisbury, the brightest star in the Tory firmament, was installed as Secretary of State. As Viceroy the Conservative choice was Lord Lytton; he had arrived in India just as Biddulph set off on his first visit to Gilgit. Lytton came to India the avowed agent of Disraeli, and his two major undertakings were entirely appropriate. The first, the proclamation and celebration of the Queen as Empress of India, was effected swiftly and occasioned widespread satisfaction. The second, the attempt to bring Afghanistan firmly into the scheme of India's defences, proved quite the opposite.

Under Northbrook the Gilgit Game had been inaugurated with

9   William MacNair (centre) in travelling disguise
with The Syed and a Pathan

10   Officers of the Lockhart mission 1885–6:
Col. Woodthorpe, Capt. Barrow, Col. Lockhart and Capt. Giles

11 Aman-ul-Mulk, Mehtar of Chitral, with some of his many children.
Afzul-ul-Mulk is in the back row on the extreme left

12 Nizam-ul-Mulk in 1885 when Chief of Yasin. The boy
on his right is the son of Pahlwan

an eye to events in Sinkiang. It was now to be subordinated to
Afghan policy. Biddulph was wasting his time harping on the pos-
sibility of an invasion across the Pamirs should Sinkiang become a
Russian supply base. The new administration's attitude towards
Afghanistan had already made the adoption of his proposals for
Gilgit a necessity. By New Year's Day 1878, as all India celebrated
the first anniversary of the Queen-Empress's proclamation,
Biddulph, back from home leave, was laying out his vegetable
plot and building his bungalow in a Gilgit orchard. The loneliest
and most vulnerable pawn on the entire imperial chess board was
digging in.

But first this other vital factor in the Gilgit Game, the Afghan
dimension. In the 1860s Afghanistan had been no more clearly
defined a territorial concept than Kashmir. And, just as the Indian
government was now finding it convenient to explore the possibilities of Kashmir's open frontier in Dardistan, so the same process,
only on a far larger scale, was taking place in Afghanistan. The
Amir of Kabul's tenuous claims to the allegiance of Badakshan,
and Badakshan's even more tenuous claims to the Upper Oxus
states of Roshan, Shignan and Wakhan, had been avidly cham-
pioned by Rawlinson when defining the extent of Afghan territory
on the Pamirs; it was a convenient way of bagging as much of the
no-man's land as possible and of interposing a friendly buffer between the likely frontiers of the two great empires.

Other tenuous Afghan claims were, however, bitterly contested
by the British. It is hard to say whether they were less valid but
they were certainly less opportune. Those to Kafiristan and to all
the Pathan states south of Chitral, for example, would have led to
the near encirclement of Dardistan. And as for the oft-repeated
claim to Chitral itself, this was clearly anathema; Aman-ul-Mulk
traditionally exercised a commanding influence over the affairs of
Yasin; acknowledging an Afghan claim to Chitral would have
meant abandoning the Hindu Kush as a British frontier. But conversely, holding the passes meant coming to an understanding
with Aman-ul-Mulk; it meant the designation of Dardistan as an
exclusively Anglo-Dogra preserve. In the light of the Russian
advance such a move might appear as purely defensive, but to the
Afghans it would appear downright offensive. And this was precisely what Lytton wanted. Biddulph's plan for the defence of the

GG—H

Hindu Kush had been adopted as a convenient means of breathing down the Amir's neck.

As so often, the one thing forgotten in all this Machiavellian theorising was the indigenous people. Forced to choose, the Dards would almost certainly have preferred the overlordship of a fellow Mohammedan from Kabul rather than one of the cow-worshipping Hindus from Srinagar. The Amir was highly revered as a religious leader and it was only sixty years since Afghan rule had stretched right across the region as far as Tibet. But ideally what the Dards wanted was neither Dogra nor Afghan. Aman-ul-Mulk, far and away the most able of all the chiefs, valued his ties with Kabul only as a means of off-setting Anglo-Dogra overtures. The harder he was pressed by Gilgit the more he turned to Kabul; but the moment Gilgit despaired of him, or the moment the Dogras were in real trouble, loud became his protestations of undying loyalty to Kashmir and cold his shoulder to the Afghans.

Just how cleverly he could play off one side against the other was to be amply tested. Lytton's endeavours to establish an exclusive British presence in Kabul would make of the Afghans first enemies, then friends, then enemies again, subjects briefly and finally suspicious allies. All this happened in the space of four years. The Dards, indeed Biddulph himself, could scarcely keep up with events. One minute the Gilgit agency and the Dogras were a vital part of India's defences and an ingenious way of pressuring the Afghans; the next it was being suggested that the agent be withdrawn, the Dogras penned back into Gilgit fort and the rest of Dardistan handed over to Afghan custody with a British agent based on Afghan soil. Aman-ul-Mulk, performing unheard-of feats of political gymnastics, seemed to change his allegiance daily and it was hardly surprising that Biddulph, faced with such a kaleidoscopic example of duplicity, totally misread its significance.

The first Gilgit agency really stood little chance. At the mercy of party politics and construed as a temporary expedient against Afghanistan as much as a permanent feature in India's defences, its early demise might be anticipated. What wasn't anticipated, however, was that the first Gilgit Agency was heading for something closer to annihilation. For this there would be many explanations but there was only one possible scapegoat.

In 1877 John Biddulph was thirty-six years old. He had been

eighteen years in India and was neither a prodigy nor a drudge. The appointment as A.D.C. to Lord Northbrook was probably more in recognition of his background than of his ability. Northbrook became a close friend and it was to this connection, plus his sporting activities in the mountains, that Biddulph owed his selection for political missions. The life clearly suited him and besides adequate reserves of discretion and initiative he displayed remarkable powers of endurance. All this was self-evident. But beyond it we know nothing of the man. To read into his handling of events in Gilgit serious failings of judgement, or to pounce on criticisms of his temperament made by men seeking a scapegoat for what happened, would be unfair. All the evidence points not to Biddulph being unsuitable but to the assignment being impossible.

The average time for the two hundred and twenty mile journey from Srinagar to Gilgit was three weeks. The track was impracticable for baggage ponies, subject to continual landslides and crossing the Great Himalaya by two highly unpredictable passes. Snow here closed it permanently for six months in the year and was liable to interrupt communications any time during the other six. As yet there was no telegraph, though from Srinagar telegrams could now be sent down to India.

Indian political agents were used to remote and solitary postings. But surely none was ever quite so isolated and quite so lonely as poor Biddulph in Gilgit. For ten months, he told Northbrook in September 1878, he hadn't seen a white face; in November he was still alone, but a Dr. Scully was on his way up, his first visitor in over a year. There was plenty to do, of course. He completed the bungalow, tended his garden, laid out a tennis court (though there was no-one to play with), studied the Dard languages, investigated their history and shot more markhor. It wasn't just a question of keeping sane; colleagues from Trivandrum to Kathmandu were doing much the same thing. On your own you couldn't afford to brood over the next move; you did what was expected and worked out a schedule that left no gaps for introspection. Even a letter from the dreaded Leitner was a welcome distraction. Apparently in code, Biddulph set it aside for an evening of close scrutiny. When he rumbled that it was written in Burishaski, the scriptless language of Hunza, he composed a friendly and appreciative reply. One of his main functions was to collect political intelligence. He organised

a network of agents that extended well into Russian Central
Asia and through the pages of the Gilgit Diary, a regular round-up
of political developments, he conscientiously relayed their reports
to the Indian Foreign Department. Perhaps he was a little too
conscientious. It would later be suggested that he placed far too
heavy a reliance on unsubstantiated rumour. But what could he do?
There was no-one to discuss things with, just the diary waiting to
be filled and the need, above all, to keep busy.

The immediate surroundings of Gilgit are almost as depressing
as the fact of its isolation. A recent traveller describes it as like
being in a cage. You feel hopelessly trapped not just by the steep-
ness of the hills all around but by their terrible tawny sterility. The
forests and mountain pastures up above are out of sight over the
horizon. In the valley it is hot and dusty all summer, cold and
muddy all winter. Every day there come stories of this road being
blocked by a landslide or that washed away by the river. The distant
crack of a rifle, the sudden appearance of some wild-looking
stranger, or just the rustle of a cold and unexpected wind feeling
its way through the orchards, sends shivers of apprehension down
the spine.

For Biddulph, of course, it was far, far worse. If he felt trapped
then so he was, not just by the terrain but by the people. In most
of India the *sahib* could expect to meet with deference if not ser-
vility from the native population; the authority of the Englishman
and the sanctity of his person commanded respect in the most
backward of the princely states. But this was scarcely the case in
Dardistan. To the hard men who thronged the Gilgit bazaar the
lone Englishman pacing his compound must have been more an
object of curiosity and contempt.

In time Biddulph would learn to distinguish one gnarled,
leathery hillman from another. The smiling, fickle Chitrali wore a
slightly different cap from that of the quick-witted cut-throats from
Hunza; the *choga*, the long buttonless dressing gown of the fanatical
Chilasis, was darker and commonly dirtier than that of the industrious traders from lower down the Indus. But each and all had the
same unkempt, piratical aspect. The open *chogas* revealed bone-
barred chests. Hideous scars and missing limbs might be the work
of a crop spoiling bear or an agitated neighbour; knives, swords
and matchlocks, like *choga* and cap, were never removed. Big

nosed men, as bony of feature as of limb, some with heads shaven, others boasting long ringlets and rat's-tails, they looked like veteran homicides from a penitentiary chain-gang. Only the eyes bespoke a fiercer pride and a nobler wit. Narrowed against the glare of rock and snow, deep-set in a web of wrinkles and jinxing with deception, they could yet deceive even such a cold fish as the solitary *feringhi*.

At the bottom of his garden Biddulph found the sculpted headstone for Hayward's grave still lying in the grass. Over the spot where Drew had read the burial service he set it up, a reminder, if one were needed, of his own vulnerability. Yet Hayward had been just an independent traveller. Biddulph's presence was potentially far more objectionable. With his authority backed by no more than a small bodyguard and a limited exchequer, he was expected to oversee a long, undefined frontier, to arbitrate in the affairs of fiercely independent tribes and to work in conjunction with an ally of doubtful loyalty whose one object would seem to be that of getting rid of him. And all this in inconceivably difficult terrain, three weeks march from his nearest compatriot and a month from a reply to the most urgent enquiry.

The wonder really is that Biddulph retained his sanity. For the second Gilgit Agency twelve years later the road would be improved, a telegraph line would be set up, the normal complement of British officers would average out at about a dozen and they would have their own troops, artillery and supply arrangements. Yet still they would find the isolation almost unbearable. So much so that the second Gilgit Agent really does seem to have taken leave of his senses.

Biddulph did two spells of duty. The first lasted nearly two years, the second only six months. When Lytton had approached the Maharaja of Kashmir with the proposed new arrangement, the latter had been happy enough about extending his rule to Yasin and happy enough about the four guns, five thousand rifles and a million rounds of ammunition made available to help him. But he had objected strongly to the corollary of a British agent at Gilgit. It was only the nomination of Biddulph, who had reported most favourably on Dogra rule in Dardistan, that reconciled him to the idea. He was still far from enthusiastic and, as Biddulph soon discovered, this hostility was in itself enough to stultify the whole scheme.

At first it was just the Kashmir governor in Gilgit who proved so difficult. Biddulph was prepared for a bit of professional jealousy and must have expected to unearth some mild peculation. But this man appeared to be in the closest collusion with his supposed adversaries, the Dards, and to be urging them to get rid of Biddulph. From Aman-ul-Mulk he was accepting bribes in the Maharaja's name and then leaning on the Chitrali to scare off his unwelcome visitor. It also looked as if it was he who had instigated Ghazan Khan of Hunza to act so menacingly during the visit of 1876. 'It is me or him,' confided Biddulph to Northbrook. Like Hayward, and Leitner before him, he believed his life to be in real danger. But when, after strenuous objections, the man was at last replaced, it seemed to make little difference. Another plot against his life came to light. Apparently he was up against not simply the resentment of an individual governor, but the policy of the Kashmir government. He who had thought so highly of Kashmir rule reckoned by the end of his first year in Gilgit that 'no native administration under British rule can be as bad or as two-faced'. At the time he didn't hold the Maharaja personally to blame, but after another two years he had no illusions. 'The Maharaja whom for years I had looked on as a weak fool in the hands of knaves turns out to be as great a scoundrel as any in Asia and disloyal to the core.'

By then, 1879, Lytton agreed. For, early that year, it was discovered that the Maharaja had been in correspondence, if not collusion, with both Russia and Afghanistan. What made this particularly serious was that by then the latter was in a state of open warfare with the British and the former very nearly so.

These were stirring times, the late 1870s. It seemed to many, and not least to Biddulph as he desperately strove to get a disloyal ally to defend an unmapped frontier, that the Great Game was about to become the Great War. Anglo-Russian rivalry in Central Asia had always been influenced by the clash of imperial interests elsewhere, particularly in the Middle East. In 1877 the Russo-Turkish war brought Russian arms sweeping through the Balkans until in 1878 they were at the gates of Constantinople. The whole crumbling Turkish empire, and with it control of the routes from Europe to India, was in danger of falling into Russian hands. Brought thus to the brink of Armageddon even Disraeli hesitated.

But the British people were warming to what seemed the inevitable; 'We don't want to fight but by jingo if we do . . .' was the hit song of the moment and accurately reflected popular sentiment. The Queen was positively horrified at the 'low tone' of her cabinet; with resignation in mind she implored them to act. At last they did. Six million pounds were voted by Parliament for military purposes, the reserves were called up, troops were summoned from India and a fleet of ironclads was sent steaming through the Dardanelles. With just the minarets and palaces of Constantinople between them, the Imperial Army faced the Royal Navy.

Russia's answer to all this was to mobilise in Central Asia. India was regarded as the most desirable and the most vulnerable of the British possessions; merely threatening it should be enough to bring Whitehall to its senses. Skobeleff, the Russian military genius, drew up a plan of invasion. Three military columns were formed and one of them in May 1878, duly set off across the Alai for the Pamirs and the Hindu Kush passes. Biddulph, if only he had known it, was within an ace of having to outshine Horatio at the bridge. But, as he could have forecast from personal knowledge, May was a bit too early to be dragging an army across the Pamirs. By the time the Russians had floundered through the snowdrifts on the Alai it was all over; far away in Berlin a congress of all the great powers had thrashed out a peace settlement.

The Russian advance on the Hindu Kush thus came to nothing, but another feature of their Central Asian offensive had far reaching repercussions. It was because of the arrival of a Russian mission in Kabul in July 1878 that Lytton had finally insisted on sending a British mission there. The Afghan refusal to receive it provided the pretext for war, and it was when the victorious General Roberts reached Kabul in early 1879 that there was unearthed the Maharaja of Kashmir's treacherous correspondence with both Afghanistan and Russia.

*   *   *

While all around was in turmoil, Dardistan confounded all predictions by remaining comparatively peaceful; neither belated reports of the Russian manœuvres on the Pamirs nor Afghan embarrassments at the hands of the infidel British sent the Dards scurrying to arms. On the contrary things were so quiet that at the height of the

drama, in late 1878, Biddulph coolly set off on his pioneering pro-
menade of Chitral and Yasin. This is not a journey that figures pro-
minently in the annals of exploration; it is a little known exploit
even by Biddulph's standards. Partly this was due to the extraordinary circumstances at the time, but it also has to be admitted
that its results were singularly negative. The first Englishman into
Chitral spent just a week there and, beyond a few strategic observations, an exaggerated estimate of Tirich Mir's altitude—'at
least 27,000 feet'—and confirmation of the extent and importance
of the valley, he added nothing to what was already known from
native accounts.

Similarly the political results were disappointing. Aman-ul-
Mulk, the chief or Mehtar, turned out to be a stocky, patriarchal
character with a wedge-shaped beard and a falcon forever on his
forearm, altogether rather like Henry VIII. He was also every bit as
astute. 'Shrewd, avaricious, unscrupulous and deceitful to an uncommon degree', thought Biddulph. The treaty by which he was
bound to Kashmir was in the process of negotiation. In return for
'Hawks . . . 2, Hunting Dogs . . . 2, Horses . . . 2', plus an acknowledgement of the Maharaja's suzerainty, he was to get 12,000
rupees a year and thus was Chitral supposed to be secured against
Afghanistan and Russia. Biddulph couldn't see it. Aman-ul-Mulk
candidly admitted that to realise that kind of money all he had to do
was sell a few Kafirs; to make his point he pressed on his visitor
a couple of doe-eyed boys dressed in nothing but their native
goatskins. He also made it clear that he would much prefer an
arrangement direct with the British, an offer made with an eye to
another and much larger subsidy. The Mehtar's sympathies
seemed to be controlled by nothing so much as the tide of battle in
Afghanistan, and the moment Biddulph turned back to Gilgit, he
was renewing negotiations with Kabul. Such a man could never be
trusted and Biddulph recommended that he was best left out of any
Anglo-Dogra defence schemes.

This seemed feasible in the light of the situation in Yasin.
Pahlwan, the Wrestler, now appeared as congenial and dependable
as Aman-ul-Mulk obviously wasn't; it was like Hayward's attachment to Mir Wali all over again. 'He took a great fancy to me', wrote
Biddulph, and appeared 'far too outspoken and straightforward for
the Kashmiris ever to understand'. To a considerable extent

Pahlwan had managed to shrug off the overlordship of Aman-ul-Mulk and he too now asked for a direct alliance with the British. Biddulph had plenty of sympathy with anyone suspicious of the Dogras and, given the strategic importance of Yasin and the good impression made by Pahlwan, enthusiastically supported the idea. Yasin at the time comprised not only the Yasin and Ishkoman valleys but also Mastuj and the upper Chitral valley. If Pahlwan's co-operation could be assured, there was no need to worry about Aman-ul-Mulk's sympathies. The Yasinis could hold the passes and, as a second line of defence, troops could always be rushed from Gilgit to Chitral by what he had found to be a comparatively easy route over the Shandur pass.

Undoubtedly Biddulph himself regarded the visit to Yasin as far from negative; only in the light of subsequent dramatic developments would it be revealed as worthless. The one remaining achievement of Biddulph's last pioneering journey—and one not to be sneezed at—was that he returned alive. From the start the Maharaja of Kashmir had strongly opposed the trip and, on previous form, might well have made it an opportunity to remove him. Aman-ul-Mulk had also objected to it and could so easily have slipped from his tightrope long enough to do Kabul the small favour of holding to ransom a British officer. Anticipating such an eventuality, the Indian foreign department had actually vetoed the trip; the news, as usual, reached Biddulph too late for him to turn back. Pahlwan would soon be revealed as having played as false as had Mir Wali before him; and in the Hindu Raj, spoiling for a chance to embarrass the Dards or to oblige the Dogras, there still lurked his brother, the dreaded Mulk Aman. Yet Biddulph sailed through. Compared to the problems encountered by both previous and subsequent travellers it was a considerable feat.

In September 1879, far from dissatisfied with his long exile in Gilgit, Biddulph returned to India. Here he found Afghanistan again in the headlines. The first British envoy to Kabul had been murdered and the troops were returning to wreak vengeance. Lytton and Disraeli faced a barrage of criticism at home; the Viceroy could scarcely be expected to give his whole-hearted attention to the far flung affairs of Gilgit. He did, however, acknowledge that the whole policy on which the Gilgit agency had been based needed rethinking. Armed with the evidence of the

Maharaja's duplicity, urged by Biddulph that the Dogras were neither capable of defending the Hindu Kush nor acceptable to the Dards, and soon freed by the fall of Afghanistan from the need to secure Chitral, he plumped for an entirely new approach. The Maharaja was 'to be relieved of all responsibilities and deprived of all powers' in Chitral and Yasin, and the agent in Gilgit would be moved to Jalalabad thence to conduct the affairs of Dardistan direct with the Dards. He was certainly right in terminating the Gilgit agency; the impossibility of Biddulph's position was conceded. But Jalalabad had yet to be detached from Afghanistan, and while serious doubts were being raised about the feasibility of this, Disraeli was defeated at the polls. The conduct of affairs in Afghanistan was the main election issue and Lytton could therefore only resign. Biddulph was left in the lurch. Failing any orders to the contrary, he returned to his post in Gilgit. He relieved Dr. Scully, his locum, in June 1880.

Though the Dards had not responded to the disturbances on the Pamirs and in Afghanistan, events were soon to show that little credit on this score could go to Biddulph and even less to the Dogra troops. Just as British schemes of defence had consistently overrated the political and military effectiveness of the Dogras, so they had underrated the obstinacy and striking power of the Dards. In the end it was not the Afghans or the Russians, and not Lytton's new schemes nor the squeamishness of the Liberals, that put paid to the first Gilgit Agency. It was the ragged matchlockmen of Dardistan itself.

As Biddulph for the third time crossed the Indus and trotted on beneath the jagged skyline into Gilgit, he seems to have sensed that trouble was brewing. Chaprot, that fortress in the Hunza gorge garrisoned by Kashmiri Dogras against attack by Ghazan Khan, was much on his mind. With rumours of a concerted Dard attack more rife than usual, there was good cause for making Chaprot independent of supplies from Nagar and of reinforcements from Gilgit. Both Nagar and Hunza were reportedly incensed by the few improvements that had been made to the Hunza road and, if this were sufficient to push them into an alliance, then Chaprot was in real danger. Rumour also had it that Pahlwan was aligning himself with Hunza. His letters to Biddulph were certainly colder than of old but, if there were any truth in his mobilising his forces, Biddulph could only conclude that he was again going to take the field against his brother Mulk Aman. Either that or possibly his paranoia about the Dogras, to whom he had ceased sending *vakils*, had put him on the defensive.

Through the long dusty summer in Gilgit tension continued to mount. Darel and Chilas were also thought to be involved in some sort of Dard confederacy and, with Gilgit under threat of complete encirclement, Dogra reinforcements were ordered up from Kashmir. Biddulph now regarded Nagar and Chitral as the real troublemakers, though he continued to see Chaprot as the likely point of attack. He himself visited the fort in July. Both the Maharaja and the Foreign Department warned against any move that might precipitate attack; Biddulph was to understand—as if he didn't already—that he was on his own. Reinforcing Chaprot was in itself provocative, but he believed its weakness was what had inspired all the trouble; it had to be done.

In early October the air was still full of rumour. Pahlwan was on the move, apparently off to visit Aman-ul-Mulk in Chitral, and the reinforcements had still not arrived. But winter was approaching and the traditional campaigning season almost over. Then, on the night of October 27th, the crash came. Pahlwan changed direction. With a force of seven hundred he swept down the Gilgit valley, overran the whole of Punial and laid siege to the fort of Sher only twenty-four miles from Gilgit. From Darel and Tangir tribesmen flocked to join him. Ghazan Khan of Hunza sent men to Sher and himself started an action outside Chaprot. Any moment the Chilasis were expected to cut the supply line at Bunji; it was highly doubtful whether postal runners carrying the desperate pleas for help would ever get through.

Biddulph assumed command of the Gilgit garrison. Without the promised reinforcements he could raise barely five hundred combat worthy troops; the rest of the garrison consisted of invalids, adolescents and dotards. When he sallied forth to raise the siege of Sher, even the chosen few melted away. He gave up the idea of taking the offensive and, abandoning his bungalow and his precious garden, he retired within the fort of Gilgit. A long siege now seemed inevitable.

As it happened the Chilasis had not fallen on Bunji. They were waiting to see if Pahlwan would take Sher or, perhaps, they were

Gilgit fort in the 1870s

just apprehensive about the approach of the Kashmir reinforcements. The postal runners got through; carrying the news relay
style over the Great Himalaya, they delivered the first grim tidings
on November 6th. 'Precedence', 'Clear the line', began the telegrams that now started to fly round India and back to London.
'Biddulph's situation may be serious', ventured the new Viceroy,
reporting to the Secretary of State. Gilgit was under siege. Each
report from there might be the last and, given the ten days it took
them to reach India, there was no telling how grave the situation
might already be. The Maharaja was to send more troops immediately, but it was unlikely that they would make it over the
passes before they were closed by the first snows; the original reinforcements, to which two British officers were now rushed, had
already been delayed by the weather. As Hayward had once discovered, mid-November was the usual closing date for the Burzil
and the Kamri. It was a grim thought, but Biddulph and the relief
of Gilgit might have to wait till the spring.

As Biddulph himself would later put it, it was 'nearly a big business'. That it was not was no thanks to the Dogra garrison, no
thanks to the reinforcements, nor to the solicitude of the government. Of all people, it was to Mehtar Aman-ul-Mulk of Chitral.
When Pahlwan had unleashed his forces down the Gilgit valley, a
Chitrali contingent had simultaneously set off via Mastuj. It was
assumed that they were coming to join the other Dards, and the
timing was of course no coincidence. But what did come as a surprise, and most of all to Pahlwan, was that this force, far from advancing to join him, was out to dispossess him. Two days after
news of the first attack had reached India, the scare was in fact
over. Pahlwan had retreated to defend Yasin and within a week he,
like his brother, was a lone fugitive in the mountains. Aman-ul-
Mulk's forces held Yasin.

Having sampled the complexity of local intrigue when examining
the Hayward case, the reader may be spared a second post-mortem
on Biddulph's moment of tribulation. What lay behind it was every
bit as mysterious. Why Pahlwan attacked in the first place, why
he was unopposed all the way to Sher, and why Aman-ul-Mulk
decided to get Gilgit off the hook, are all questions that have never
been fully answered. Biddulph was inclined to blame the only
parties who would obviously gain from the affair—Aman-ul-

Mulk who had re-established his supremacy over Yasin and would get his subsidy doubled, and the Maharaja who would now have the satisfaction of seeing the Gilgit Agency withdrawn.

But no-one now paid much attention to Biddulph. Northbrook had admired him. Lytton had merely tolerated him, but Lord Ripon, the new Liberal Viceroy, was positively horrified by him. Biddulph had got everything wrong; Pahlwan, his friend, had proved to be the rogue while Chitral and Nagar, whom he distrusted most, proved his staunchest allies. When he threatened to organise punitive raids, Ripon shuddered and ordered the agent back to Simla. There it was decided to close the Agency down. The Maharaja was to understand that the government reserved the right to re-open it if ever the situation demanded; but in 1881, with the experiment having proved such an unmitigated disaster, it was hard to envisage any circumstances that might justify such a move.

7. Out in the Cold

The failure of the first Gilgit Agency did not signify a dwindling of British interest in Dardistan. The years 1881–89, during which the Agency was in abeyance, witness further exploratory activity, though of a more covert nature. It is interesting that these years also coincide almost exactly with the brief period during which Rudyard Kipling worked in India. No-one did more than Kipling to popularise the notion of the Great Game; in *Kim* he created an underworld of spies and travellers engaged on momentous and mysterious assignments that was all vastly more exciting than strategic theory and diplomatic manœuvrings. Whether, in reality, there existed such a sophisticated espionage network is still open to debate; but certainly, during the 1880s, there was enough clandestine trans-frontier travel, enough anxiety about Russian intentions and enough concern with intelligence work to suggest such an operation.

Kim was not written till long after Kipling had left India; only two or three of the characters can be tentatively identified and the events are entirely fictional. But it is worth noting that not only do Kipling's dates coincide with what would prove to be the most undercover phase of the Gilgit Game, but also that Kipling's India, i.e. the Punjab, was that of the frontier and the mountains. The newspaper for which he worked, *The Civil and Military Gazette* of Lahore, was the descendant of that founded by Leitner; and the journal to which Kim's Bengali colleague submitted his scholarly monographs was Leitner's *Asiatic Quarterly Review*; almost certainly Leitner and Kipling were acquainted. When not in Lahore, Kipling was chronicling the official and social life in Simla; here the policies and attitudes to be adopted during the final phase of the Gilgit Game were being formulated, and the men involved were being trained. It is no coincidence that suddenly the Gilgit story is full of Kipling associations.

The mysterious journey of William Watts MacNair and the Syed (note the overtones of Kim and the Lama) begins, fittingly, on the Grand Trunk Road at Nowshera, a staging post between Rawal Pindi and Peshawar. In March 1883 MacNair, a surveyor who had been mapping in Afghanistan in the wake of the second British occupation, had applied for a year's leave; it was granted. On the night of April 9 he rode into Nowshera—and promptly disappeared.

No-one noticed. The survey of India was dominated by English officers; MacNair, though, was a civilian and 'country bred', that is born and educated in India; he had never been to England. Thirty-three years old and still only a surveyor third grade, he was not the sort to occasion much attention. He was unmarried and on leave; it was up to him how he spent his spare time. Nor was there any reason for his superiors to be suspicious of his wanting a whole year off. The most conscientious of employees, he had shown wayward tendencies only in his relations with women; no doubt a few delicate enquiries as to any young widows being in station would reveal his whereabouts. As for political interests he had none. The Game, to him, meant not the undercover world of *Kim* but the equally topical obsession of cricket. It was said a scratch XI would materialise and disperse to fielding positions at the sound of his voice; MacNair was a slow bowler, tricky and devastating in the best Indian tradition.

His only other passion was his work. He had joined the Survey of India when he was eighteen and would remain with it till his death. He loved the precision of maps and he loved the travel though not, as some, for the solitude it offered but for the society. Merchants and pilgrims met along the road, peasants across whose fields he carried his survey, and village greybeards who volunteered the names for his maps—these were the men who intrigued him. MacNair had a genuine affection for Asiatics. A *sahib* credited with an understanding of the native mind was usually one who could get a single Indian to do the work of ten; rare indeed were those who really relished the native way of life. The idea of Hayward, for instance, or Leitner successfully carrying off a disguise is preposterous; both were far too overbearing. But MacNair was different.

At Nowshera on the night of April 9 he set about proving it. First he packed his two compasses—magnetic and prismatic—into a *gooda*, a sheepskin sewn up to form a bag with the wool inside;

for a planetable he butchered a large tome on Islamic physic, retaining just the cover and a few pages of prescriptions, and devoting the rest of the book to paper holders and rulers. Then, leaving his beard to grow, he carefully shaved his whole head; skin colouring was achieved with 'a weak solution of caustic and walnut juice applied to face and hands'. By 3 a.m., dressed in the heavy turban and loose robes of a Kaka Khel Pathan, he was ready. As Hakim (doctor) Mir Mohammed he headed north for the mountains.

His rendezvous was for the 13th at Ganderi just beyond the British frontier. He arrived undetected on the appointed day; waiting for him were two genuine Kaka Khel Pathans who traded regularly between Peshawar and Chitral, a Kafir lately converted to Islam, and the Syed, the originator of the whole scheme. Syed Shah had been MacNair's assistant during the recent operations in Afghanistan. Probably he actually was a *syed* or Mohammedan holy man; such a profession, entailing a good deal of travel, would have particularly recommended him to the Indian Survey; he was in fact being trained with a view to joining that most select corps of native travellers known to history as The Pundits. Since the 1860s these men, under the auspices of the Indian Survey, had been making secret route surveys beyond the northern and north-western frontiers; much of what was now known of the routes through the Western Himalayas and into Central Asia—and nearly all of what was known of Tibet—was the result of their work. Operating under code names or initials—the Mullah, the Havildar, A.K., etc —they included Buddhists and Hindus as well as Mohammedans; C23, otherwise the horse-dealer Mahbub Ali in *Kim*, was inspired by what Kipling could glean of their activities.

In attempting now to make a route survey from the Punjab to Chitral and Kafiristan, the Syed was doing just what he had been trained for. The trouble was that this particular assignment had not been officially commissioned and that, anyway, Pundits were not supposed to be accompanied by their British colleagues. Under the cautious Lord Ripon, Dardistan was strictly out of bounds to all government servants; as for an Englishman going there, the visits of Hayward and Biddulph furnished eloquent testimony of both the dangers and political embarrassments that could result. Both men were therefore risking not only their lives but their

GG—I

careers. MacNair makes it clear that the original idea was the Syed's; no doubt this can be ascribed to the over-enthusiasm of a new recruit. But no such excuse can be made for MacNair himself. He admitted joining the Syed on his own insistence, but is mysteriously silent about what prompted him to take such a dangerous and uncharacteristic step.

From Ganderi the party crossed the Malakand pass into Swat and headed for the Lowarai pass into Chitral. This was the route that Hayward had originally hoped to follow, the most direct line between British India and Dardistan. MacNair was the first European to see it. Diligently he observed the height of the passes and the width of the rivers. He had no experience of the higher ranges of the Western Himalayas but, by any standards, this was not a difficult route. The Malakand was open throughout the year and mules could cross without having to be unloaded. By pretending to wander off in search of roots and herbs for his patent medicines, MacNair was able to continue his mapping. Once he was all but surprised; four armed men caught him poring over his planetable; just in time he shot the ruler up his sleeve and heaved shut the book of remedies. On the whole the disguise was working well. He had grown proficient at eating with his hands and could crouch for hours native style. His companions, of course, knew his true identity but in Dir, where he treated a stream of patients, no-one else seems to have guessed that he was other than a respected *hakim*.

It was thus extremely unfortunate that he was given away not by any slip on his own part but by a malicious, and probably purely speculative, rumour. Floated by a bitter rival of the two Pathan merchants, this rumour had it that both the *hakim* and the Syed were British officers in disguise. With an outright denial, the Khan of Dir sprang to their defence; it was sufficient to secure their immediate immunity. But the rumour surged ahead of them over the Lowarai into Chitral and Kafiristan. The latter, their original destination, could only be reached by passing through a belt of fanatically suspicious Mohammedans. Letters arrived from this quarter warning them to steer well clear, and below the snow-choked Lowarai, the southern gateway to Dardistan, MacNair hesitated.

If he had turned back now, he might well have made it back to

British territory without trouble. The Government need never have known of his transgression and his career would not have been compromised. But of MacNair's many endearing traits, a lack of professional ambition is one of the most notable. To him, as to Kim, the game was far more important than the prize. When credit was due elsewhere he paid it, regardless of how his own reputation might suffer. Few public servants, and certainly no other explorer, ever presented an account of his achievement that both began and ended by awarding the full credit for the whole enterprise to his native companions. A senior of the R.G.S. would call it 'one of the most adventurous journeys that has ever been described before the Society'. Yet, when all he got for his pains was an official reprimand, MacNair would show no resentment; he simply 'never troubled his head about promotion or preferment'. So it was at the foot of Lowarai. Having got this far he was certainly not going to play safe. If they couldn't make direct for Kafiristan, they could still press on for Chitral and there trust to Aman-ul-Mulk's good services.

The Lowarai, over 11,000 feet high, proved very different from the Malakand. Though rugged and steep the latter is essentially a desert pass like the not so distant Khyber. It can prove formidable enough when defended, as the next British party to tackle it would discover; but it is rarely affected by snow and too low to pose altitude problems. The Lowarai, on the other hand, is a true, if modest, Himalayan pass. The winding approach leads up through fine stands of conifers, haunt of the marauding bear; from boulders on the grassy banks of mountain torrents redstarts bob and flutter. Higher up, the trees give way to close cropped mountain pasture which for half the year is buried beneath the snow. For a comparatively dry area, the Lowarai boasts an impressive snowfall; telegraph poles get buried to within a foot or two of the wires and the avalanches are some of the most lethal in the Himalayas. In April, as MacNair discovered, the snow still lies for several miles on each side of the saddle; all his party's baggage had to be transferred to porters and much of the track consisted of snow slides or steps cut in the ice. It was truly a gateway into the mountains and, if he and the Syed now felt safe from the interference of government, they were also beyond its assistance.

To Aman-ul-Mulk, MacNair made no secret of his real identity;

if they were to enter Kafiristan from Chitral it was essential to have his co-operation. The Chitrali responded favourably enough; 'Mr. William', as he called him, could go wherever he wished, even into Kafiristan; but what he must not do was take his companions with him. Relishing the role of the righteous, Aman-ul-Mulk refused to believe that MacNair was anything but an official British emissary or that the Syed was any more than his guide. He insisted that since the Syed did not know Kafiristan, the *sahib* would be better served by one of his own trusted agents who did. Moreover, he also secretly wrote to the Indian Government to apprise them of the safe arrival of their man.

Pondering their next move, MacNair and the Syed made an excursion up the Ludkho valley to view the Dora pass leading into Badakshan. It seems that they didn't actually climb the pass, but MacNair had no doubt about its significance. 'I can safely pronounce it to be the easiest of all routes leading north from Chitral.' Here was news for the Indian foreign department; it was almost as much of a bombshell as the 1874 discovery of the Baroghil and Ishkoman. And whilst these latter had proved to be less vulnerable than was at first thought, the Dora was destined to remain a source of concern until the end of the century; this was the pass used by Kim's colleagues to penetrate into Central Asia.

Meanwhile, what to do about Kafiristan? MacNair was loth indeed to go anywhere without the Syed. Yet duty as much as inclination demanded that no opportunity of getting a man into Kafiristan should be passed over. This strange land lying between Chitral and Afghanistan was the only sizable slice of territory south of the Hindu Kush watershed that remained totally unexplored. On the maps it was not quite a blank. Peaks up to 16,000 feet gave some idea of the ruggedness of the place, and a number of unconvincingly dotted rivers suggested habitable valleys. There were also a few outlandish place-names—Kam, Wai, Shu—contributed by the likes of MacNair's Pathan companions. But as yet no European had ever managed to enter the country.

The people were even more of a mystery than the geography. In the racial jigsaw of the Western Himalayas, Kafiristan was a piece that simply did not fit, and the Kafirs had been an enigma to just about every branch of the social sciences for half a century. Reputedly as primitive and unapproachable as the Bushmen, they were Asia's greatest ethnological mystery. Leitner, with uncharacteristic candour, admitted that in calling them Dards he was doing so simply out of convenience; in fact their languages, religion and customs appeared to have nothing whatsoever in common with any of the Dard peoples. Surrounded by tribes once influenced by Buddhism but long ago converted to Islam, the Kafirs seemed to have been bypassed by every religious and cultural development since the stone age. They worshipped spirits, wore goatskins, and hunted with axes or bows and arrows. To look at they were almost as fair and fine featured as Europeans; Sir Henry Rawlinson had seen a Kafir girl whose long blonde hair formed a veil that reached to the ground; she was the loveliest oriental he had ever come across. But they were also said to smell quite abominable and to indulge in orgies of unspeakable obscenity. Sir Henry Yule, who with Rawlinson umpired the exploration of Asia, summed up the situation: once Kafiristan had been explored the R.G.S might close its doors; it was the last big mystery. MacNair could scarcely shy off just because he felt the prize not rightfully his.

Accordingly, on April 23 he parted from his companions and headed west in the company of a lone Kafir. Two guides, he later concluded, would have been a better arrangement, one to find the way, the other to help him along it. The paths were terrifying. They ascended one of the valleys that opens onto the Chitral river and were soon among faces 'pink rather than blond'; blue eyes were occasionally encountered and golden hair was quite common. These, however, were the Kalash Kafirs, a rather debased variant of the true Kafirs and subservient to Chitral. Independent Kafiristan began over the Shawal pass. MacNair pushed ahead and two days later breasted the pass after seven hours' toil in the snow.

> The view on the *kotal* as the sun was rising was a sight never to be forgotten; near and around us the hills clad in white with different tinges of red showing, and clouds rising in fantastic shapes, and disclosing to view the blue and purple of the distant and lower ranges.

For the surveyor this was a chance not to be missed; rapturously he sketched in the features of this hitherto unseen land. 'Picturesque, densely wooded and wild in the extreme', it had all that the romantic pioneer could wish for. At the first villages in the Lutdeh valley he was well received, and, when the weather deteriorated, happily settled down to observe Kafir life. Observation, for MacNair, meant participation. He was soon joining in the Kafir dances, sampling their wines and cheeses and visiting their shrines. His hosts looked pretty wild. For one thing they shaved the whole of their heads except for a small patch on the crown whence streamed a long, never-cut rat's-tail. The women wore an elaborate cap from which two, sometimes four, long horns of hair protruded. But 'all were exceedingly well disposed towards the British'; MacNair 'might venture further and state that they would not hesitate to place their services, should occasion require, at our disposal'.

What a thing it would have been to present the government with the unsolicited and unconditional allegiance of the whole of Kafiristan. In a short story entitled *The Man who would be King* Kipling chose Kafiristan as the primitive mountain kingdom where two British 'loafers' were deified by a credulous and savage people. That the Kafirs looked on the British as long lost brethren who would deliver them from the oppression of their Islamic neighbours, even that the Kafirs were anxious to adopt Christianity as a first step, were more than rumours in the Punjab cantonments. But it did not fall to MacNair to exploit this situation. In fact his visit was about as short as it could be; within a day or two of crossing the Shawal, Aman-ul-Mulk summoned him back to Chitral; fearing for the safety of his colleagues, he obliged. Meanwhile, showing a different face to the Government of India, the Mehtar boasted of the special favours he was showing to the government's representative; a case of breechloaders, he hinted, would do very nicely as a mark of gratitude. (Instead, there eventually arrived three antique brass mule guns.)

So short, in fact, had MacNair's visit been that neither of the two British travellers who followed him to Kafiristan before the country's tragic demise would concede that he had really been there. Sir George Robertson, who admittedly acquired a deeper knowledge of Kafiristan than anyone, insisted that though MacNair travelled among the Kalash Kafirs he could not have crossed the Shawal pass into the Lutdeh valley; he had heard from a Chitrali who claimed to have accompanied MacNair that he did not cross the pass, and all the customs described by MacNair related only to the Kalash.

In the light of the later dismemberment of the Kafir country, much importance was attached to the distinction between the Kalash, who came under the administration of Chitral, and the true Kati Kafirs of what had been independent Kafiristan. In MacNair's day the distinction was less noteworthy, and he might well have crossed the Shawal without appreciating the extent to which it was a political and ethnological watershed. Equally, since he makes no mention of him, it seems unlikely that he had a Chitrali companion. But MacNair, unfortunately, was dead by the time these accusations were made public; in seeking to deprive such a modest character of his one outstanding achievement, Robertson was probably displaying as much professional pique as sound judgement.

After his recall to Chitral, MacNair must have been close to despairing of the whole expedition. There was no chance of returning to Kafiristan, and there would have been little consolation in knowing that only two years would elapse before another expedition, spurred on by his own partial success, would complete his work. The most that could be salvaged from the trip was to complete the circuit of Dardistan and return to India via Gilgit and Kashmir. This, after acrimonious exchanges with Aman-ul-Mulk, MacNair and his companions achieved. They reached Srinagar at the end of June. A journey for which they had allowed a whole year was over in three months.

As soon as he had scrubbed off the walnut juice and confessed to the name of William Watts MacNair there came a summons from Simla and the stiffest possible reprimand. It was lucky he couldn't care less. Unsubdued and with nine months leave to squander, he promptly set off on another journey of discovery; he sailed for England. There the R.G.S. sprang to his defence. He was a guest of honour at their anniversary dinner and received the coveted Murchison Award. His brief and modest account of the journey was shown to great advantage by the discussion that followed. First Leitner launched himself from his chair with a long and ungracious outburst about the presumption of anyone visiting Dardistan without inviting along the foremost exponent of its languages or at least devoting some attention to them. This was a bit unfair; he hadn't seen MacNair's confidential report in which the traveller had made a very creditable attempt to follow the doctor's example. He had collected a useful little vocabulary—the Kafir for salt was 'o' and for water 'w'—and had illustrated it with ethnographical dialogues and a delightful section on Kafir recipes.

Next came Rawlinson with the absurd pronouncement that the route which for twenty years he, in his wisdom, had recognised as the 'great natural high-road' from India to Central Asia had at last been opened up. Great natural high roads were one of his specialities; ten years before he had been saying the same thing about the so-called Changchenmo route from Ladakh to Sinkiang. As to how a man travelling in disguise and in fear of his life could be said to have opened it up one doesn't ask. MacNair, anyway, didn't bother. Perhaps after a consolatory visit to Lords Cricket Ground, he returned to India and there, still a surveyor 3rd Grade, he died of fever while planetabling in Baluchistan in 1889.

* * *

Like Kafiristan, MacNair doesn't really fit. Amidst the collection of rabid careerists and brooding romantics who dominate the Gilgit story, his sheer normality amounts to a delightful distinction. One wonders how on earth such a man ever got involved. Why did he, in fact, take that fateful step in Nowshera on the night of April 9, 1885? The reader of *Kim* will naturally suspect a secret motive; and he will not be surprised that till his dying day MacNair refused to reveal it. But it is more significant that Mac-Nair's contemporaries also found his explanations somewhat lame. They suspected that there was more to this improbable journey than met the eye; and the Indian papers in particular thought they could detect the influence of none other than the Quarter Master General of the Indian Army, Sir Charles Metcalfe MacGregor. MacNair staunchly refused to acknowledge any dealings with 'old Mac'; to have done so would obviously have compromised the Q.M.G. who would soon be in dire enough trouble anyway. But opinion at the time was in no doubt that, if MacGregor hadn't actually urged MacNair to go, he had certainly known in advance what was planned and had indicated approval. Moreover he alone is on record as welcoming back the disgraced surveyor 'with open arms'. The visit to Kafiristan thus looks like the first of many exploits in Dardistan that would be inspired by the thinking of this most controversial exponent of the Great Game.

Though founder of the Indian army's Intelligence Department, MacGregor was scarcely the mastermind of an espionage network. A soldier, simple and brave, 'a big bluff gruff man' according to Younghusband, he was also a far cry from the shady and devious Lurgan Sahib of *Kim*. If indeed he served Kipling as a model at all it was more probably for one of those self-seeking government servants satirised in *Departmental Ditties*. So much has now been written to eulogise and glamorise the everyday work of the men who ruled India that it is easy to forget more objectionable details like the system, if one can call it that, of promoting one's career. To anyone with an ambitious streak, the normal channels of advancement proved far too sluggish. The ladder was there not so much to be climbed as to be by-passed. For soldier and civilian alike this meant getting onto someone's personal staff, joining the political service or being co-opted for a special assignment. The way to set about it was by cultivating one's connections. Cut-throat lobbying and manoeuvring were as universal as the obsession with rank and the craving for honours that prompted them. Biddulph had owed everything to his Northbrook connection, and many another would never have seen the Western Himalayas but for the workings of patronage; similarly, but for the prospect of medals and promotion, many another would never have wanted to.

MacNair, far from ordinary in this respect, was the exception that proved the rule; MacGregor was the classic example. As a subaltern his zeal to catch the eye of his superiors had been legendary. He drilled his men to distraction and then turned to his horse, perfecting parade-ground feats straight from the circus ring.

> He clubbed his wretched company a dozen times a day;
> He used to quit his charger in a parabolic way;
> His method of saluting was a joy to all beholders
> But Ahasuerus Jenkins had a head upon his shoulders.

Kipling's man chose the easiest way up; he wooed Cornelia

Agrippina 'who was musical and fat' but who 'controlled a humble husband who, in turn, controlled a Dept.' MacGregor just kept on trying. He bombarded the press with letters, invented a new type of saddle and, at the despairing suggestion of his colleagues, bought his own trumpet and learnt to blow it—anything, in fact, to bring his name to notice. As a matter of course he volunteered for every expedition under the sun, including Forsyth's to Sinkiang. But better by far was a military expedition; a V.C. would mean a degree of recognition by no means beyond the dreams of his ambition. Friends were the first to concede that he was not an easy man to get on with. He was too grim and self-absorbed; only in the heat of battle did he become relaxed and good company. True to the traditions of Rob Roy, a supposed ancestor, he faced the bullets with a tartan plaid over his shoulder and a massive claymore in his hand. 'One of the most fearless men in the Indian Army', it was thought, but he was also one of the most blood-thirsty—and one of the most ambitious. 'Oh for a campaign', he cried, 'a long one and a fierce one. One that would put me in my grave or place me above injustice.' Injustice, of course, meant simply a lull in his promotion prospects. In the conduct of India's external relations every official attempt to negotiate rather than fight was viewed as an unkind thrust in the path of his career.

Another favourite ploy of the ambitious was the writing of anonymous and unsolicited reports. MacGregor had been a great one for this, tackling subjects that ranged from *On Clandestine Prostitution* to *On The Storing of Supplies in Abyssinia*. The idea was that the moment one was known to have been read with approval by someone in authority, forward would step the none-too-bashful author to acknowledge his work. Nauseating it may have been, but that was the way to get ahead. And for MacGregor it had at last worked. As Quarter Master General from 1880–85, he had already been knighted. He was only a step away from a generalship and he had a good chance of realising his ultimate ambition – Commander-in-Chief of the Indian Army.

But MacGregor, in the end, wrote one report too many. His longing for a campaign led him to take a passionate interest in the Great Game. Whilst his contemporaries were inclined to argue the Central Asian question as if it were some kind of academic dis-cipline, he took the view that the Russian menace was not a question but a fact. The army as a whole were naturally more 'forward' in their views than their civil equivalents; but even by their standards MacGregor was way out ahead. In all these articles and reports alarm-mongering had been his speciality and, while under Lord Ripon the Russian threat was officially played down, MacGregor conceived it as his personal mission in life to keep the flame burning. He cared little if he was more often ridiculed as a fire-eating prophet of doom; somehow the administration just had to be brought to a true realisation of India's imminent peril.

In his youth he had travelled widely in Afghanistan and Persia and there formed his views on India's vulnerability. But it was not as a traveller that he impinged on Gilgit; nor as a military reformer, in which role some claim he deserves recognition as the father of modern India's army. Rather, and more modestly, it was as the man who selected and coached the Gilgit Game's most distinguished players. His was the thinking that guided them and his the personality that influenced them. Within the Q.M.G's department he devoted his considerable energies to the creation of an Intelligence Branch for collating and analysing reports from across the frontier; MacNair's was one of its prize exhibits, Younghusband one of its most distinguished graduates. On the question of Afghanistan he badgered the Commander-in-Chief to get the troops sent back there a third time with the object of establishing a permanent hold on Herat and the middle Oxus. He also, with more success, urged on Ripon and the British Foreign Office the necessity of demarcating the northern boundary of Afghanistan. In his case it was not so much a question of showing the Russians just where they must draw the line in their advance through Central Asia, as of getting the despised 'politicals', and the equally contemptible Viceroy, to commit themselves to a line which, if encroached on, would mean war. Simultaneously information was amassed about the likely strengths and deployment of both Russian and Indian troops in the event of war breaking out. The results of this last were embodied in the fatal report, *The Defence of India*, published secretly in 1883, soon after MacNair's return.

In his blunt military way MacGregor set down, by numbers, the troops that would be available to both sides and the objectives they could reasonably attain during the first ninety days of hostilities. The Russians would probably launch a five-pronged attack, three columns being aimed at Kabul and Herat, one at Chitral and one at Gilgit and Kashmir. Without advance warning he thought it doubtful whether, in the present state of India's defences, any of these places could be saved. To occupy them in advance of hostilities was therefore a basic precaution. But this in itself was not enough. The expected assault would for the first time embroil British troops in a major continental struggle along a landlocked frontier. British resources in terms of manpower were not up to such a challenge; but India's were. The Indian army should be reorganised and expanded to constitute a major fighting force of continental proportions.

Lord Ripon was a great admirer of Sir John Lawrence, the originator of the policy of 'masterly inactivity'. In the light of recent Russian behaviour which included the capture of Merv just beyond the Afghan frontier and another spate of activity on the Pamirs, this policy could scarcely look less appropriate. Moreover MacGregor didn't hide the fact that his paper was not just an academic exercise; it was a polemic designed to arouse the administration or, failing that, to create such a wave of Russophobia that the administration would be discredited.

'I solemnly assert my belief', he concluded, 'that there can never be a real settlement of the Russo-Indian question till Russia is driven out of the Caucasus and Turkistan.' This was going too far. Turkistan was virtually the whole of Central Asia. Russia's advance, it seemed, was not to be held up but to be reversed, war not shunned but invited and the frontiers of India pitched deep into the heart of the continent. Such intemperate rantings did his cause no good at all. But it was not this that caused all the trouble; MacGregor was entitled to his own views. Where he went wrong was in promulgating them while Quarter Master General and in allowing the press to see a paper that was supposed to be strictly confidential. Such indiscretion looked too much like the attempt it obviously was to pressurise the government. Gladstone regarded it as a direct criticism of Liberal policy and demanded an explanation. The Q.M.G. was allowed to retain his post but the suppression of *The Defence of India* and the reprimand that followed spelt death to his future prospects.

In disgrace he saw out his term of office as Q.M.G. and in 1886, a sick and embittered man, accepted a vastly inferior posting. The following year he was gazetted a Major-General on compassionate grounds; he was a dying man. Sadly the news of his promotion arrived a fortnight too late. The irony of such an intensely ambitious man realising one of his greatest dreams two weeks after being laid in the grave is rivalled only by his disgrace coinciding with a period during which all that he stood for was coming back into favour.

In December 1884 Ripon resigned as Viceroy and was succeeded by Lord Dufferin. Again this was Gladstone's choice; but Dufferin was altogether a more flexible and outward looking statesman. He had once been a Tory, his background was diplomatic including a spell as Ambassador in St. Petersburg, and, in India, foreign affairs would remain his speciality. Which was just as well; for, three months after taking office, he was faced with a major war scare as grave as that of 1876. MacGregor had urged the idea of demarcating the north-western section of the Afghan frontier as a way of getting a timid administration to commit itself to a line that it would be bound to defend. Ripon went ahead with the scheme confident that a well defined frontier would reduce the risk of war. In the event it all but precipitated it. Staking out a prior claim to the Panjdeh oasis, Russian troops coolly routed an Afghan detachment. Immediately British troops in India were put on the alert, Gladstone secured a vote of credit for £11 million and Dufferin began seriously to consider sending the army to hold Herat. Had the Amir taken the matter to heart as much as the British, these preparations would have been more than justified. But probably he had never heard of Panjdeh and it was his total indifference to the affair which more than anything cooled the atmosphere. Nevertheless MacGregor's grim forebodings appeared to have been partially vindicated; clearly it was high time that the merits of a 'forward' policy were reconsidered.

When a great man's career was in eclipse, or when the policy for which he stood was out of favour, the long appendage of subordinates who had pinned their colours to his standard lay low in the regimental lines, biding their time. Then, the moment the climate seemed to change, out they all came brandishing their connections and clamouring for promotion and appointments. In 1885 MacGregor himself was out of the running, disgraced beyond redemption; and the change of government that usually heralded such a move actually followed it. Otherwise the signs were unmistakable. General Frederick Sleigh Roberts, the go-getting 'our Bobs' of Kipling and a comrade and admirer of MacGregor's, was appointed Commander-in-Chief. About the same time, April 1885, Dufferin chose as his Foreign Secretary the young Mortimer Durand. In his 'forward' outlook Durand was altogether more subtle and realistic than MacGregor, but he was still MacGregor's man; he had once shared a house with him and was now his brother-in-law. Then in June 1885 Gladstone resigned and Lord Salisbury, Disraeli's successor as Tory Leader, formed his first ministry. It was pure coincidence, though not one without significance, that on the very day that he did so the first ever major British mission to Dardistan marched out in a long column from Srinagar. It was headed by Colonel William Lockhart, MacGregor's closest friend and his deputy in the Intelligence Branch.

The Lockhart Mission was conceived primarily as an expression of this new climate of opinion; its roving character, its varied objectives and the whole conduct of the exercise will bear this out. However it had to have some specific points of reference and this was where MacNair came in. His modest little journey had raised four intriguing questions; could the direct route from Peshawar—or Nowshera—to Chitral be opened for British use; could the 'well-disposed' Kafirs be incorporated into the scheme of India's defences; was the Dora pass really another of those alarming backdoors into India; and had Aman-ul-Mulk of Chitral changed his tune since the days when Biddulph had virtually written him off? In *The Defence of India* MacGregor had emphasised the importance of Chitral by awarding it the attention of a whole Russian column. MacNair had no good opinion of Aman-ul-Mulk but he did report that the old chief was seriously exercised about Russian activities on the Pamirs; in 1883 one group of Russian explorers had reached Shignan and another, surveying, had touched Wakhan. The latter had given it out that they were hoping to reach Chitral and Kafiristan. In fact Aman-ul-Mulk understood that they were empowered to make him an offer for the Ludkho valley leading down from the Dora or the Darkot valley where Hayward had been killed. 'Shall I kill them or make prisoners of them or send them to Your Excellency?' he had asked Lord Ripon.

Lockhart was to advise him; indeed the need to secure Chitral was now considered so great that terms of friendship were to be established regardless of the Mehtar's known duplicity. No longer was this all just a reflection of British anxieties about Afghan dealings with Chitral; rather it was a straightforward attempt to thwart Russian ambitions. Lockhart and his men were cautioned about leaking news of the expedition to the press; 'the less the public hears of it the better'. It was recognised that news of a British visit to Kafiristan would bring a protest from the Amir and perhaps even an attack on the Kafirs. But the reason for designating the rest of the mission's itinerary as top secret was simply to steal a march on what Kipling called 'the power to the North'.

Since the closure of the Gilgit Agency four years earlier, the Dards and the Dogras had been left to themselves; Biddulph's bungalow stood empty, goats grazing the garden. This was not because Ripon had evolved some new policy for guarding the Hindu Kush routes. On the contrary he had still relied on the Dogras doing the job for him, and this in spite of the fact that they were clearly incapable of exercising any influence beyond Gilgit and were scarcely more trustworthy than the perfidious Dards. However, the country had remained at peace. The Maharaja, now an old man, knew from bitter experience just how far he could go. Sensibly he refrained from pushing the likes of Ghazan Khan or Aman-ul-Mulk. The subsidies were paid out, the *vakils*, with their scrawny sheep and their little bags of gold dust, trooped in, and high in the Hindu Raj, well out of harm's way, the final act in the saga of the Yasin brothers was played out; Pahlwan was gunned down by his equally outlawed brother, the dreaded Mulk Aman.

Life in Dardistan was hardly idyllic but it was as settled as it had ever been. So much so that Leitner would soon look back on this period, the lull before the storm, as a sort of golden age. Dogra rule, compared with what was to follow, did not seem such an unmitigated disaster as he had once thought. Its sheer ineffectiveness meant that the Dards at least maintained their independence and their unique way of life. Increasingly it seemed that the real irritant was the arrival of a British officer. Like a wasps' nest the Hindu Kush was quiet enough until stirred into frenzy by the meddlings of a Biddulph or a Hayward. Or indeed a Lockhart.

8. The Lost Brethren

From Srinagar the new mission followed the usual route over the Great Himalaya. Losing two weeks waiting for the Kamri pass to open and several days ferrying their baggage across the Indus at Bunji, they reached Gilgit in late July 1885. Biddulph's bungalow was commandeered by the officers—'a capital house' thought Lockhart—and Dr. Giles, the mission's surgeon and geologist, set up his dispensary. If the presence of the mission was not immediately resented it was largely thanks to the doctor's dexterity in the matter of restoring noses; plastic surgery had a great future in a place where the normal punishment for the pettiest of crimes was mutilation.

Meanwhile Lockhart took stock of his party. Undoubtedly there had been a good case for getting away from the clandestine one-man-shows that had previously represented British attempts to explore Dardistan. The Lockhart mission, however, went to the other extreme. There were four British officers—Lockhart, Giles, Colonel Woodthorpe in charge of surveying, and Captain Barrow also of the Intelligence—each with two ponies and three or four servants. Then there were five native surveyors, a military escort of Sikhs and a baggage train of 300 mules laden with beads for the natives that included an arsenal of breech-loaders. Mortimer Durand, the new Foreign Secretary, almost certainly wanted it this way; the unspecified object of the mission was to give the Dards some inkling of the true prestige and might of British India.

Lockhart, too, doubtless relished the kudos such a mighty force conferred on its leader. But already he was becoming aware of its drawbacks. In the recent hostilities in Afghanistan he had been Q.M.G. to General Roberts' force and had thus played an important part in the famous Kabul–Kandahar march. He seems, however, to have had no previous experience of the Himalayas. Nor had he apparently sought Biddulph's advice. For he, surely, would have stressed the idiocy of taking a mule train into Dardistan; in fact his own solution to the problem of mountain carriage had been a flock of pack-bearing sheep as used in Tibet (they didn't need feeding and, when you had eaten their loads, you could always eat their mutton). Other travellers had equally imaginative solutions; Hayward was a yak man—it was the only beast that could match his own powers of endurance; and Younghusband, introducing the idea of supply dumps along his proposed trail, plumped for the high load factor of the Bactrian camel. Lockhart presumably thought that in adopting the mules that had performed so well in Afghanistan he was playing safe. But the parapets and rock staircases of Dardistan were not built for quadrupeds that could not be carried; and hauling several hundreds of them up and down on ropes was a slow process. Accordingly, at Gilgit, he took on two hundred porters and reduced the mules to sixty. Or rather, fifty-nine. For on the first day's march out of Gilgit a significant portion of the mission's exchequer, 4,000 rupees in silver, plus the mule to which it was tied, plummeted down a sheer cliff face into the river. A day was wasted, fishing fruitlessly, and for the whole year that the mission would remain in the field Lockhart would be desperately scrounging cash from anyone willing to advance it. It was a bad start.

From Gilgit he headed west for Chitral via the direct route over the Shandur pass. Woodthorpe and Barrow, meanwhile, were sent round via Yasin to study the Darkot and Baroghil; in the process they recorded that transfiguration version of the Hayward martyr-dom. The passes, or rather the approaches to them, were less impressive. The Baroghil was all that Biddulph had said; it presented 'the most curious and startling feature in this part of the world; the mighty range suddenly sinks down abruptly into absolute insignificance'. But how deceptive this was. For an invading force, once across the pass, had either to climb up the Darkot into Yasin or down the glaciers into Chitral. Woodthorpe tried both. In each case his men were severely frost-bitten and the party all but benighted; and this was in August, supposedly one of the best months for travel in the Hindu Kush. A platoon of marines might get through but an army with artillery was out of the question. Without extensive road building the danger was one of infiltration, not invasion.

Oddly, the only pass in the region that would ever see the passage of artillery was that which Lockhart was negotiating with the baggage. The Shandur is neither very high nor steep and its position between transverse valleys well south of the Hindu Kush watershed relegated its importance purely to that of internal communications. Lockhart preferred to call it a plateau rather than a pass. He got his party across without mishap and agreed with Biddulph in regarding it as an excellent corridor by which the route down the Chitral valley could be commanded from Gilgit. But ten years later an ageing Irish colonel with a desperate band of followers would beg to differ. In mid-January with the snow shoulder deep and the temperature well below freezing, the Shandur was a nightmare. Guns could neither be dragged over nor ponies manage to carry them across. To the men who finally shouldered the heavy steel-rimmed wheels, the icy barrels and the boxes of ammunition, Lockhart's name would be one best not mentioned.

On September 2 Woodthorpe and Barrow rejoined the main party at Mastuj and the mission started down the Chitral valley to the capital. The road was execrable. Then as now, each little group of hamlets in its green oasis was cut off from the next by miles of sizzling rock. The foaming river monopolises the narrow valley floor forcing the track to switch-back relentlessly up and down the steep and dusty bluffs. Here the only thing that grows is artemisia, a desert shrub that fills the air with an astringent, thirst provoking aroma. The colours too are desert colours, brown rock, pale sand, white sky. In the higher side valleys there is timber and grazing but along the channel gouged by the Chitral river the aspect of parched austerity is more Afghan than Alpine; lizards cock their horny heads just out of reach, while tumbleweed and will-o-the-wisps make fair play on the gentler slopes.

The contrasts, too, are typically those of desert lands. An irrigation channel crossing the face of a hill draws a straight line between Sahara and garden. In one stride you pass from glare and dust into the rich green of rice fields and the scent of wild roses. On one side not a tree, not a blade of grass; on the other chenars, poplars and acacias, and below them a tangle of fruit trees, apple, pear, peach and pomegranate. Golden orioles flash through the branches and asparagus, introduced by a grandson of Aman-ul-Mulk, grows wild in the grass.

Lockhart and his men took eight days over a journey of sixty odd miles. In spite of Biddulph and MacNair no-one had really explored Chitral; the new mission now made good the deficiency. Giles was a geologist and something of a naturalist. With his help and that of Woodthorpe and his surveyors, Barrow was able to compile the first gazetteer for the whole valley. Tirich Mir, 'looking like a mass of frosted silver' according to the poetically inclined Lockhart, turned out to be rather lower than Biddulph had estimated, about 25,000 feet, and no other serious rivals to Everest or K2 were spied. But the oases were every bit as populous and prosperous as Biddulph had hinted. Chitral was at last revealed as much the largest and most important of all the Hindu Kush valleys—as well as being the most vulnerable.

As the mission approached the largest oasis, which even today hardly justifies the name of Chitral town, Aman-ul-Mulk's letters became increasingly frequent. This was presumably a good sign though, as they were written in rhyme, it was hard to tell; even the versifying Lockhart could make nothing of them. Four miles from his fort, where the valley opens out, the Mehtar was waiting for them. Extending a fist like a prizefighter's he grasped the colonel's fingers and, 'according to the very disagreeable custom of the country', continued to fondle them as they rode side by side. Across the river, Chitrali irregulars were drumming and shouting for all they were worth, horsemen in garish robes swept back and forth blazing away with their matchlocks while from the fort an artillery salute, 'most irregularly fired', boomed across the valley; 'the effect was good'.

As a centrepiece, the Mehtar and the colonel hand in hand could hardly have been bettered. Lockhart was cut out to be an imperial figure. Hooded eyes and droopy moustaches gave him a St. Bernard's look of noble imperturbability tinged with a hint of disdain. Big by any standards he stood patrician head and mighty shoulders above the tallest Dard and required six strong men to hoist him onto his pony. (In Chitral it was not customary for the mighty to mount unaided.) But the Mehtar was also a six man proposition. Not so tall, he was broad almost to squareness. Lockhart guessed 'the old fox' was knocking 70; he was also toothless which made it hard to follow his mumbled Persian. But there was no denying the nobility of bearing. Nor the 'determined cast of countenance' characterised by a scimitar of a nose, fair skinned and bony, cleaving the face between turban and henna-red beard.

Eleven o'clock next day official exchanges began. The officers swopped their battered tweeds for dress uniforms and their walking sticks for swords. Tents were so arranged that a long street ran through the lines to a flagpost before a brightly coloured awning. The Union Jack was raised, the Chitralis were welcomed by a guard of honour, a salute was fired and official introductions were performed with due ceremony. It might have been the beginning of some grand durbar, except that there then followed a sticky snack of 'tea, coffee, cake, chocolate and toffee'. Just why Lockhart should bother to report to Durand, the Foreign Secretary, in such detail about a minor matter of decorum is not explained. But it's good to know that the Mehtar then 'filled his mouth with snuff, slowly chewed it and spat the result into the turban of one of his officers'. Lockhart should have been warned. The veneer of propriety and cordiality was both thin and deceptive.

More probably the colonel was simply amused. The son of a landed Scots minister, he would eventually realise MacGregor's ambition of becoming Commander-in-Chief in India; he was a good, even a great soldier whose manipulation of the strings of patronage won him remarkably few enemies and many intensely loyal friends. 'His heart was as sound as his head' according to an obituarist, and for once this wasn't just an epigraphic platitude. But hard-headedness to the point of insensitivity and stalwart determination to the point of obstinacy were not what was required of a political officer negotiating with the treacherous Dards. Nor were geniality, inoffensiveness and the best will in the world much better. It is impossible to avoid the impression that Lockhart, and the rest of his staff, handled the Chitral situation with incredible naïvety. What they wanted was some sort of guarantee that, in the event of a Russian move from the north, Aman-ul-Mulk would hold all the key gorges into Chitral and allow free passage for British troops. Given the now acknowledged difficulty of the Hindu Kush routes, such an attack could only be small scale. The Chitralis, whom Lockhart reckoned 'perhaps the best men any-where up or down a precipice', should be well capable of with-standing it until British troops could storm up by MacNair's route from Peshawar and finish the enemy off. Imagine, then, Lockhart's delight when the Mehtar unasked, offered to do just that. All he wanted in return was the willingly given guarantee that Chitral territory should descend intact to his heirs. Barrow could hardly draw up the treaty quick enough.

But then 'the old grasper' raised the question of his subsidy. From Kashmir, in return for a few hawks and greyhounds, he was now getting 16,500 rupees a year. How much more might he expect in anticipation of these new services? Lockhart had already presented his own little trousseau of Sniders, revolvers, broadcloth and 'a miscellaneous assortment of tools, combs, looking glasses, knives, scissors, thread, buttons, braids and toys' valued at 5,000 rupees, not to mention much of his camp furniture (some of it is still to be found about the valley today). He was not empowered to offer more, and the fact of the matter was that Aman-ul-Mulk would defend the whole of India on these sort of terms; he was also happy to sign treaties to that effect. But it didn't mean that 'we now have a hold of Chitral' as Lockhart triumphantly announced to Durand.

The question of the subsidy was left to be sorted out by one of Aman-ul-Mulk's sons who would visit India for the approaching winter. Lockhart noticed no obvious decline in the Mehtar, but the next visitor to Chitral would find him semi-senile. At all events he couldn't last much longer and it was vital to sow the seeds of future friendship with his heir. For this, six months of V.I.P. treatment in India was reckoned the best possible grounding. The only problem was to decide who should receive it, and again Lockhart made a hideous blunder.

Aman-ul-Mulk was reputed to have sixty sons of whom three or four were regarded as serious contenders for the throne. There was Amir-ul-Mulk, an unpredictable youth of psychopathic tendencies who had already objected to his share of the mission's bounty. Then there was a child of five whom the mission had passed on the road from Mastuj riding on a white pony. This was Shuja-ul-Mulk, a very long shot indeed for the succession though, in the end, the only one to survive the impending bloodbath. Much better known to Lockhart were the two most serious contenders, Nizam-ul-Mulk, the playboy chief who had been installed in Yasin, and his deadly rival Afzul-ul-Mulk, the quiet athletic chief of Mastuj. It seems pretty clear that already Nizam was considered the senior in precedence. There was no simple rule of primogeniture but he was the older and both as ruler of Yasin, the more important dependency, and as the companion of his father during the official welcome given to the mission, he looked to be the favourite.

Lockhart chose to ignore this. Afzul was the better man so Afzul should be the British candidate. Nizam was all that he couldn't stand, 'a greedy beast' who exhausted the mission's supply of sugar, tried to make off with their mess-tent and pestered Giles for his Arab and his retriever. He was also a homosexual and his rowdy parties with a troupe of dancing boys kept the mission awake half the night. If Afzul should 'deprive him some fine day of his sleek, curly head', Lockhart for one would have no objections. 'Dear Afzul', he was altogether different; strong, manly, generous and without a sweet tooth in his head. His comrades adored him and so did Lockhart. 'Will you please be very civil to young Afzul'. he told Durand. 'I mean exceptionally civil. He is worth it.'

Durand, however, had scarcely heard of Afzul. Nizam was the heir presumptive and it was to Nizam that he had just sent the official invitation. Informed of this, Lockhart was all for sending both men to India; the government could then judge for themselves. But their father thought otherwise; Lockhart might choose, but only one son might go. 'Of course Nizam must go,' he replied, furious at having been made to look such a fool. Worse was to come; the following winter in Gilgit he found himself having to act as the gay young chief's chaperone. With his usual gang of musicians, dancers and hooligans Nizam descended on Kashmir territory, determined to whoop it up all the way to Simla. 'The young barbarian' set fire to the hospital, smashed up the telegraph office (there was an office but no line back to Kashmir as yet) and demanded 'the fattest sheep, the finest flour and [inevitably] the most expensive sugar'. He was petulant in the extreme when Lockhart had to explain that the Dogra troops were not willing to dance for him; and he left in a huff, with the boys still pirouetting and the bands still playing, on New Year's Eve.

Aman-ul-Mulk's main interest in the whole affair had been to leave as open as possible the selection of his heir. Patricide was the first thought of any Dard crown prince and the Mehtar's best chance of dying a natural death therefore lay in seeing that none of his sons acquired pre-eminence in his lifetime. Lockhart's adoption of Afzul must have seemed a heaven-sent opportunity of redressing the senior status enjoyed by Nizam. Although the trip to India would seem to have given Nizam another advantage, Lockhart would see to it that Afzul was not forgotten; in 1887 he too received the V.I.P. tour. The result was that, when the crisis finally broke, the Indian government would be in the embarrassing position of having two rival candidates.

Lockhart had been invited to choose who should go to India and so he had done so. He had been offered assurances about the defence of Chitral and he had accepted them. Gullibility wasn't in it. He had also been told that Chitral was his; he might go wherever he pleased, even east into Dir or west into Kafiristan. He determined to do both. To Durand he wrote that 'it would be a great thing to get hold of Dir as we now have hold of Chitral'. Except for a narrow belt of Pathan country between there and Peshawar, this would effectively open up MacNair's route from British territory. However Aman-ul-Mulk knew this too; he had no intention of seeing it opened up, nor of incurring the hostility of his Pathan neighbours by doing so. Every political initiative in this direction, including Lockhart's, came to nothing and it would eventually take a corps of fifteen thousand to force the Malakand and open the Lowarai. The nearest Lockhart's mission got was to Drosh on the Chitral side of the latter.

As regards letting the mission cross into Kafiristan, the Mehtar also had second thoughts. He made much of the difficulties of the country and of the savagery of its people. And he insisted that, if the British party went ahead, he be relieved of all responsibility for their safety. Lockhart agreed, giving him a signed paper to that effect. This was extremely dangerous; 'the old fox', armed with such a carte blanche, could dispose of the mission whenever he felt so inclined. But the Dora pass had to be visited and it was essential to explore further the political sympathies of the Kafirs who lived in its vicinity. On September 19, abandoning the last of the ill-fated mules, the mission headed west up the Ludkho valley.

*   *   *

When, before the R.G.S., Leitner had savaged MacNair for entering Kafiristan with neither a linguist nor an ethnologist, he had actually made a good point. The great interest of the country was, after all, its people. Kafirs reaching the slave markets of Bukhara invariably caused a sensation. One Russian authority had

actually claimed that they were Slavs—which might sound absurd
but, given the tempo of pan-Slavism in the Balkans at this time,
had ominous implications. The Russians had noted not only that
Kafiristan was a racial anomaly but also that it was the one place
along the whole mountain frontier that had had no diplomatic
dealings with either the British or their feudatories; it just might be
the long sought chink in India's defences.

Lockhart, though he too lacked the services of an ethnologist,
was immediately impressed by the Kafirs' willingness to accept
the British as long lost brethren. To their Mohammedan
neighbours both races were *Kafirs*, i.e. infidels, and to them it was
a source of malicious glee that the savages of Kafiristan honestly
believed that they shared a racial heritage with the mighty *sahibs*.
When the ever co-operative Afzul had procured a few Kafirs for
Lockhart's inspection, their first reaction had been 'to give out
quite proudly that they are of the same race as the English and
expect to be treated as such'. Like some rare pedigree of dog en-
countering one of its own species for the first time, the Kafirs were
consumed with a curiosity that far exceeded that of their visitors.
The tweed of the Norfolk jackets was closely examined, the heavy
boots sniffed and weighed and, to make sure that the newcomers
really were white all over, the Kafirs craned their necks to view
down a shirt front and jerked at a passing trouser leg. Lockhart
endured the scrutiny with his usual strained geniality. He certainly
appreciated that in encouraging this supposed relationship lay the
simplest means of winning the Kafirs' loyalty. One wonders, though,
whether he appreciated its corollary; that if the Kafirs regarded
the British as brethren because they were white and non-Islamic,
they might think exactly the same about the Russians.

The importance of such a consideration was heightened by what
the mission discovered about the Dora pass. 'Could rapidly be
made fit for wheels', wrote Lockhart. Some of the party had
ridden to the top without dismounting and the approach from the
Badakshan side looked just as easy. Having now inspected most of
the other passes into Dardistan they were confident that this was
much the most vulnerable. It was higher than the Baroghil and,
where the track skirted a lake (now renamed Lake Dufferin),
could easily be barred. So could its approaches near the mouth
of the Ludkho valley where the path wound through a mountain

crack four hundred feet deep and no wider than a country
lane. But Lockhart's point was that if the natives co-operated with
the aggressor this route, and this route alone, posed no serious
obstacles to the passage of artillery and substantial numbers of
troops. There were no glaciers, little snow and therefore predictable river crossings. The Dora to Lockhart would become what the
Baroghil had been to Biddulph, the reason for, and focus of, a
scheme for the defence of the whole of Dardistan.

But first the Kafirs. From the Dora the mission struck south-
west into the bewildering mountain network to which this strange
race owed its survival. All seemed to go well. The high valleys
offered a wonderful contrast to the heat and dust of Chitral. Woods
of evergreen oak, cedar and pine, sparkling streams at the foot of
grassy slopes and the cool bracing air from the snowfields above
reminded Lockhart of the Alps. Though still accompanied by a
party of Chitralis, pressed on them by Aman-ul-Mulk, they had no
difficulty finding Kafir guides and at the first village were again
welcomed like long-lost prodigals. To the village shrine they were
taken to be reconciled with Imbra, the great spirit supposedly
common to all white peoples. Lockhart emptied his pockets of
small change, the priest addressed a large boulder and Imbra was
reported to be gratified.

'The Kafir religion', according to a later visitor, 'is a somewhat
low form of idolatry with an admixture of ancestor worship and
some traces of fire-worship.' Lockhart missed the fire-worship but
the ancestors were everywhere; he was introduced to a fresh clump
at each village. The Kafirs' greatest artistic endeavours were lav-
ished on the carving of these effigies of the dead. Some were as
much as fifteen feet tall. Seated, standing or mounted on horse-
back the ancestors were positioned in sociable groups; there, time
and the prevailing wind would gradually loosen their foundations
till they keeled over like drunken sailors. But the hard cedar wood
and the dry atmosphere militated against decay. They remained
straight-backed and beetle-browed like pieces of a giant's chess set,
even when flat on the grass. Lockhart was making the acquaintance
of the accumulation of centuries, much of which is now dispersed
through the world's museums. Along with some low straight-
backed chairs, a few carved timbers, some weapons and imple-
ments, they represent the pathetic legacy of a now defunct people.

As the mission penetrated deeper into the country they, like MacNair, were gradually initiated into the local specialities, the wine, the cakes that tasted like plum pudding and, above all, the dancing.

It was a mixture of country dance and Highland Schottishe. Advancing and retiring in lines, intermingling in couples, they kept excellent time to the music of reed pipes and two small drums, and marked points in the dance by ear-piercing whistles on their fingers and by brandishing their axes. The red firelight, the savage figures, and their fierce but perfectly timed gestures, presented a weird spectacle, which it would be difficult for the on-looker ever to forget.

No women took part because, as the menfolk explained, it would be degrading in the presence of outsiders like the accompanying Chitralis. Lockhart and company were relieved; the women were proving a sore trial. 'To judge from their manners their morals cannot be very high. To put it in the mildest language they cannot have much modesty.' Precisely what Lockhart was trying to imply is not clear. Was it just their lewd gestures that so upset him or was he being importuned in more direct ways? The only subsequent European visitor to Kafiristan was invited to consummate the reunion of the races by taking a Kafir maiden to bed. But it looks as if the colonel and his men had to resist more than just an invitation.

Lockhart might draw the line at seduction, but nevertheless he acquired a son. Gumara was a man about the colonel's own age. He was also 'strong and had a reputation for bravery (having killed twenty-nine Mussulmans), so it seemed that his adoption as a son might be of use to the party and the proposal was agreed to'. The suggestion had come from the Kafirs; Lockhart had no idea what was involved other than that he would acquire a useful ally and oblige his possessive hosts without betraying Mrs. Lockhart. In the event he may well have regretted such solicitude for his spouse. The adoption ceremony started reasonably enough. A sheep was sacrificed, its kidneys removed, lightly toasted and passed to the two principals on the point of a knife. Between mouthfuls father and son stood a foot apart and blew kisses at one another. Then the surprise. Lockhart's coat and shirt were torn open, butter was rubbed on his left nipple and the Kafir hastily applied his lips. Gumara sucked like a vampire, the colonel winced in pain and the reunion of the races was at last achieved; the long lost Kafirs of Gish, the great war god who was supposed to have deserted Kafiristan for London, were reconciled with their Kafir brethren, the children of Imbra.

Gumara proved to be a model son. He carried his father across every stream and generally tried to be of use about the camp. But back in Chitral his anxiety to be never more than kiss-blowing distance from the colonel grew wearisome. Communication was impossible after they had parted from their bilingual guides and the poor Kafir had to be abruptly orphaned. It was a pity Lockhart didn't remember Leitner's Lahore home for the strayed and unwanted of the Hindu Kush.

Gradually the mission's policy of humouring their hosts seemed to pay off. The Kafir chiefs were eating out of Lockhart's hands and Barrow was instructed to draw up what must surely be one of the British Empire's most bizarre defensive treaties.

Covenant made between Colonel W. S. A. Lockhart on the part of the British Government, and the following chiefs of the Bashgal tribe:
1. Mara
2. Malik
3. Gulmer
4. Chandlu, son of Mara
5. Merig, son of Malik
6. Shtaluk, son of Gulmer

In the event of an enemy of Great Britain approaching the frontiers of Kafiristan, the above-named will send all available men of their own to the threatened quarter, to hinder or repel the invader. In return I agree, on the part of the British Government, to pay the several chiefs mentioned the sum of ten rupees per mensem per man placed in the field, and to provide arms for them; the chiefs on their part agreeing to receive one British officer per 500 men so raised, as instructors and leaders. This agreement has been sealed by the ceremony of sharing a goat's heart between myself and the above-mentioned chiefs.

W. S. A. Lockhart. Colonel.

The treaty was dated 1st October 1885. Lockhart, like an eager
Monopoly player collecting his set, was confident that he had now
got hold of Kafiristan too. Before passing on the good tidings to
Durand, however, he had cause for second thoughts. At 9 a.m.
the following day the mission's path was barred by a crowd of
excited Kafirs brandishing their axes. A Chitrali sent forward to
parley was pitched over a cliff and a Kafir who remained loyal to
Lockhart was hit on the neck with an axe handle. The situation
looked extremely nasty. The Sikh escort were instructed to loosen
cartridges and the Chitralis were ordered back out of the line of
fire. This last move, however, abruptly cooled matters; it was clear
that it was the Chitralis whom the Kafirs found so objectionable.

'Go away now by the Shawal pass,' the Kafir spokesman commanded. 'Don't be angry; we are your friends but are determined
not to let the Chitralis remain another day in the valley. Come
back in the spring but come without the Chitralis and you can go
wherever you like.'

Lockhart replied that he would do just that; he might try to
engineer an approach from Badakshan in which case he would not
be travelling under the auspices of Chitral. The Kafirs were
satisfied. They kissed his hands and again begged him not to be
angry.

Peeved rather than angry, Lockhart headed back to Chitral along
the route taken by MacNair. On the Shawal pass he found a
couple of tarns by which to commemorate his old friend—they
became the MacGregor Lakes—and reached Chitral on October
7. Aman-ul-Mulk's reception of the mission was less enthusiastic
than in the previous month; his one ambition was to send them
packing before they devoured the valley's entire supply of winter
fodder. Lockhart took the point, sending the baggage straight on
to Gilgit and himself following as soon as all outstanding business
had been completed. In early December he reached winter quarters
in Biddulph's bungalow.

Here two interesting bits of news awaited him. The first was
that he had just narrowly escaped being waylaid by the dreaded
Mulk Aman, last of the three Yasin brothers. As in the past,
rumour had it that the Kashmir governor in Gilgit had paid Mulk
Aman to stir up trouble for the mission. So reminiscent of
Biddulph's and Hayward's vicissitudes was this that Lockhart

too conceded that the Dogras were just a liability; they should be sent back to Bunji and the east bank of the Indus. During the long Gilgit winter he brooded over a new scheme for the defence of the Hindu Kush which, for the first time, excluded Kashmir completely. He recommended not so much the reopening of the Gilgit Agency as 'the acquisition of Gilgit'. He might disguise it simply as a reinstatement of the arrangement that had led to Biddulph's appointment; but the nineteen British officers he wanted at Gilgit were to have administrative and revenue duties as well as the purely military. The mountain battery and the twelve companies of infantry were to consist of Dard levies and men recruited from 'a good man-producing part of the Punjab'; their diet was to include huge quantities of beef, anathema to the Hindu Dogras. To Lockhart's way of thinking, the beauty of the scheme was that by doing away with the Dogras the main source of friction in the area would have been removed; all his predecessors in Dardistan would have agreed. However they would surely have had reservations about his corollary; that Dard treaties and Dard troops were infinitely more trustworthy. The cornerstones of Lockhart's scheme were his new alliance with Chitral and his conviction that the Dards, helped by British officers and arms, could defend their own passes.

The other bit of news that awaited him in Gilgit would eventually result in a second and rather different conclusion being drawn about how best to defend the Hindu Kush. A lone *farangi*, it was said, had arrived in Shignan on the upper Oxus, having crossed the Pamirs. 'An Englishman from Yarkand', apparently, 'a middle-sized man, clean-shaven, with his following and baggage all on ponies'. Who is he, asked Lockhart in a letter to Durand? And what is he doing here? The description gave nothing away except that the stranger must be a trifle eccentric; baring one's chin to the razor in the below-freezing temperatures of the Pamirs could better be described as masochistic. No British traveller had been that way since Gordon and Biddulph in 1874. And since Lockhart himself was toying with the idea of heading for the Pamirs as soon as conditions permitted, he was sorely troubled by the identity of this unfortunate interloper.

His mind was hardly put at rest when the answer finally came. It took the form of a letter not from India but from Zebak in

Badakshan; and on the face of it was a matter-of-fact request for news and medicine. But to men who had just spent six hard months establishing for themselves a reputation as travellers and explorers the signature at the end was the ultimate put-down; they must have felt like venturesome seagulls sighting their first albatross. It was signed, in an infuriatingly neat hand, 'Ney Elias'.

9. Too Old and Too Broken

The dedicated scientific explorer is a notoriously difficult beast to interpret; but surely none was ever more dedicated or more baffling than Elias. The problem is not a lack of evidence, as with Biddulph, nor of credibility, as with Leitner. Neither is Elias merely unexciting like Lockhart. Quite the contrary. In his lifetime he was both legend and enigma. To all who followed him into the heart of Asia his very name was an inspiration. Yet few knew his precise itineraries, fewer had actually seen him and scarcely any, had they done so, would have recognised him. Younghusband was an exception. He found himself sitting next to the slight and self-effacing hero on a train to Simla in 1889; he also had access to the secret itineraries. Not a man to diminish the pioneering content of his own work, he would later concede, in a remote corner of the Pamirs, that 'Mr. Ney Elias has travelled in this, as he has in almost every other, part of Asia'. In fact Younghusband did as much as anyone for the Elias myth; who, his wide public would wonder, was this elusive figure with the peculiar name to whom even the great Younghusband was anxious to bend a knee? And why, if he was such a giant among explorers, was he a plain 'Mr.' with neither rank nor honours? Nowadays the legend is badly in need of rehabilitation, but the enigma is as puzzling as ever. In an exhaustive and faithful study his recent biographer finds him still mysterious, still riddled with contradictions.

Wintering in Gilgit in 1886 Lockhart simply wanted to know what this celebrity was up to, trespassing on his sector of the frontier. In no mood to make allowances, he interpreted the short note from Zebak as a personal challenge; it was just what one might expect from another intensely ambitious explorer. One of the perks of travel was that of impressing lesser mortals by date-lining one's letters from the back of beyond; and the business of emerging, unannounced and ever so casually, from the unknown was a cherished vanity. Younghusband would be as bad as Leitner at bursting in, travel stained, weather scarred and all but forgotten, on unsuspecting dinner parties. Stanley erupting from the Dark Continent, Burke crawling in from the Outback or Philby looming out of the Empty Quarter, this was the stuff of travel, moments to be carefully managed by the explorer and long treasured by his fans.

But Elias, announcing himself from the wrong side of the Roof of the World? One can't be sure. It could have been the grand gesture; he certainly had plenty to crow about. While Lockhart and his battalion had been slogging laboriously from Srinagar to Kafiristan and back to Gilgit, a distance of about seven hundred miles, Elias with just four servants had whizzed right round him like an orbiting comet. Starting almost simultaneously, but from Simla, he had covered more like two thousand miles and had crossed in the process five of the world's grandest mountain systems (the Pir Panjal, Great Himalaya, Karakorams, Kun Lun and Pamirs). He had also found time to clarify that vexed question of the source of the Oxus, he had come up with some new and constructive observations on checking the Russian advance to the Hindu Kush, and he was now evidently blazing a trail round Badakshan. Lockhart, in spite of Woodthorpe's surveys and Barrow's political work, could scarcely compete; his mission had been eclipsed.

The whole thing was made much worse from Lockhart's point of view by the fact that no-one had ever bothered to tell him that Elias was in the field. It was one thing to be shown up as an amateur, quite another as a fool; to have had to wait for the 'clean-shaven Englishman' to reveal his identity had added insult to injury. For once he reacted with energy. No civilian explorer, albeit one working as a government agent, could be allowed to run rings round a highly organised military mission. His instructions had made no mention of the Pamirs or the Afghan provinces and, as for that idea of reaching Kafiristan from the Afghan side, it had been little more than a pipe-dream; the Afghans were not even supposed to know of his dealings with the Kafirs let alone provide him with access to them. But now, under the impetus of Elias' letter, the dream became a pressing resolve. With or without official sanction, Lockhart determined to force a path through Hunza, muscle in on Elias' achievements on the Pamirs and continue through Badakshan into the Kafir country. Showing all the

13 Ney Elias

14 Francis Younghusband in 1887

15 Col. Grombtchevski

16 Col. Algernon Durand

17 The famous meeting of Younghusband and Grombtchevski
at Khaian Aksai. Younghusband in bush hat,
Grombtchevski in uniform

18 Safdar Ali, Mir of Hunza, photographed when he was
an exile in Sinkiang

do or die competitiveness of the last phase of the Gilgit Game he was out to get his own back.

But was this being fair to Elias? If Lockhart had been less pre-occupied with the reputation of his own mission he would surely have conceded that Elias was not a man for gestures of one-upman-ship. The letter could simply have been written to warn him of the other's whereabouts and thus forestall any conflict of operations. Elias shows none of the dismissive conceit of the great explorer. 'That mute inglorious Milton', was how a contemporary described him; 'invincible modesty alone prevented his being known as one of the greatest English travellers'. His obituarists would all agree; he was morbidly sensitive about self-advertisement; none did so much and talked so little about it; and 'his true distinction was to die undistinguished'. Not, surely, the sort to cock a snook at any-one.

That Elias was one of the greatest of English travellers ought to be beyond question. In 1868 he had surveyed the mouth of the Yellow River in northern China. In 1872, making one of the most adven-turous solo journeys of the century, he had crossed the Gobi desert, the Mongolian steppes and most of Asiatic Russia en route from Peking to Moscow. For this marathon he was awarded a gold medal by the R.G.S. in 1873; the other, that year, went to H. M. Stanley for his discovery of Dr. Livingstone. Early in 1875 he had taken part in a mission from Burma into western China. In 1876 he had been appointed as British Representative at Leh, the capital of Ladakh, and from there had made two journeys across the breadth of the Western Himalayas into Sinkiang. He still pined for a chance to explore Tibet proper, but he was already regarded as the greatest Asian traveller of his day. At forty-one years old he might reason-ably have settled for the Pamirs as the crowning achievement of an outstanding active career.

However, besides the modest retiring nature, Elias had another much commented on trait; he was never satisfied. A degree of rest-lessness is essential to the make-up of any traveller; but this was something much more intriguing. His portrait gives a hint of the trouble. The fashionably lush moustache successfully hides the tell-tale line of the mouth; yet the eyes are arresting, a little too wide and intense, the eyebrows ever so slightly raised. A man of discern-ment, one feels, high-principled, aspiring. In fact he was all that and more; he was a perfectionist. His goals and his standards were ever the most ambitious conceivable. Yet, travel and government service being what they were, his achievements consistently fell short of them. A report from Elias on one of his journeys always begins with a catalogue of failures; even the great crossing of Asia is portrayed as a saga of frustrated plans and missed opportunities. Colleagues, when he has any, prove incompetent and irksome, his official instructions either incomplete or misdirected. And always there is some vital line of enquiry, some unmeasured peak, some unseen ruin or some untrodden path, that he has failed to pursue. A gratifying discovery is no consolation; it just serves to remind him of all the others he has missed. Perhaps it can be explained by the perfectionist's anxiety to anticipate every possible criticism. But the suggestion has been made that this determination to denigrate was the product of some far deeper psychological exigency bordering on masochism. One certainly wonders whether that famous modesty was not something far more complex. The man who acknowledges only his own standards can afford a certain detachment about his public image; but what others take for humility is really the outcome of an impossible vanity.

As a traveller he was the most professional and exacting imaginable. Observations for latitude and longitude, for altitude and temperature, distances and bearings were as essential to his progress as the availability of carriage and supplies. As a schoolboy, his diary had amounted to little more than a careful daily log of the weather and, now as then, his journals rigorously excluded all personal detail. In blizzard or sandstorm, on a mountain pass or in a Simla office his handwriting remained impossibly neat, his prose concise, his calculations meticulous. And always—proof surely of a relentless professionalism—written in indelible pencil on the flimsiest of paper. Other travellers might indulge in the odd luxury; Leitner found pocket space for his Bovril and Younghusband was wont to squeeze in a bottle of sherry; missions like Lockhart's boasted tinned foods from Fortnums and a veritable cellar of claret and madeira. Not so Elias. If there was room for a bottle of sherry he would have filled it with a spare sextant.

Not surprisingly he was also a loner. His passionate belief in small unencumbered expeditions looked sensible in the context of deserts and mountains where supplies were hard to come by; and in the Pamirs it would be dramatically vindicated. In fact Lockhart's extravaganza would be the only one of its kind to enter Dardistan; Younghusband would revert to the one-man show of earlier days. But in Elias' case the belief was also prompted by personal predilection. He found it extremely hard to work with others, a feeling that was no doubt reciprocated. Durand, the Foreign Secretary, later described him as 'a very difficult kind of creature'. Any companion would not only have to work to his impossible standards but also put up with a highly irritable temper and rough it to an extent that only Hayward would have appreciated.

How the unusual name of Ney came into his family is not known. As a boy it must have taken some living down, but if he had now come to terms with it and even perhaps relished its distinction, this was certainly not true of the Elias. His parents had actually given up the Jewish faith and young Ney was brought up a Christian. But they didn't change their name and nor did Ney. Instead he suffered agonies of embarrassment; to be dubbed 'the wandering Jew' would have filled him with horror. That a man with such a name and so acutely sensitive could have failed to come to terms with his ancestry is another of his baffling contradictions. Again it hints at some psychological chastisement, some need to punish his spirit in the same way that his travels punished his physique. Allied to the more predictable traits of the outsider, domineering mother and eccentric overseas education, it resulted in an inability to confide and a horror of sentiment. A classic introvert, he remained a bachelor, shunned society and knew neither friends nor loved ones.

For such a man travel in empty places had much to be said for it, and had he possessed the wealth and influence of contemporary aristocratic travellers he might, in time, have come to terms with his own personality. As it was, the Eliases were Bristol merchants; their second son started his travels with a posting to the Shanghai branch of the family firm. His expeditions to the mouth of the Yellow River, though of considerable scientific merit and conducted with true professionalism, were in the nature of holiday excursions. The marathon across Asia, made in his early thirties, was also on his own initiative and at his own expense. To the extent that he was at last recognised as one of the most scientific and determined

explorers, the investment paid off; he attracted the patronage of
Sir Henry Rawlinson. But it didn't ensure a succession of geographical assignments such as Elias had hoped for. Rawlinson, no
doubt recalling the Hayward fiasco, played safe. He recommended
him not to the R.G.S. but to the foreign department of the Government of India. If Elias wanted to go on travelling he was going to
have to operate as an official government agent.

This he accepted. He never enjoyed political work and continued
to regard it as less important than geographical and scientific discovery. Yet he proved one of the ablest and most dedicated of India's
select band of trouble-shooting emissaries. His grasp of the political and strategic requirements of the country's defence was second
to none and, perhaps a little surprising in a man so different from
the rest, his views were fully in tune with those of MacGregor's
'forward' disciples. On the other hand, where he failed was in refusing to fall in with the prevailing esprit of the political service. Durand
complained that he would not learn the work of the department
and was thus a bad political officer. All the evidence suggests that he
just failed to conform to the way in which the department operated.
To a man like Elias the system of patronage and promotion that
nurtured MacGregor, Lockhart and Durand himself must have
been horrifying indeed. He would remain in government service
for most of his career, always the most perceptive and dependable
of agents, yet he still refused to identify with the service. He stood
apart, aloof, his recommendations either ignored or appropriated
by others, his reputation as much above censure as commendation,
and his career uniquely static. When he later heard of Lockhart's
scheme for the re-opening of the Gilgit Agency he ventured to
Durand, 'Would I do for it or it for me?' No heavy lobbying, no
long-winded report on the subject, no mustering of qualifications
and years of service—just this quiet diffident little hint. Needless to
say it cut no ice with the Foreign and Political Department.

A sad man, lonely and ultra-sensitive, disgruntled in his professional life and disturbed within himself, he was also, by 1885,
a sick man. He probably never knew precisely what was wrong, but
it can be taken that that request from Zebak for medicine was
genuine enough. Dyspepsia and anaemia figured on the medical
report which had invalided him home in the previous year. A liver
condition had also been diagnosed and it was this, exacerbated by

dysentery—both the lightning bacillus and the nagging amoeba—
that was undermining his constitution. Throughout the Pamirs
expedition his health would continue to deteriorate. Worry no
doubt contributed to his physical decline but it was also intensified
by it. To a man such as Elias nothing can have been more upsetting
than the slow realisation that this was likely to be his last major
expedition.

When he had returned from sick leave in 1885 he had immediately
volunteered to return to Leh, 'if not a mountaineer a man for the
mountains' according to his biographer. Dufferin and Durand had,
however, a far more attractive proposition; and with Elias in
Simla and available at just the right moment, for once the most
qualified and able of the usual herd of applicants got the job. He
headed north across the mountains on May 29. He had been
offered the services of a doctor but, preferring as usual to be the
sole European, had opted for just a native medical assistant. A
touch of 'the gravel' in Kashmir and one of his 'attacks' in Ladakh
were ominous send-offs.

*   *   *

Not even a fire-eater like Charles MacGregor could complain that
Dufferin was not making the most of a Tory ministry at home. In
spite of the Panjdeh crisis the Afghan boundary commission, now
under Colonel Sir West Ridgeway with 35 British officers and over
1,300 native assistants, was still inching its way east towards the
middle Oxus. In Dardistan Lockhart and his men seemed to be
securing the country piecemeal and, though no-one would have
mentioned his name in the same breath, it was about now that the
government commissioned Dr. Leitner to compile his Hunza–
Nagar Handbook. That took care of half the crescent of buffer
lands between the Indian and Russian Empires; it left Sinkiang
and the Pamirs for Elias.

The Viceroy and his Foreign Secretary might have preferred
something a little more imposing than the solitary explorer and his
meagre following; but the uninhabited character of the Pamirs
and the sensitivity of the Chinese ruled it out. In fact, at the last
moment, Peking withheld the official accreditation for the mission.
Elias thus found himself in the extraordinary position of leader of

an official mission which, the moment it crossed into Chinese
territory, was downgraded to the status of 'a party travelling for
pleasure and instruction'. This was precisely the sort of mix-up
that the perfectionist found intolerable. Of the four written objectives of the mission the first two, to do with improving political
and trading relations with the Chinese authorities in Sinkiang,
depended entirely on his being able to negotiate from a position
of authority; nowhere did rank and face count for so much as in
the Chinese empire. Moreover, even if the Chinese did show
willing to treat, they could be expected to come under strong
pressure from a fully accredited and immensely influential Russian
consul already installed in Kashgar. He had just succeeded in
running Andrew Dalgleish, the only British subject in Sinkiang,
out of the country and was sure to try the same again with the
newcomer.

Yet here was Elias, expected to take on the indifference of the
Chinese and the hostility of the Russian consul with no more
authority than that of a tourist. With justifiable indignation he
pounced on the absurdity of the situation and, one feels, was almost
gratified to find the Chinese not only unwilling to negotiate but
refusing to admit that there was even common ground to discuss.
Algernon Durand, the Foreign Secretary's younger brother and a
man with a big part to play in what he christened the Gilgit Game,
would later maintain that Elias was the 'only Englishman that the
Chinese funked'; 'they sh-t when they think of him' was how one
of his spies put it and there can be no doubt that in 1885 Elias
pushed matters as hard as he knew how; the mission would entail
enough reverses without his needing to invent any. Nevertheless,
having started with a resounding failure, having vented his dis-
gust at the way the mission had been despatched and having
emphasised the utter hopelessness of his situation, Elias could turn
to his other objectives with an altogether freer hand.

These were less specific and therefore more intriguing. He was to
take up George Hayward's mantle and explore the Pamirs and
Upper Oxus with particular reference to the territorial status of
the region. He was also to monitor Russian movements in and
around it. One thing his Chinese passport did specify was that he
was to be allowed to leave Sinkiang by way of the Pamirs. The
Afghans had been told to expect him from this direction and had

agreed to assist him. He was further armed with a letter of
introduction from the Aga Khan which was evidently Leitner's
idea; the doctor had long ago noted that many of the peoples
of Dardistan and the Upper Oxus were Ismaili Mohammedans; with their spiritual leader happily settled in Bombay it
was only common sense to enlist his support. Elias found no fault
with these arrangements and resumed his journey heading west
from Sinkiang on September 30, the day Lockhart was negotiating
his treaty with the Kafirs.

British geographers of the day laboured under a misapprehension about what they called 'The Pamir'. They imagined it was a
steppe or plateau, elevated but not especially mountainous. It was
rectangular in shape which was unusual for a mountain system,
and it was boxed in on all but one side by true ranges with peaks
up to 25,000 feet. They also knew that the Arabs had designated
it 'the Roof of the World' and a roof, to an Arab, would have been
something flat. Finally, according to every authority since Marco
Polo, a Pamir was a strath of high-altitude grazing. Lord Curzon,
later Viceroy of India, who made a determined effort to clear up
the misapprehension, reckoned that there were in fact eight true
Pamirs. He also emphasised that though they were wide, level
and, in summer, well grassed, they were not plains nor even
plateaux; they were valleys. Furthermore, although the most
distinctive feature of the region, they were hardly typical. The
Pamirs as a region was a mountain maze. In fact here was a true
mountain system as formidable as any of its neighbours. Geo-
logically speaking it was far older, which accounted for the filling
up of some of the valleys and the rounding of the peaks. But
geographically it was as much part of the West Himalayan
mountain knot as the Hindu Kush or the Karakorams.

The Russians appreciated its character rather better than their
British rivals. Indeed, by the time Elias set foot in the area, they
had already explored it. Since 1870 botanists, surveyors and
military spies had been pushing south from Khokand over the
Alai and Trans Alai ranges or east from Bukhara through Karategin
and Darwaz. In 1883 a party of Russian army mapmakers reached
the northern slopes of the Hindu Kush and were all for crossing
into Chitral and Kafiristan; it was rumours of this that had so
alarmed Aman-ul-Mulk at the time of MacNair's visit. The same

group had also carried their survey to points that the Survey of India had already plotted, thus rendering the Pamirs no longer a geographical void. The whole story, though a minor one compared to the penetration of the Western Himalayas to the south, would no doubt repay research. Here it is sufficient to note that in 1886 Elias was not embarking on *terra incognita*. The Russian authorities were altogether less secretive about the work of their explorers. The R.G.S., for instance, had a correspondent in Paris who kept them posted month by month on the movements of Russian travellers; reports presented to the St. Petersburg geographical society were quickly translated and printed in the Society's journal. Elias owed a great deal to his rivals and would derive much satisfaction from magisterial corrections or commendations of their work. But, if not a pioneer, he was the first to cross the area from east to west. He was also the first to put it into the context of the Western Himalayas and of India's defence.

The journey from Yangi-Hissar in Sinkiang to Zebak in Badakshan took just over two months. In that time Elias crossed or reconnoitred more than a dozen passes of over 13,000 feet and discovered a peak of over 24,000 which even the Russians appeared to have missed; he named it Mount Dufferin.* The valleys were indeed as bleak, empty and featureless as the high plains of Western Tibet, the passes never as difficult as those he had crossed in the Karakorams and Kun Lun. But still these were definitely not steppes. True to his ideal of the scientific explorer, he suppressed any mention of the difficulties of the journey. The intense cold and appalling wind of a Pamir winter have to be inferred from a chance remark about four consecutive nights of heavy snow, or the exquisite comfort of finding shelter behind a cliff face, or the joy of descending to an altitude where the temperature at midday was above freezing. (The contrasts between shade and sun were equally dramatic; the following year a traveller recorded simultaneous readings of 100° F in the sun and 35° of frost in the shade.) In the summer the thermometer could fall forty degrees in as many minutes, and during the course of a day might show a variation of

*The name did not stick; the peak is usually known as Mustagh Ata. A discussion of its nomenclature and of its confusion with the neighbouring mountain of Tagharma or Kungur can be found in Gerald Morgan's *Ney Elias*, London, 1971.

ninety degrees. In winter it was less volatile; if the mercury didn't freeze solid, it was distinctly sluggish. Elias says nothing about his own precautions, but on Lake Rangul he noted how the geese had to keep flying round all night to avoid being frozen in.

The only other wildlife on the Pamirs were the packs of wolves and the herds of Marco Polo sheep. These sheep, almost legendary beasts, stood five feet high and their curled horns, to judge by skeletons strewn about the slopes, grew up to six feet in length. Biddulph, who in 1874 had vowed to bag the first, never got within range of one. Elias was slightly luckier; he had one shot. But his aim, though good, was not quite good enough and the wounded beast made off. Pursuit was hopeless—another failure to add to the record. Whether his disappointment was on humane grounds or whether because of the loss to science is not clear; he was certainly no trophy hunter. Nor was he yet so gloomy as to read any personal significance into the incident. But could there be a better analogy of his own circumstances than this crippled specimen of an elusive and incongruous beast limping off into the mountains?

Actually, Elias had long been of the opinion that high altitudes were good for his condition; it was partly on health grounds that he had volunteered to return to Leh, 11,000 feet above sea level. Descending from the Karakorams and Kun Lun into Sinkiang his irritability had returned with a vengeance. But now, up in the Pamirs at an average of 12,000 feet, he regained peace of mind and body; total absorption in his work was the surest sign that Elias was in good heart. The strain, nevertheless, began to tell. Anyone who shaved every day in those sort of conditions must have had a truly spartan regimen. For hours he would stand braced against the icy blast while he took his readings; then sit up half the night to observe his position from the stars. And there could be no delay. Winter was about to close the high passes, rendering any movement between the various Pamirs impossible. If he was sustained by the altitude he was also fascinated by the emptiness, the wilderness; to the scientific explorer as much as to the tortured introvert it was an inspiration. Ahead, the low lying and populous regions of Badakshan and Kateghan presaged nothing if not the severest reaction.

Just as he was leaving the upper Oxus the first mail since Sinkiang caught up with him; it had taken two and a half months from Simla. Long-awaited instructions from Durand as to what he should do next were not included, but there must have been mention of Lockhart's winter quarters for immediately, on December 6, Elias penned his note to Gilgit. By the 26th, before the letter had even arrived, he was fretting about having had no reply.

He was also sinking fast. It shows clearly in his journal which suddenly becomes uncharacteristically personal; scientific enquiry gives way to morbid vitriol, the people are loathsome, the country depressing, the expedition a disaster. 'How sick and tired', he writes on entering Badakshan, 'one gets of everlasting hills, brown, rocky, barren and snow-topped, and of deep, narrow valleys.' It was no better when the hills gave way to the plains of Kateghan, 'a dreary, gloomy land and one that depresses the spirit more than any place I know of'. The native Uzbegs were 'like savage curs muzzled by their Afghan rulers . . . surly and sullen . . . . an ill-favoured, coarse, Chinese race with bad features and bad characteristics stamped upon their faces'. Here it was wet as well as cold. 'Civilised domestic animals would not be able to live in this climate unless better cared for than an Uzbeg.'

Far from blazing a trail, as Lockhart imagined, he was limping along on his last legs. At Taliq'an on January 8 he felt 'very unwell' and had to rest up. 'It has been the most dreary and uninteresting journey I have ever made.' He wrote to Ridgeway of the Boundary Commission asking for a doctor to be sent to his aid. He was still waiting for Lockhart's reply, and the next letter from India, only twenty-nine days out from Sinkiang, again failed to include Durand's promised instructions. In his reply he asked for the doctor who had been offered when the mission first set off. Ridgeway had now told him that he could not detach his own doctor and that if Elias wanted treatment he had better come and get it. That meant crossing the breadth of northern Afghanistan. It also meant the indignity of throwing himself on Ridgeway's mercy and, worse still, it was likely to jeopardise the continued existence of his mission. Elias knew nothing of Lockhart's plan to take him in the rear, but he did know that Ridgeway was anxious to lead all or part of his Commission to the upper Oxus. Needless to say, he strongly advised against it. With no further instructions from Durand, it looked suspiciously as if there were some scheme afoot to put his own party at Ridgeway's disposal. His best chance of continuing on his own therefore lay in remaining in the field and as far from the big battalions as possible. Always assuming, of course, that his health bore up.

Sadly it didn't. On January 28, after a brief recovery he was again struck down. 'The cutting wind or some other cause has made me unwell again.' The weather had indeed deteriorated. It was as bad as anything he had experienced on the Pamirs. Finally, on January 31, the day his letter actually reached Lockhart, enfeebled and desperate, he threw in the sponge. Whatever the price to his dignity as an explorer, to his independent survival as a political mission and to his ebbing state of health, he must cross Afghanistan and seek out the Boundary Commission.

Illness will not allow me to go any further without medical aid. I must try and reach there [the Commission was near Maimana] or not at all. This is a sad end to all my labours and upsets all my plans for the future. The expedition has been a bad business from the beginning ... and no doubt I was too old and too broken ever to have undertaken it ... To have broken down after all and to have to leave the work unfinished and plans upset is a bad business.

His mind was rambling, and when he finally succumbed to a stretcher he felt it was 'the beginning of the end'. Four weeks later, in late February, his sorry little party fell in with a survey group from the Commission.

One can scarcely expect Elias to have relished being back among his own—mortified would have been nearer the mark—but one good thing about contact with Ridgeway, and at last news from Lockhart, was that he could afford to take a less gloomy view of his own achievements. In terms of the ground covered he had, of course, outmarched and outsurveyed everyone. The first Englishman to cross the Pamirs, he was also the first actually to visit the Afghan dependencies of Shignan and Roshan about which there had been so much political heartache, and he was the first to inspect, in Roshan, the vital confluence of the two principal upper Oxus tributaries. Geographically, this last was the most significant achievement; for after careful measurement of the flow of the two

rivers and after exhaustive enquiries, he felt confident in reversing
the 1874 verdict of Gordon and Biddulph. There was precious
little in it but in terms of annual volume of water the Panja, and
not the Bartang-Murghab-Aksu made the greater contribution and
was therefore the true Oxus. Up to a point, and quite fortuitously,
Sir Henry Rawlinson had been proved right after all. Although
there still remained the vexed question of which of the Panja's
feeders was the principal one, Elias had at last disposed of the
thorniest problem.

On the political front his main contribution arose from an unexpected discovery concerning the territorial status of the Pamirs.
There was no new Russian advance to report and, according to an
informant in Sinkiang, the Russians were more exercised about his
movements than he about theirs. If this were true they must have
wondered over Elias spending as much time quizzing the Kirghiz
nomads as he did assessing the military capabilities of the passes.
But unlike Biddulph or Lockhart, Elias was a civilian. He was less
concerned about how the Russians might overrun the Pamirs,
more concerned about whether they had any right to.

In the squabble for this inhospitable core of the continent, the
Great Game is revealed in its most fatuous aspect. If the Pamirs
had to be parcelled out, surely the only logical way to do it was
along the parallels of latitude. For here, excluding more favoured
districts along the encircling arms of the upper Oxus, was the pro-
verbial howling wilderness, a mountain tundra fashioned and
governed by the cruellest wind outside the polar circles. Its domi-
nant race consisted of wolves; in vast packs they tore across the
frozen wastes snapping at the heels of some prodigious ram.
Man scarcely counted. In 40,000 square miles there was one
indecipherable inscription, a couple of derelict mausolea and a
few makeshift sheep-pens. If a Kirghiz family elected to see out the
winter with their yaks in the mountains they still lived in tents—
scarcely a settled population. The history of the region was just as
sparse, amounting to some Chinese legends about dragon infested
lakes, a dubious account of the flight and pursuit of some luckless
rebels and two pages of wide-eyed wonderment in Marco Polo.
Nothing here to assist the diligent Elias trying to establish a traditional carve-up. Nor was the geography any more helpful. The
headwaters of the Oxus tributaries trickled from icy tarns or gushed

from cavernous glaciers to wander in easily forded rills that in winter disappeared beneath a foot or two of ice. Their very direction of flow was sometimes hard to ascertain. As Rawlinson now admitted, they were not much good as frontiers. But then neither were the mountains. Ill-defined ranges with comparatively gentle passes they posed no barrier to the indiscriminate grazing of the Kirghiz herds and marked no major watersheds. In desperation Elias at one point toyed with the idea of a 'bazaar-shed', a line based on the shopping habits of the nomads, as the only logical solution.

Dr. Leitner, as usual, had a better one. 'Left as a huge happy hunting ground for sportsmen, or as pasturage for nomads from whatever quarter, the Pamirs form the most perfect neutral zone imaginable.' The problem of their status, 'created by the conjectural treaties of diplomatists and the ambition of military emissaries' would attain the heights of absurdity if territorial claims were to be based on the wandering propensities of nomads; 'neutralisation' was the ideal solution. Unwisely he prefaced his comments with a reference to the neglected wisdom of all his earlier prognostications and duly committed this one to oblivion; 'whoever does not belong to the regular military or civil service has no right to know or to suggest'.

In fairness, it was also too late for such a Utopian solution. The Indian government had sponsored the Afghan claim to Shignan, Roshan and Wakhan and now accepted that these states extended across Rawlinson's Oxus frontier and onto the Pamirs. In fact Elias' investigations were regarded as a necessary preliminary to the Boundary Commission continuing its demarcation of the Afghan frontier as far east as it could be made to run. It was in this connection that he had made his most important discovery. The Afghan frontier, he reported, could be continued right across the Pamirs till it touched territory claimed by the Chinese on the north-east bank of the Murghab-Aksu tributary. This would create a belt of neutral buffer territory right across the region and thus effectively screen the whole of the Hindu Kush and Dardistan from direct contact with Russia.

Elias' authority for this highly satisfactory discovery was the word of the nomadic Kirghiz. Although few and far between in the heart of the Pamirs, their black domed *yurts* were comparatively plentiful around Rangkul and the Murghab. The gnarled little men Elias found 'vain and fickle like all nomadic races'; they tended to offer allegiance to whichever power was likely to trouble them least. But even around Lake Karakul, which his map designated as Russian territory, they welcomed Afghan suzerainty. This was in marked contrast to the settled populations of Shignan and Wakhan who heartily detested the Amir and his deputies. No doubt the Kirghiz too might change their minds when they had a better idea of Afghan dominion; but in Elias' view this should not discourage the government from urging the Amir to establish garrisoned outposts right across the region.

One can imagine how the Russians felt about this. In 1873 they had agreed to an Afghan frontier that stopped at what Rawlinson had designated as the Oxus. Subsequently the Indian government had discovered that the states awarded to Afghanistan on the basis of this agreement stretched at least thirty miles across the river; they had asked the Russians for a new definition taking this into account. Now Elias, finding Kirghiz nomads on the other side of the Pamirs who professed some shadowy allegiance to Shignan—and hence to Badakshan and thus to Kabul—urged that this elastic Afghan arm be extended a further hundred miles to the east. At this rate St. Petersburg might reasonably have looked to the day when a British agent, making confidential enquiries in the Kun Lun, would make out a good case to wrench an Afghan finger to the threshold of Tibet. It might all be done in the spirit of defence but to an outsider it looked scarcely less acquisitive than Russian claims to the whole of the Pamirs; deriving from traditional Kirghiz links with Khokand, they too were 'based on the wandering propensities of nomads'.

The significance of Elias' new discovery was, as usual, not immediately appreciated. In 1886 Durand was increasingly preoccupied with an Amir who had suddenly become hostile to the whole concept of frontier demarcation. It was only after Elias had retired from the field that his discovery was suddenly pounced on and elevated to a cardinal feature of British policy towards the Pamirs. The Wakhan corridor, though narrower than he would have liked, exists to this day and is Elias' peculiar legacy.

In the spring of 1886 there was also the possibility that all his recommendations would at any moment be superseded. His mission was, after all, a reconnaissance; a more detailed and thorough appraisal was expected from the Boundary Commission. With Ridgeway about to move in on the whole upper Oxus region, with Lockhart about to extend his operations to Wakhan and with Elias himself anxious to get back to the Pamirs, it seemed sense to wait on events. If all went to plan the Pamirs would be overrun with surveyors, a satisfactory boundary would emerge, the Marco Polo sheep would be decimated, and the whole country be reduced to a weighty gazetteer and a large scale map.

Oddly none of this came to pass. Throughout 1886 not a single British boot left its mark on the virgin Pamir snows. What amounted to the best ever chance of gaining the topographical knowledge vital to a settlement of the Pamir question was passed up. Afghan hostility was partly to blame and so too was the disinterest and bungling of the Foreign Department. But what finally put paid to this golden opportunity was the intense personal rivalry of the three principals, Lockhart, Ridgeway and Elias.

*   *   *

Surprisingly it was Colonel Lockhart and his companions who alone in 1886 broke new ground. Emerging from winter quarters in Gilgit on April 16 they made straight for Hunza. 'It is doubtful whether I am not guilty of disobedience,' wrote Lockhart in his diary. A frantic exchange of letters between Gilgit, Simla and Kabul had still not elicited permission for the party to enter Afghan territory; in fact Durand had just ordered him not to start until the position had been clarified. Lockhart wouldn't wait. Every day the Hunza river was rising with newly melted snow; if he delayed he would miss the opportunity of by-passing the worst of the parapets by taking to the river bed.

As it was, the road proved 'the worst in our experience this trip'. But, after an exact repeat of Biddulph's difficulties over eliciting hostages from Ghazan Khan, he successfully negotiated the gorge and, dodging past the avalanches thundering down the flanks of Rakaposhi, reached the Mir's eyrie. En route he received news that his plans had finally been accepted by the Amir and sanctioned by Durand. The gods were on his side and Lockhart beamed on Hunza with a warm and wondrous eye.

Only one slight doubt ruffled his calm self-confidence. Durand had taken the opportunity to request that he make supply arrangements for the Boundary Commission's movement through Wakhan or Chitral. A more acute mind than Lockhart's might have already guessed that the new itinerary had only been approved because it might serve the interests of the more important Commission. Always more sensitive in matters of seniority, he did however realise that he, like Elias, was in danger of being placed under Ridgeway's orders. His protest to Durand produced an assurance that no such move was intended but that Ridgeway's work took precedence and he must co-operate. Then, and throughout the next two months, Lockhart's reaction was to keep the Commission at arm's length. He could cope with Elias, but not with the favoured Ridgeway. Every request from the latter regarding supplies or routes was met with dire warnings about the difficulties and shortages likely to be experienced if the Commission came anywhere near Dardistan or the upper Oxus. He might also have mentioned that such supplies and goodwill as did exist would be more than exhausted by the passage of his own party.

Encamped amidst the apricot blossom on the ledge of Hunza, the mission continued with a virtual re-run of Biddulph's trials of ten years before. Ghazan Khan, 'sixty, fat, blackish, ugly but with rather a merry eye' welcomed them effusively. Well he might; four British hostages afforded even better prospects of realising his long-cherished dream for the restitution of Chalt and Chaprot. These two strategic forts in the Hunza gorge were still held jointly by the Dogras and by the Mir of Nagar, his deadly rival. Lockhart, learning nothing from his predecessor's experience, had walked into precisely the same trap.

'A hitch', he called it when first wind of Chalt and Chaprot being the price of the mission's further progress reached him. Next day he was calling it 'a facer', and the day after he was in despair; it was 'the collapse of all our fine plans'. He could do one of three things: retreat, fight or capitulate. The first would involve an unacceptable loss of prestige, not to mention the personal ignominy. The second, though he reckoned that they could give a good account of themselves, was appallingly risky and might involve the government in a rescue operation beside which the one that had recently failed to save Gordon in Khartoum would look like child's

19 Chitral Fort

20   Baltit, home of the Mirs of Hunza

play. That left capitulation. 'Give me Chaprot and my people shall carry you through the Killik snows [the Killik was the pass he intended to follow from Hunza to the Pamirs] as if you were women', declared the Mir. With the merry eye there went a colourful turn of phrase. He proceeded to emphasise the strategic importance of the forts; they were 'as dear to him as the strings which secured his wives' pyjamas'. Sadly, though, the forts were not Lockhart's to give. They belonged to Nagar and the garrison arrangement with the Dogras was considered vital to Gilgit's security.

In the end two things happened. First Ghazan Khan modified his demands. According to later information gleaned by Elias, he had recently strengthened his ties with the Chinese in Sinkiang to the extent that Hunza was now regarded as 'an outlying district of the Chinese empire'. On hearing of Lockhart's proposed visit, the Mir's new suzerains had despatched an officer with two cannon to help him keep the British out. It was the news that the guns had just been abandoned in the snows of the Hindu Kush that now dramatically weakened the Mir's bargaining position.

The other development was that Lockhart had second thoughts about capitulation. He slept on the problem, then sat for a long time gazing forlornly across the Hunza valley. On all sides the avalanches boomed like distant artillery; the vista was one 'which cannot, I think, be beaten in the whole world'. But, far from subscribing to the usual reaction of an overwhelming sense of insignificance, Lockhart emerged from his reverie more determined than ever that, regardless of consequences, the mission must succeed. He couldn't transfer the two forts, neither could he bid the Dogras relinquish them; but he might just risk an official wigging to the extent of dispossessing the chief of Nagar. This temporarily satisfied the chastened Mir and was most acceptable to the Dogras who would undertake the expulsion. He also committed the British government to the extent of seeing that Nagar received some financial compensation.

It was not a good idea to give in to a man like Ghazan Khan, nor was this a nice way to treat Nagar, the most loyal of all the Dard states. In fact for a British officer who prided himself on his sense of justice, it was downright shameless. But Lockhart looked on the bright side. No force was to be used against the Nagaris and

Durand was to understand that the forts would still be held by
Kashmir. 'I don't think I have sinned ... I don't think I could do
anything else than what I am doing.' Face had been saved and,
'in spite of many predictions to the contrary', a British mission
was about to traverse the whole of Hunza. 'No one will ever want
to come up this way again,' he wrote, the inference being that it
scarcely mattered if he had trodden on a few toes. From someone
who two months before had been recommending the virtual subjugation of Hunza and Nagar as part of his scheme for the new
Gilgit Agency, it was an odd remark. Predictably, from now on,
Nagar would resist as staunchly as Hunza any overtures from
Gilgit. The next party to enter the country would have to fight
every inch of the way.

Lockhart pushed on to further tribulations. Whatever else
one can say about the man he was certainly resilient; he was on new
ground now and nothing was going to stop him. Not even the
Killik pass which proved a nightmare. Two porters died from
exposure, nearly all the party suffered from snow blindness, frostbite or both, and Lockhart's pony had to be abandoned in a snow
drift. When they struggled into the first outpost in Wakhan they
had been without food for two days. They congratulated themselves not, as they might, on being the first Europeans ever to cross
the watershed of the high Hindu Kush, but on their luckiest of
escapes. Had the pass been tackled a day earlier or a day later, they
would have perished in one of the heavy snowfalls. Had they taken
a day longer, they would have starved.

As the mission settled down to a cauldron of boiled mutton
provided by their new Afghan hosts, Lockhart was again convinced that their troubles were at an end. Woodthorpe's men had
continued their survey right across the watershed and would soon
be swarming along the sides of the Wakhan valley. Besides satisfactorily puncturing Elias' monopoly of the upper Oxus they would
also be forestalling the Boundary Commission. No need now for
you to visit Wakhan, Lockhart wrote to Ridgeway; the surveying
would be done by Woodthorpe and he couldn't recommend the
place for 'sight-seeing or pleasure-making'.

Nor, much longer, for hospitality. The Afghan reception proved
cordial indeed compared with Hunza's; but it was short-lived.
For one thing it transpired that the mission was expected to pay

cash, on the nail, for all supplies. Ever since losing the treasure chest nearly a year before, Lockhart had been short of funds. He had managed to borrow from the Kashmir governor in Gilgit but this money was now exhausted and the next cache was not till Badakshan. Thither it was his intention to proceed as rapidly as possible but it also now transpired that the Afghans had no intention of allowing him to do so. The Amir had in fact withdrawn the permission to enter his territory within days of granting it. Lockhart was therefore trespassing. He should retrace his steps and, if he couldn't afford to pay for his supplies, he would do well to move off immediately or again suffer the pangs of hunger.

For two weeks he stalled. Fuming over this 'most monstrous piece of impertinence', he waved the telegram from Durand that had given him the all-clear. He accused his immediate adversary, the governor of Badakshan, of disobeying the Amir's instructions, and he finally sent him a copy of a fabricated letter that logged all the governor's misdeeds and advocated his removal. He also complained that his mail was being withheld and his funds sequestered —Elias had written that there were indeed 14,000 rupees awaiting him in Badakshan. It cut no ice with the governor. 'I cannot allow you to either advance or remain on the border without His Highness' permission'. What made it still worse was that the wretched governor kept quoting Elias at him. Elias had come with the requisite permission and Elias had been treated with due honour. 'Had you been similarly authorised, I should have treated you with the same distinction.' Lockhart had been told by Durand how well the great explorer had hit it off with the governor. He also knew that Elias was then in Badakshan. Why wasn't he doing something?

On June 4, after a third ultimatum, Lockhart formed up the mission and set off—forward. With his Sikh escort primed for action he expected trouble at every bend of the road. So did the Dards just across the watershed. According to news received by Leitner, Nizam-ul-Mulk, the gay young chief of Yasin had a force waiting on the Baroghil to whisk Lockhart back to safety. Whether the Afghans even knew of this is doubtful, but the people of Wakhan itself were sufficiently disenchanted with Afghan rule to see that Lockhart was not starved or waylaid in their valley.

By the time he reached Badakshan, where he was potentially

more vulnerable, the dust seemed to be settling. Elias, only a day's journey away, excused his inability to help by explaining that no-one in the country would admit to knowing the mission's whereabouts or intentions. From this it appeared that Lockhart was to be allowed to slip quietly through. There came also a note in cipher from Durand which confirmed that Anglo-Afghan relations were under strain and advised Lockhart to repay Afghan restraint by slipping quickly away. Above all he must abide by their demand that he refrain from revisiting Kafiristan. It was now clear that the Amir's suspicions centred on his dealings with the Kafirs. If not exactly Afghan subjects, they were traditional Afghan prey and the Amir was highly resentful of direct British dealings with them.

Thus Lockhart now had every reason to retire with good grace. To the chorus of those demanding such a move were added the voices of Ridgeway and Aman-ul-Mulk of Chitral. The former claimed that the advance of the mission had forfeited the goodwill of his hosts and brought the whole Commission to a standstill; the latter begged him to retire simply for his own safety. Lockhart, congratulating himself on being able to take a hint and glowing with a sense of having done the magnanimous thing by Ridgeway, withdrew.

Before he did so, on June 11 at 12.00 noon, and at, of all places, Zebak, 'Mr Ney Elias appeared'. That's all Lockhart records of the meeting and, indeed, it is his last mention of the explorer. Elias for his part is equally reticent; when it was decided that he should travel back to Chitral with Lockhart he significantly opted to follow in his wake rather than march at his side. Two more dissimilar characters it would be hard to imagine; the one a transparent careerist, hearty, well-met, insensitive and unstoppable, an extravagant traveller, a gullible political agent and an overbearing soldier; the other a slight, tight, prickly introvert, racked with self-doubt, obsessive and impossible; yet a shrewd and unshakeable negotiator, a scrupulous explorer and a man to whom travel was life. Only in their work might they have found common ground but of that the one was too jealous, the other too embittered, to speak.

Lockhart plodded over the Dora pass dutifully averting his gaze as he skirted the inviting passes into Kafiristan; even to the entreaties of Gumara—his adopted son, who had reappeared—he turned a deaf ear. Mild disappointment, but no more, was his only reaction to being denied what was supposedly the goal of the whole contentious journey. In the last six months he had stirred up more trouble than any previous visitor to the region—and that was saying something. Nagar was alienated, Hunza encouraged, the Afghans antagonised and the Kafirs disappointed. To this tale of woe Aman-ul-Mulk added a postscript by irritably hustling the mission from the one state in which they felt they had really gained ground. Lockhart found the Mehtar much aged and wondered how long this pillar of his whole defensive scheme for Dardistan could survive. Yet failure he would never concede, remorse he wouldn't have recognised. He had confounded the sceptics by entering Kafiristan and by passing through Hunza; he had thus completed the exploration of Dardistan. He had also inspected both sides of all the main Hindu Kush passes and had arrived at the reassuring conclusion that, with the exception of the Dora, none would admit anything more formidable than a small exploratory party.

Simla evidently concurred with this highly favourable summary of his work; before the mission left Chitral on the road back to Kashmir, Lockhart received an urgent summons to drop everything and hasten home to take over from MacGregor's successor as Quarter-Master-General. The mission had served its purpose; Lockhart's future looked rosy. Ten years later as General Sir William Lockhart he was appointed Commander-in-Chief in India.

'Too old and too broken', the tired melancholic explorer who followed him back to Simla went unnoticed. Six weeks' winter convalescence with the Boundary Commission had restored Elias' strength only temporarily. He was still a sick man and, if possible, an even more embittered one. Exhaustion and hypochondria had been all the Commission's medical officer had made of his condition; after such a diagnosis it was hardly surprising that the patient proved a difficult one. Equally predictable had been Ridgeway's reaction to his presence; he sought instructions that would place Elias under his command. Whether Durand agreed to this is not clear; Ridgeway thought he had, Elias that he hadn't. But in the end it made no difference. The official go-ahead for the Commission to continue its work into Badakshan and the upper Oxus region rendered Elias' role superfluous. He had intended to complete his work in Badakshan and then return to the Pamirs. If the only way he could do this was by accepting the invitation to join one of Ridgeway's survey parties he rightly preferred to decline. To a gold medallist of the R.G.S. and the greatest Asiatic explorer of his day such an offer was positively insulting.

In May he had headed slowly back across northern Afghanistan. Though surprised not to be overtaken by the advance party of the Commission, he was so confident that they were hard on his heels that he did not recommence his survey. In Badakshan, where the governor still treated him with kindness, he was bombarded with requests from Ridgeway, as well as from Lockhart, about supply arrangements and itineraries. The Commission's daily requirements included half a ton of fire wood, five hundredweight of flour, a ton of grain and two tons of hay. 'There will not be much of Badakshan left uneaten,' he complained and he emphasised the appalling strain of such a vast procurement and the near impossibility of getting the stuff carried up into the Pamirs. It was no wonder the Afghans were having second thoughts about the whole business of boundary demarcation.

It also looked as if Lockhart's battalion from the east and Ridgeway's from the west were set on a collision course. Neither man would back down and Elias, like a nettled policeman in the middle, desperately tried to fend them off. If Lockhart was really storming through Wakhan then Ridgeway had better forget Wakhan and the Baroghil and send his forces round via the Dora and Chitral. 'It will have a bad political effect on Chitral and Badakshan if the *Sahibs* are seen to be opposing each other. You could make much better *bandobast** that way and if you had to come face to face with Lockhart you would not be so much at his mercy as if you left him uncontrolled on your flank.'

Meanwhile his own remaining ambition was, as he put it to Durand, 'to try to elbow my way through the crowd of commissioners and surveyors and get back by Kabul or Chitral(or wherever famine has not set in) and hand myself over to you for disposal'. He had already approached Aman-ul-Mulk about passing through Chitral and, although Lockhart's decision to take the same route

*Bandobast is a word with wide connotations; the nearest English equivalent is something like 'organisation' or 'arrangement'.

almost dissuaded him, he was still anxious to see the Dora and to form some idea of Dardistan. No doubt he was also anxious to be the first traveller to complete the circuit of the Western Himalayas by adding the Hindu Kush to his tally of ranges. He succeeded, but as he squelched to the top through the mud and snow churned up by Lockhart's men, triumph can seldom have tasted so bitter.

The pass itself he reckoned far too defensible to warrant Lockhart's alarm. Similarly his verdict on Aman-ul-Mulk was one in the eye for the colonel. 'No guarantee given by an irresponsible barbarian of this kind could ever be effective, and no semblance of a reasonable or continuous policy could ever be hoped for.' He approved wholeheartedly of Biddulph's appraisal of the Mehtar, 'avaricious, unscrupulous and deceitful to an uncommon degree'. adding only that he was now also senile and thus still more unpredictable; he was 'best left out of the account altogether'. As if bent on a thorough demolition of Lockhart's work he went on to recommend that the way to secure Chitral was not by subsidies and treaties but by intimidation. With remarkable foresight he suggested that Chitral would not be safe until it could be controlled not from Gilgit but by way of MacNair's route from the Punjab.

On this combative note the official report of his 1885–86 journey ends. It was not however the end of his disappointments; the last were in many ways the cruellest. In the first place, unbeknown to him until he reached Gilgit, Ridgeway had abandoned his attempt to survey the upper Oxus. In other words Elias could after all have completed his work there; indeed the Commission's withdrawal would have made his further work doubly valuable. It seems unlikely that the objections raised by the Amir to Ridgeway would have applied to Elias and, with the prospect of another sojourn in the wastes of the Pamirs, even his health might have improved.

But it wasn't to be; and the reason, quite simply, was that no-one had told him. Ridgeway's problems had begun in May but, for what one can only assume to have been reasons of personal jealousy, he failed to tell Elias. Likewise Durand; he capped his long history of neglecting Elias by failing to pass on the information. When word did reach him, he was halfway back to India and desperately longing for a rest. He naturally assumed that the failure in communications reflected the government's lack of interest in the matter; they had shown little appreciation of what he had done already, so it was no surprise that they should have no desire for him to continue.

Such pessimism seemed fully warranted when in October, after seventeen months and three thousand miles, he finally reached Simla. Ridgeway had got his knighthood while still in the field, Lockhart's came soon after his return, Elias' never came. Nor was there even the customary letter of thanks from the Viceroy. An invalid again, he sailed for England wanting only to forget the whole business. In this there should have been no problem. His report was so secret that only thirty copies were printed. He was forbidden to lecture or publish anything about the journey, and only the barest of itineraries ever became public knowledge. To those who knew anything about the region his feat seemed improbable; though it fuelled the Elias legend, it brought little acclaim.

And so it should have ended. But if Elias was obsessed by his failures it was partly because others would never allow him to forget them. A year later there came a devastating reminder; he was gazetted a Commander of the Indian Empire. Then, as now, there were honours and honours. A C.I.E. to one of the greatest English travellers for his last marathon was, as the papers put it, like 'throwing a bone at him'. Mischievously, or possibly mistakenly, Ridgeway had once given him the initials when they were communicating about the supply of a doctor. Making his feelings plain enough, Elias had then inveighed against the whole honours system and described the C.I.E. in particular as 'that damning mark of faint praise'. True to his principles he now took the unprecedented and highly controversial step of returning the medal. The newspapers drew in their breath and officialdom frowned in disapproval; Mr. Ney Elias could now be pretty certain of remaining a plain Mr. however long and distinguished his subsequent career.

In fact he had only ten relatively unremarkable years ahead. But the really interesting aspect of this *cause célèbre* is the light it throws on his personality. He was more than justified in returning the medal, but was this the action of an excessively modest and retiring nature? It won for him a notoriety that almost overshadowed his reputation as a traveller. Modesty would surely have dictated a more supine reaction. Again one suspects that he fought shy of recognition not from modesty but either because he scorned all opinion other than his own or because he knew too well how honours were customarily acquired; probably both.

10. The Exploring Spirit Was Upon Me

On one point Lockhart and Elias had been in rough agreement; MacGregor had got it wrong when he predicted that the Russians would send part of any invasion force across the Pamirs and over the Hindu Kush. The thing was impossible. Devoid of supplies, unbearably cold and mountainous throughout, the Pamirs could be crossed only by small reconnaissance parties operating between July and December. As for the Hindu Kush, just one route was still canvassed as suitable for troops, that via the Dora, and to reach this an invader would first have to wrest Badakshan from the Amir. The notion that the Gilgit Game had to do with holding the northern gates of India against invasion would be a long time dying; too many statesmen continued to ignore the geographical realities, too many soldiers could think only in the broadest strategic terms and too many political officers had a stake in seeing that the region retained its priority. But it is true to say that as a rationale for a British interest in Gilgit the defence of the passes would no longer do.

However, as the Russians had protested when justifying earlier advances, 'in the East it is impossible always to stop when one wishes'. Translated into a British context this might have read, 'it is impossible always to withdraw when one ought'. Leitner, not without justification, put it more crudely, 'the devil finds work for idle hands'. New 'forward' policies had a way of emerging before the old ones had been dismantled, and once a new threat had been identified, proof of its plausibility was soon to hand. Invasion could be discounted; but what about infiltration and subversion? Kipling certainly saw the Russian threat in these terms; in *Kim* pseudo-sportsmen from across the frontier slip through the Hindu Kush passes to woo 'the five kings' who are clearly the Dard chiefs. The reality in the 1880s differed only to the extent that the Dard chiefs appeared to need little wooing. A Russian reconnaissance party had, it was argued, only to cross the Hindu

Kush for the whole of Dardistan to explode like a keg of gun powder. Disaffection in Hunza and the near certainty of a disputed succession in Chitral, plus the traditional weakness of Kashmir's hold on Gilgit, amounted to an open invitation. In 1883 Russians had reached Wakhan; it was only a matter of time before some Tsarist agent with a pocket full of roubles and a caravan of breech-loaders would come glissading down the glaciers on the wrong side of the frontier.

Sure enough, in May 1888, less than two years after Elias, Lockhart and Ridgeway had fled the field, the first party arrived. Preceded by wild rumours of a whole Russian detachment, it materialised as three dazed and desperate intruders straggling down from the Baroghil pass. At Mastuj, Nizam-ul-Mulk was waiting for them. Displaying considerably more sense than Lockhart had ever credited him with, he promptly arrested them and wrote to Simla for instructions.

It was a false alarm. Nizam reported that his captives admitted to coming from Russia but he was surprised that they brought neither presents nor promises; indeed they appeared to be totally destitute. They also claimed to be not Russian but French. So they were. Telegrams in cipher from Simla to London elicited from the Russian ambassador that they were 'bona fide French geographers'. To Gabriel Bonvalot and his two companions thus falls the honour of first bridging the Pamirs gap between the British and Russian empires. Though an experienced traveller who had already traversed most of Central Asia, Bonvalot tackled the Pamirs on the spur of the moment. He was no Anglophile and found much to criticise in the excessive liberality of previous British visitors to the region. But he was also no Russian agent. The most in the way of political significance that could be extracted from his achievement was that the journey from Russian to British territory was tougher still than had been anticipated. Lord Dufferin, who got Nizam to send his prisoners on to Simla, listened with sympathy to their tale of suffering and deprivation; they had been benighted on the Alai, snowed in on the Pamirs and robbed in the Hindu Kush, they had lost the whole of their baggage train and were lucky to get away with their lives. But, to Dufferin's mind, this was 'excellent news'. It confirmed that for at least six months the frontier was firmly closed.

It was in the following year, 1889, that the real thing came; a Russian political officer with a Cossack escort entered Hunza. Dardistan did not exactly explode but the welcome accorded this Captain Grombtchevski was in marked contrast to the treatment meted out to Biddulph and Lockhart. Offers of money and arms appear to have been accepted. In return the new Mir of Hunza, Safdar Ali, son and murderer of Ghazan Khan, gave permission for a Russian post to be set up on his territory and agreed to seek Russian aid in repelling any further aggression from Gilgit. These arrangements for long remained a matter of speculation in Simla, but the mere fact of a Russian entering Hunza, when seen in the light of recent developments, had the most sinister implications.

For one thing it could hardly be a coincidence that in the same year Safdar Ali assumed the offensive. He recaptured Chaprot and Chalt, and Hunza forces got to within striking distance of Gilgit. Again the Kashmir troops proved incompetent and badly officered; defeat was staved off by suing for peace; it was an ignominious and all too familiar predicament. But what made it worse from a British point of view was an untimely reminder from the Chinese. As Elias had reported, they were taking an unusually lively interest in 'their outlying dependency' and, when Safdar Ali was pressured into surrendering his recent gains, they demanded an explanation from the British representative in Peking. Dufferin provided it. In categorically repudiating all Chinese claims on Hunza, he insisted that the place was a vital dependency of Kashmir. As he explained to the Secretary of State, whatever the legality of China's claim, it was totally inadmissible on the grounds that if, as still seemed likely, Russia should annex Sinkiang, then she would inherit the claim.

The whole question of the Hunza–China connection was also highlighted by Safdar Ali's other move. He reinitiated the traditional Hunza pastime of raiding caravans on the Ladakh–Sinkiang road. The 1888 attack took place between the Karakorams and Kun Lun on what was supposed to be Sinkiang territory. Amongst those who were captured and ransomed were some Kirghiz of the region. They appealed to the Chinese but, receiving neither redress nor sympathy, turned to the British agent in Ladakh. It could be argued that if the Chinese failed to restrain one lot of doubtful subjects and failed to protect another they could scarcely aspire to sovereignty over either. But more intriguing from a British point of view was how the Hunza highwaymen had managed to get undetected from one end of the Western Himalayas to the other. Lockhart had explored only the Killik pass out of Hunza; there were evidently others both to the north and the east, plus a corridor of unexplored territory that ran the length of the Karakorams. As so often, unexplored meant unappropriated. This corridor started from that part of the Pamirs which neither Chinese nor Afghans effectively controlled. If the Russians grabbed the one they would grab the other, and a wedge of Russian territory might suddenly be driven not just south to the Hindu Kush but east between Kashmir and Sinkiang.

Lord Dufferin's Viceroyalty terminated in December 1888. In the previous year Mortimer Durand had argued strongly for the reopening of the Gilgit Agency; he paid little attention to Lockhart's grandiose scheme for 'the acquisition of Gilgit' but he believed firmly that, with the western sector of Afghanistan's frontier now defined, Russian pressure would move east to the undefined Pamirs. Grombtchevski's appearance in Hunza convinced Dufferin that his foreign secretary was right. Accordingly Captain Algernon Durand, younger brother of 'Morty', was despatched to Gilgit to draw up recommendations for the reopening of the Agency. These were ready just before Dufferin left India, but the decision on whether to implement them was left to his successor, Lord Lansdowne. It was a mere formality. The new man, as nominee of Lord Salisbury and the Tories, was as much obsessed with the needs of imperial defence as his Tory predecessor, Lord Lytton; within two months of his arrival in India he was talking of 'the necessity of assimilating the frontier tribes', and within six months Algy Durand was on his way back to Gilgit as agent. His first job was to beard the lion in his den; he was to visit Hunza and get Safdar Ali to abandon his raids and forswear all dealing with Russia and China. As an incentive he was to offer a greatly increased subsidy.

So much for the diplomatic response. The other obvious need was for military intelligence. Someone must explore the country behind the Karakorams and around the perimeter of Hunza; and in the process he must stand by to counter any further Russian or Chinese overtures towards Hunza. This mission, even by the standards of the Gilgit Game, called for quite exceptional talents. Hayward, who back in 1868 had made a short foray west of the Karakoram pass, had reported on the appallingly difficult nature of the country. Rock-choked rivers swirling through beetling ravines formed the valley gutters between the Karakorams and Kun Lun. One either scrabbled and waded through their icy depths or climbed to the moraines and glaciers that spewed chaotically from the greatest cluster of peaks in the world. To negotiate such terrain called for the skills of a mountaineer. The desolation of the country and the duration of the enterprise demanded a traveller fitted by both temperament and experience to survive long spells of hardship and solitude. And the delicate political eventualities necessitated someone utterly dependable but more tactful and resourceful than many of his predecessors. The man chosen was barely twenty-six years old, a captain in the 1st King's Dragoon Guards, by name Francis Edward Younghusband.

For the next five critical years Algy Durand, the Gilgit Agent, and Frank Younghusband, the roving explorer, would epitomise the Gilgit Game. In character they were almost as wildly dissimilar as Lockhart and Elias. Yet they worked tolerably well together, kept their suspicions of one another out of official correspondence and, coincidentally, shared two points in common. In the first place both had ties with the same part of England, Northumberland. Durand had spent much of his childhood at the ancestral home of the Dukes of the county and Younghusband could trace his ancestry through eleven generations of Northumbrians. They regarded themselves not as British but as English and Durand, at least, rejoiced in traditions of repelling Scottish incursions; as Gilgit Agent he liked nothing better than to be described as the warden of India's northern marches. Younghusband, for his part, always pointedly excluded the Scots from his eulogies on English rule and civilisation. Each thus saw himself as continuing a family tradition in an imperial setting. It imparted a depth of dedication to their work which few of their contemporaries can have shared.

They were, on the other hand, nothing if not typical in both being intensely and unashamedly careerist. The carrot of a medal and the plum of promotion were sustenance to all, and it made little difference that Durand chose to disguise his ambition as a desire to live up to the expectations of his distinguished brother; or that Younghusband sublimated his pursuit of personal recognition in some wider civilising crusade. Yet the odd thing is that five years of distinguished service on the Gilgit frontier brought to neither the conventional success he sought. Younghusband unlike his father, two uncles and two brothers, never attained the rank of general; when he left Dardistan he determined to resign from active service altogether. Durand, unlike his father and two brothers, failed to get a knighthood and he, too, resigned from government service soon after leaving Gilgit. The explanation for this lack of recognition has nothing to do, as well it might, with some official sense of remorse for the politics pursued in Dardistan. Nor is it any reflection on the conduct of the two men; both, in fact, were popularly regarded as heroes. But what happened is that the experience changed them; in the mountains Durand discovered his limitations, Younghusband found a new vocation.

* * *

As he rode out of Leh for Hunza and the Karakorams in July 1889, Younghusband's reputation stood high but precarious. Recently elected the youngest Fellow of the R.G.S. he was better known than Elias. Yet his fame rested on just one great journey; addressing the R.G.S. he had been conscious of his lack of geographical training, and in government circles he was still handicapped by having had no political experience. The new mission struck him as a perfect chance to flesh out his reputation. It also accorded exactly with his personal inclinations; as he later put it, 'the exploring spirit was upon me'.

'I wonder', he had told his sister four years before, 'if I shall ever really settle down in any place for more than a few months at a time.' He had been reading through the papers of his uncle, Robert Shaw, the man who with Hayward had made the first successful journey to Sinkiang. He had also just had his first taste of the mountains, making a brief trek to Kulu and Lahul. Travel, and particularly mountain travel, had suddenly become his one passion in life. But with his enthusiasm so often doused by 'pigheaded red-tape men', he was seriously considering resigning his commission and travelling freelance.

It was Lockhart who changed this. He claims to have been the first to have spotted Younghusband's talents as a political officer; 'I picked him out in '85 as just the man required for the Intelligence Branch explorations.' He got him transferred to the Q.M.C's department, but then refused to take him on the mission to Dardistan. Instead it was MacGregor who gave him his first break. 'Damned rum name that,' MacGregor had commented on first being introduced to Younghusband and, though the new recruit had since learnt the whole of *The Defence of India* by heart, he still held the Q.M.G. in great awe. With trepidation, therefore, in 1886 he proposed that he should undertake a mission to the mountains of Manchuria. 'If the Indian Empire is to be saved,' he tried to convince MacGregor, 'I must at once be sent on duty to Manchuria.'

Manchuria lies between Mongolia and Korea. It was not self-evident even to MacGregor that India's security was endangered by any developments in that quarter. But he had to admire the boldness of Younghusband's thinking. The government could hardly be expected to pay for such a trip, nor could it possibly warrant eighteen months' absence from duty. Six months, though, he could arrange; Younghusband was launched.

The Manchurian journey afforded experience of travel in the remote parts of China; but as an expedition it paled into insignificance beside its sequel. For instead of returning to India by sea, Younghusband grasped the opportunity of an overland journey across the breadth of the Chinese empire and through the Western Himalayas. Elias, rather than Shaw, was his inspiration as for weeks on end he urged his camels across the Gobi and on to the oasis cities of Sinkiang. A lone European travelling by night through the star-filled immensity of the Central Asian deserts, he felt the stirrings of a spiritual curiosity that would transform his travels into a symbol of a more vital journey, that of inner exploration. It all began with little more than a naïve sense of wonder. He experienced a sense of deep humility in the awareness of a man's insignificance beside the silent immeasurable vastness of Nature (always with a capital N); at the same time, and seemingly in complete contradiction, he was filled with a fierce pride in the authority and stamina that enabled him, a stranger and a youth, to prevail over men of other races and over terrain as hostile as could be imagined.

What was the lesson of Nature's perfection and what the secret of human ascendancy?

The onward journey from Sinkiang to India provided a still sterner test and hinted at some of the answers. His commanding officer in the Intelligence Branch had suggested that the greatest value would accrue from his expedition if, instead of following the usual trade route from Sinkiang to Ladakh, he were to strike out for the central Karakorams and investigate a pass called the Mustagh; Colonel Henry Godwin-Austin had attempted it in 1861 and, though unsuccessful, had reported it as being in regular use.

Younghusband was compelled to differ. The challenge of the unknown route was irresistible but the pass proved a death-trap. The glacier ascent defeated his baggage ponies and the crest, at 19,000 feet, gave onto an almost sheer ice face; only a well equipped mountaineer could hope to get down it. Younghusband knew nothing of climbing; he couldn't even assess the degree of danger. But by now he was committed to the mountains. His initiation was over; it was time for the baptism of fear.

This quasi-religious language may sound fanciful, but that undoubtedly was how Younghusband saw the Himalayas. Not for him the *sangfroid* of Elias, the stern detachment of Biddulph or the genial exasperation of Lockhart. The Hindus regarded the mountains as the abode of the gods and no-one of average sensitivity could deny that this was an appropriate and inspiring notion; it was high time someone treated the world to a taste of their majesty and mystique. After all, the traveller for sport could have done better in Africa, an ethnologist like Leitner might have been happy in the Levant, and those like Elias for whom travel was some kind of personal exorcism might have satisfactorily wrestled with their problems in a desert. Only for the explorer who sought not man, not beast, but God, were the mountains unique; or, put another way, the traveller who would love the mountains and understand their allure must also be a seeker. Younghusband, earnest and impressionable and already dissatisfied with the narrow credo of an evangelical upbringing, responded to the Himalayas with a long sigh of recognition.

I lay down on the ground and gazed and gazed upon the scene, muttering to myself deep thankfulness that to me it had been [given] to see such glory. Here was no disappointment—no trace of disillusionment. What I had so ardently longed to see was now spread out before me. Where I had reached no white man had ever reached before. And there before me were peaks of 26,000 feet, and in one case 28,000 feet, in height, rising above a valley bottom only 12,000 feet above sea level. For mountain majesty and sheer sublimity that scene could hardly be excelled. And austere though it was it did not repel—it just enthralled me. This world was more wonderful by far than I had ever known before. And I seemed to grow greater myself from the mere fact of having seen it. Having once seen that, how could I ever be little again.

A wiry but slight five feet six, he was here inviting ridicule. But cynicism, whether directed at his competitive outlook, his intellectual naïvety or his biblical prose, was something to which he was all but impervious. In earlier days, happily and proudly, he had risen to the bait of every test of stamina his schoolfellows and regimental colleagues could devise. No man ever cared less about making a fool of himself; the important thing was to welcome each challenge, to forge ahead and to excel, regardless.

So it was with the Mustagh pass. The thing was impossible, therefore he would do it. Knotting turbans and reins for ropes, hacking steps in the ice with a pickaxe and trusting to a grip from frozen, bootless feet, he managed what the great Swedish explorer, Sven Hedin, would call 'the most difficult and dangerous achievement in these mountains so far'; it was hardly surprising that at the time he believed Providence guided his every step and was preserving him for some still greater feat.

Not only Providence but the eyes of the world seemed to be forever on Frank Younghusband. Embarking now on the new mission to Hunza he marvelled at the trust bestowed on him and was overwhelmed by the need to do well by his country. No pious claptrap this; Younghusband was too direct, too honest. He lived in the awareness that men hung on his every deed and that civilisation waited with bated breath for his revelations. The rapt attention of family, superiors and country made every trial a Herculean challenge and every achievement an occasion for profound analysis. Moreover, in the glare of the footlights, there was no place for self-doubt. His judgements must be unassailable, his courage inexhaustible. Supreme self-possession became the Younghusband hallmark. It might rile his colleagues and amuse his superiors, but to his juniors and more particularly, to his native followers, it amounted to charisma.

An instructive comparison might be made with Lawrence of Arabia; each in his day captured the popular imagination and was hedged about with romance, each was controversial and each mystical. Yet where Lawrence was cold, tortured, tragic, Younghusband was all warmth, simplicity and good cheer. The man from the deserts stood aloof and impossible; the man from the mountains was down to earth, almost endearing. In fact they were about as different as could be, and nowhere does this show better than in their charismatic appeal. Lawrence secured the loyalty of his Arabs by becoming one; Younghusband won the devotion of his guides and porters by doing exactly the opposite. He remained obtusely English. He baulked at native dress and could speak no Asian languages other than the obligatory Hindustani. Faced with someone who clearly understood not a word he was saying, he was most likely to repeat himself in English, slowly and ever so distinctly, rather than lend his tongue to some foreign inflection. Yet, through a barrage of interpreters, his self-assurance, his transparent honesty and his genuine solicitude for others somehow shone through. For all his Englishness and his sense of superiority, he was fascinated by the small hardy men of the mountains. He admired their courage, he valued their companionship and, to an extent that only the mountaineer can appreciate, he trusted them. The *sahib* of his day might have offered rupees to the man who could find a way down from Mustagh—or have berated the man who had led him to such an impasse. Younghusband had done neither; he had held his tongue and waited; with a sidelong glance at their imperturbable leader, the men had set about risking their lives for him. Whether Balti porters, Ladakhi guides, Gurkha soldiers or Yarkandi ponymen they became very much a part of the whole mountain experience that so thrilled and troubled him.

Even the Kirghiz, about whom he was even less complimentary than Elias, were roused from their spineless stupor by his confidence and determination. The first object of the 1889 mission was to rendezvous with the men who had fallen foul of the Hunza raiders. He was to reassure them about the government's efforts to protect them and thus secure their co-operation in exploring the route by which the raiders had come. After 185 miles travelled in six days including three passes of around 18,000 feet, Younghusband reached the Kirghiz camping grounds at Shahidulla. His offer of money to repair the abandoned fort there and of a small Kashmir garrison to hold it, together with his irresistible air of authority produced a dramatic effect. The cowed nomads forgot their fear of Hunza's retribution and agreed to betray the unknown route. In fact they were so taken with their obliging visitor that they were all for tendering allegiance to Kashmir and thus to British India.

What made Younghusband's performance particularly impressive was the awkward fact, which gradually dawned on him, that Shahidulla and its Kirghiz residents were none of India's or Kashmir's business. His uncle, Shaw, had been the first to make the point when he had observed that 'the Maharaja [of Kashmir] has no more right to Shahidulla than I do'. The frontier lay several marches south on the crest of the Karakorams. If the official justification for claiming Hunza was that it lay on the Indian side of the main watershed, then, by the same coin, Shahidulla, north of it, must be Chinese. Younghusband was poaching; yet awareness of his weak ground cramped his style not a bit.

For someone with such a deep respect for the local peoples, his insensitivity about the rights of other administrations is surprising. For most of the next two years he would be roving about beyond the British frontier; yet in marked contrast to Elias he never approached an understanding of the motives and fears of the two principal authorities, the Afghans and the Chinese. He saw things exclusively in terms of the great imperial struggle and is not without blame for the upheavals that occurred in his wake, most notably on the Pamirs. His temporary adoption of the Kirghiz of the Kun Lun had typically disastrous consequences. The Kashmir soldiers were in due course withdrawn; the Hunza raiders relieved the Kirghiz of the rupees before they could rebuild the fort; the Chinese demolished the rest of the old fort and built a new one much closer to the frontier; and three years later the Kirghiz leader, with whom Younghusband had hit it off so well, was still paying for his pro-British sympathies in a Chinese prison.

Younghusband, however, was content to have secured the immediate objective, the co-operation of the Kirghiz; 'the real excitement of the expedition was now to begin'. On September 3 accompanied by his escort of six Gurkhas, a Pathan surveyor—he was still weak in this department—two Ladakhis, two Baltis and five Kirghiz, he headed west for Hunza. The pass by which the Hunza raiders crossed the main range was reputedly called the Shimshal and lay on the eastern edge of Hunza territory. Between there and Shahidulla the nimble-footed Dards threaded trackless defiles and cluttered gorges for some two hundred miles. The Shaksgam and Raskam rivers that drained these gloomy gutters had to be forded five and ten times a day. From their waist-deep waters Younghusband's ponies now emerged festooned with icicles; the men clung to their tails to avoid being swept under by the current or knocked down by the icebergs that bobbed along in it.

It was hard, cold and unrewarding work. A spare figure at the best of times, Younghusband lost weight so dramatically that his signet ring slipped from an emaciated finger. A later traveller would be constrained to wonder whether 'such an inhuman mass of snow, lifeless mountain and ravine was not meant to be denied to mankind'; even the view was 'frustrated on all sides by stark black mountains imprisoning the stone-filled valleys'. Young-husband felt much the same; but after a hard day's march he would make a point of shinning three or four thousand feet up the nearest precipice just to glimpse the view. The sight of those peaks and glaciers refreshed his spirit. All that white untrodden snow and those curling swelling glaciers hypnotised him; they were a challenge and something more, a message perhaps, a mystery.

Twice he found a pretext for breaking the monotony of the grim battle in the gorges and again exploring the snows. The first was the rumour of another pass which, like the Mustagh, debouched into Baltistan; a traveller in the 1830s had called it the Saltoro and had made an unsuccessful attempt on it, the map-makers later dutifully recorded it and Algy Durand, a few months before, had tried to get a look at it from the south. The second was purely wishful thinking on his own part; approaching Hunza and fearing that the Shimshal would prove a disappointment he chose to ignore his guide's advice and explore the conjectural position assigned to it on the map. On both attempts he forced a path up the glacial moraines, crossed onto the main glacier 'and made good progress over the ice till brought up short by impassable crevasses—'great staring rents in the ice fifty or sixty feet deep'. Though a mountaineer at heart and now with as much Himalayan experience as any contemporary climber, he still had neither the equipment nor the occasion for a serious mountaineering enterprise that might keep him amongst the snows for weeks rather than days.

If this was a disappointment the two excursions were not altogether fruitless. Officially he could justify them as affording conclusive proof that the central Karakorams were watertight; barring mountaineers, no expedition from the north could hope to reach India that way. 'The fact is that from the Karakoram pass to the real Shimshal there is an immense glacier region equalled in extent by no other glacier region in the world; the mountains are of most stupendous height and rugged in the extreme; and between the two passes mentioned above the range . . . for practical military purposes is impassable.'

But it was on a personal level that these new tussles with the mountains made their greatest mark. If the Mustagh pass in 1887 had been his baptism, the Karakorams in 1889 were his first communion. At last he could feel the mystery, he could read the message. The same factors as in 1887 worked to heighten his spiritual perception. On the Saltoro pass he again looked death in the face and came away unscathed. Dawn on September 16 had found his small party blundering through a heavy snowstorm just below what they took to be the pass. They seemed to be beyond the worst of the crevasses and were cutting their way up an ice slope before descending into the ravine that led to the pass.

. . . suddenly we heard a report like thunder, and then a rushing sound. We knew at once that it was an avalanche; it was coming from straight above us, and I felt in that moment greater fear than I have ever yet done, for we could see nothing, but only heard this tremendous rushing sound coming straight down upon us. One of the men called out to run, but we could not for we were on an ice slope, up which we were hewing our way with an axe. The sound came nearer and nearer and then came a cloud of snow-dust, and the avalanche rushed past us in the ravine by our side. Had it happened a quarter of an hour later, or had we started a quarter of an hour earlier, we should have been in the ravine and buried by the avalanche.

As if this were not enough, a second avalanche promptly thundered across the path they had just cut, obliterating all trace of it. 'We have to trust to something higher than man to lead us through everything safely,' he had written in his diary. Now he had the desired proof that Providence was still on his side.

On what he designated the Crevasse Glacier it was not the danger but the spectacle that impressed him.

When I can free my mind from the overpowering sense of grandeur which the mountains produce, and from the thoughts of the stern hard work we had to go through in those parts, I think of the beauty of that glacier scenery, the delicate transparency of the walls of ice, the exquisite tinting of the blues and greens upon it, the fairy caverns, the deep crevasses and the pinnacles of ice, as forming a spectacle unsurpassed in its purity of loveliness. Other scenes are beautiful and yet others are impressive by their grandeur. . . . But it is high up among the loftiest mountain summits, where all is shrouded in unsullied whiteness, where nothing polished dares pollute, that the very essence of sublimity must be sought for. It is there indeed that the grand and beautiful unite to form the sublime.

The searing whiteness of those snowy realms, the hard dazzling purity of ice, the unsullied unpolluted virginity of it all, these are what impressed him most and the same themes occur again and again in all his mountain descriptions. Not the savagery of wind or the brute force of avalanche or even the eerie silence which makes man feel an impostor. On the contrary, Younghusband felt at home; he was being vouchsafed a foretaste of heaven and a vision of how the world should be; he was being commissioned to go forth and make it so.

Each excursion was followed by a period of rest during which he retired to his tent for a couple of days to read. His library was small but amidst such awesome scenery and following such traumatic experiences, each word took on a heightened and personal meaning.

'As I read the thoughts of men on the deepest meanings of it all, I was unwontedly elated. I seemed to be on the brink of discovering a new religion. All the inessentials were fading away. And before me was appearing a religion so clear, so true, so convincing that when men saw it they would surely leap to seize it.' It was like K2 with the clouds suddenly being torn from its summit. A work on Buddhism caused him to reflect on his followers, not just on their performance but on their innermost aspirations. Whether Buddhist, Mohammedan or Hindu they too believed in living the good life and, when under great stress, they too turned to their gods. This common ground impressed him to the extent that he found conventional Christianity too exclusive; the innermost meaning of all things, the eternal truths of which his new religion would consist, must be readily acceptable to all creeds.

On the other hand he couldn't but be struck by the superiority of Christianity over all rivals. This, it seemed to him, explained the ascendancy of the white man in India. On a personal level it accounted for his own success in getting his men to follow him to the ends of the earth. Applying Darwinian theories of evolution to religion and ethics he saw the races of mankind at different stages of development on the ladder of moral awareness. The Hindu and the Chinese might be intellectually smarter, the Sikh and Mohammedan braver, but the English Christian occupied the top rung in moral ascendancy. The teachings of his religion imbued him with a greater resolution, a greater self-denial and a deeper sympathy. And this, moreover, was the way ahead, not bigger brains or tougher skins but warmer hearts.

Elitism is no virtue; Younghusband was later ashamed of presuming that Providence had singled him out. He must also have been relieved that he had not drawn the obvious parallel between moral superiority and the attainment of great physical altitudes, or that he had not suggested that his personal single-mindedness was somehow being rewarded by a glimpse of Nature's purity. Yet, at th time, he was not innocent of such vanities. He would look back on this spell in the Karakorams as the turning point in his life and, as if afraid to pursue the logic of his awakening, would prefer to regard the whole thing as a mystical experience. One would shudder were it not for his disarming naïvety and for the unquestioned sincerity of his subsequent retraction.

About October 12, brimming with new found resolve, Young-husband ascended the real Shimshal pass and came face to face with the dreaded Hunza raiders. Throughout the previous weeks he had set a watch day and night in case of attack. Now news reached him that Algy Durand, although not actually manhandled, had found Safdar Ali in a truculent and unpredictable mood; the Mir had been warned of Younghusband's approach and the new subsidy was not to be paid out till he was safely through Hunza territory. It was not, however, clear whether the chief would co-operate or whether he had agreed to Durand's stipulation about no more caravan raids. If he hadn't then resistance might well be offered to any British officer snooping at the vital pass by which the raiders went; the Dards were not unnaturally jealous of the few geographical secrets that remained to them.

After two hundred miles of uninhabited wilderness the first evidence of human endeavour was predictably grim. A square stone tower, windowless and forbidding, hove into sight. It stood on the end of a bluff that formed the farther wall of a deep ravine cutting clean across the valley floor. At the other end of this wall, where the ravine tucked itself into the sheer mountain side, there was another tower with a large gaping door; between the two towers ran a high stone rampart. With the unfordable river on one side and the mountains on the other, the only possible access was down the ravine and up the zigzag path under the rampart to the open doorway. All was peaceful; just a thin plume of smoke betrayed that the position was held.

With a couple of men to interpret, Younghusband plunged into the ravine; he left the Gurkhas to offer covering fire if needed. Half way up the other side the silence was suddenly shattered by a loud report; the door in the tower had been slammed shut. Then waving figures, brandishing matchlocks and shouting, appeared along the rampart just fifty feet above him; at that range stones, let alone bullets, could have annihilated his party. With the cool of a man who felt himself indestructible, Young-husband halted and quietly signalled for someone to come out and parley. His serenity was infectious; the shouting died away, the door opened a crack and two wild looking Dards obeyed his summons.

Though jittery and as uncertain of their chief's intentions as they were of their visitor's, the garrison lapped up his self-confidence. By nightfall the long haired and heavily armed raiders were sharing a fire with their timid Kirghiz prey. The grave Pathan surveyor, the sturdy Gurkhas and the long suffering Baltis and Ladakhis stood amongst them. And the solitary Englishman could not but again marvel at 'the extraordinary influence of the European in Asia'.

Next day it transpired that Safdar Ali had indeed acceded to Durand's demand in the matter of arranging for Younghusband to continue to the Hunza valley; he therefore proceeded on up the Shimshal pass. He still hoped for another glacier-bound wilderness like the Saltoro or a knife edge like the Mustagh but, from native report, was not altogether surprised to find a gentle snow-free ascent and a crest as open and level as a pamir. It was so easy that, like Biddulph with the Baroghil or Lockhart with the Dora, he was inclined to draw the wildest conclusions about the vulnerability of Dardistan. Study of the reports of his predecessors should have warned him that the difficulties were to be expected not on the pass but amongst the gorges and glaciers beyond it.

These he did not explore. Having reached the top of the pass he surprised his Hunza escort by promptly turning about and heading back the way he had come. While Safdar Ali was on his best behaviour pending receipt of the subsidy, Younghusband would take the opportunity of visiting the other passes between the Shimshal and Lockhart's Killik. Both debouched onto the Pamirs and therefore he would continue round the Hunza perimeter along the Raskam river.

There was however another considerably more pressing reason for delaying his entry into Hunza proper. At least four other parties of Europeans were taking advantage of the favourable autumn conditions of 1889 to explore neighbouring valleys on the Pamirs and Kun Lun. One consisted of two English sportsmen combining a bit of surreptitious surveying with the pursuit of the Marco Polo sheep; from them Younghusband had just learnt that Grombtchevski, the Russian agent who had reached Hunza in the previous year, was again in the field and was now lurking somewhere in the Raskam valley.

To what extent the movement of Russian travellers dictated his own is not clear, but in retrospect Younghusband liked to look back on the whole 1889 mission as an elaborate game of hide and seek. 'The game was on', he wrote when, soon after leaving Ladakh, he had learnt that a large Russian expedition was refitting in the northern foothills of the Kun Lun. At Shahidulla he had kept an anxious eye on their activities and at one point thought that they were stockpiling supplies for some sort of invasion. They also had 'road-making equipment' (spades?) and had enlisted the services of a Frenchman with wide experience of the Kashmir side of the passes. One is reminded strongly of the climax in *Kim*; the players and the setting of the 'game' are enough to establish that Kipling knew his Younghusband. The plot, however is quite different. This Russian expedition had no designs on India. Too big for espionage and too small for an invasion force it was actually a scientific and military undertaking commanded by a disciple of Przhevalski, the greatest of Russian travellers, and was continuing his work along the Sino–Tibetan frontier. As for the Frenchman, this was M. Dauvergne, an expert on carpet manufacture who was under contract to the Kashmir government. Also a sportsman and an inveterate traveller, he soon parted from the Russians, continued on to the Pamirs and thence crossed into Dardistan. He was probably no more in the espionage business than Gabriel Bonvalot.

Younghusband's suspicions were however justified in the case of Grombtchevski. Lord Curzon would soon identify him as the 'stormy petrel of Russian frontier advance', and there can be no question that his travels were politically motivated. With regard to Hunza he had been actively engaged in intrigue and he had also tried to enter Chitral and Kafiristan undetected. Even Dr. Leitner, who from the Oriental University Institute, Woking, took up Grombtchevski's case with some vigour, seems to have concluded that a bona fide representative of the Imperial Geographical Society had no business to be crossing frontiers in uniform and with a military escort.

Anxious to get further news of this notorious figure, Younghusband chased after the two English sportsmen. A week after leaving Shimshal he received a letter written in Turki from the man himself; he was waiting at the next camping ground. Thus, at a spot called Khaian Aksai, British and Russian agents for the first time came face to face. It was almost as if the place had been chosen. One march to the north the Raskam river disappeared into a gorge that divided the Kun Lun from the Pamirs; a similar distance to the west the Karakorams merged into the Hindu Kush. Inacessible it was, yet strategically valuable and surprisingly fertile—in Younghusband's view alarmingly so; for the waving grass and grey willows, so inviting beside the brown desolation of rock and scree, were a true no-man's land, unknown and unclaimed. The Russian had as much right to hoist his flag there as the Englishman.

Considering the veil of secrecy that would be drawn over all Younghusband's activities in 1889 not the least improbable feature of the occasion was that it was recorded on film. Grombtchevski had a camera and the following year he obligingly sent Young-husband, then in Kashmir, a print; this was reproduced only twice before being lost to posterity. It was never a great picture and on the one occasion that it appeared in a British publication the rough handling across Asia, as well as the loss of detail in reproduction, did not improve it. Yet as a remarkable record of a celebrated and desolate encounter it can scarcely be equalled; imagine the excitement if a photograph of Stanley's meeting with Livingstone ever came to light.

Instead of the conventional studio portrait, here we see the explorer in action. Bearded and in a battered bush hat, with one hand on hip and the other on his gun, Younghusband at last looks convincing. The jaunty air bespeaks a dauntless physique and one can sense the assurance that so impressed his followers (here ranged on his right). No doubt that pile of sticks and tree trunks in the foreground was their doing. The Gurkhas were uncomfortably aware of their lack of stature beside the burly Cossacks and had already begged their leader to explain that they were in no way typical of their regiment; he was to tell the Russians that most Gurkhas were a good six foot six. Aware too that their commander was somewhat undersized they appear to have got him to climb on top of something and then to have concealed the object behind the unlit bonfire. Younghusband thus stands shoulder to shoulder with the massive Grombtchevski, a man of six foot two with a frame to match.

Though now a Lieutenant-Colonel in the Imperial army—and

wearing a uniform to prove it—Grombtchevski was a Pole by birth. He was ten years older than Younghusband and had served with distinction in the Imperial Bodyguard and under the vaunted Skobeleff in Turkestan; he was now designated a Special Frontier Commissioner for the province of Ferghana, previously Khokand. As one of Russia's most experienced travellers he had attracted the patronage of the Tsar and was regarded as the natural successor to the famous Przhevalski. Besides the journeys of 1888 and 1889 he had been the first, in 1885, systematically to explore Sinkiang and in 1886 to work up the Naryn river into the Tian Shan.

In the present year he had left his Russian base on June 1, and accompanied by seven Cossacks (standing behind him in the photo) and Dr. Conrad, a German entomologist (seated on his left) had again set off for Kafiristan. In Roshan and again in Shignan the Afghans had performed with zeal the role envisaged for them by Elias; they refused to let him pass. Hunza would therefore have been the next logical step and it seems that Safdar Ali did invite him back. But for some reason he declined. Even to a would-be protector the Hunza chief could be a sore trial, but more probably Grombtchevski, still with no more than promises, hesitated to compete with both Durand and Younghusband. He had therefore turned to the exploration of the Raskam valley and the chance of a battle of wits with a British agent on neutral ground.

Actually the meeting turned out to be a most dignified and amicable affair. Younghusband inspected the Cossacks and Grombtchevski the Gurkhas; they exchanged invitations to dinner and the Russian officer plied his guest with vodka; doing his best to reciprocate, Younghusband broached his one bottle of brandy. The Englishman was impressed and delighted to find his opposite number such 'a very good sort of fellow'; though rivals and soon perhaps enemies they yet, as individuals, had much in common. Grombtchevski was equally gratified; here was a young man who truly appreciated the extent of his travels—something no-one seemed to understand in Russia—and the hardships they involved. He had expected a challenger and he had found a disciple. As icy gusts felt their way down from the Pamirs to tug fiercely at the guy ropes, the affable Pole and the irrepressible Englishman clinked glasses, huddled deeper into their sheepskins and mulled over the future of Asia. Combining the incongruous, the momentous and the romantic in equal measure, it is perhaps the most representative and memorable vignette in the whole of the Great Game.

Two days later they parted. The Gurkhas presented arms and the Cossacks drew swords. Grombtchevski pressed on Younghusband a fine sheep and made a little speech about how he hoped they would meet again 'either in peace in St. Petersburg or in war on the Indian frontier'. Younghusband repaid the courtesy by presenting the Russian with his book on Buddhism—he had finished it anyway—and left him with what he would have regarded as a magnanimous parting thought; 'we are both playing at a big game and we should be not one jot better off for trying to conceal the fact'.

They actually met again rather sooner than anticipated—in Yarkand the following summer (1890). By then they had every reason to distrust one another but again they got on famously. After going his separate way from Khaian Aksai, Grombtchevski had sought permission from the British Resident in Kashmir to spend the winter in Ladakh. The predictable refusal of such an unprecedented request was a long time coming and while the Russian cooled his heels in Shahidulla, the Kirghiz suggested an exploratory foray east towards the Tibetan frontier. Younghusband claims to have put them up to this, the idea being to cause the Russian 'extreme hardship and loss'. If such a plot existed, it worked. Grombtchevski leapt at the idea of seeing the eastern extremity of the Kashmir frontier, and the Tibetan plateau did the rest. At an average height of 18,000 feet, without water, fuel or grass, the party was soon in trouble. Tears caused by the icy wind got no further than their eyelashes before freezing solid. The baggage ponies went down one by one and the Cossacks became too weak to carry their rifles. They all suffered severely from frostbite; a year later Grombtchevski was still on crutches. When they made it back to Shahidulla they had lost all their ponies and all their belongings.

Grombtchevski never suspected Younghusband of such a wretched prank; he held the Kashmir Resident responsible, by his refusal to allow him across the frontier. In a sense, though, he got his own back. For when Hunza raiders returned to relieve the

Kirghiz of the money given them by Younghusband in the previous year, he was on hand to point out the lesson of his rival's empty promises. So much so that the Kirghiz agreed to betray to him, too, the route by which the raiders came.

But at Khaian Aksai some sort of gentleman's agreement seems to have been reached whereby Grombtchevski would in future steer clear of Hunza and Dardistan in return for a free hand north of the watershed. Safdar Ali's affairs were therefore of less interest and, besides, the expedition was in no fit state to take up the Kirghiz offer. When the two men met in Yarkand in 1890 Grombtchevski thus had a clear conscience. Younghusband kept quiet about his own role in the Russian disaster and they again parted the best of friends. Two years later it was reported that Grombtchevski kept a photo of Younghusband on his bedside table and nearly thirty years later, in 1925, Younghusband received a letter from his old rival. But by then the genial Pole was a decrepit and dying man. He had risen to the rank of Lieutenant-General, had been imprisoned in Siberia by the Bolsheviks and was now bedridden and destitute in Warsaw; he died the following year. With the letter there was an account in Russian of his travels. It included the only other known reproduction of that remarkable photograph.*

*This account of Grombtchevski's travels has not been traced.

PART THREE

Vici

11. Looking for a Pretext

To Dr. Leitner, now setting up home in Woking, the re-establishment of the Gilgit Agency was, of course, a hideous mistake. But worse still was the assumption that for the Agency to be effective it was necessary for the Dards to be subdued. In Leitner's view the military roads that would open up the Dard valleys amounted to crude provocation, the engagements that would ruthlessly suppress Dard independence amounted to atrocities, and the promotion-crazed soldiers who would run the country were no better than vandals. Instead, Dardistan should have been left as a kind of nature reserve in which the Dards could roam at will, living in their traditional style, speaking their ancient tongues, and visited only by scientists observing them from a discreet distance. This was not only the most morally acceptable solution but also the most politically expedient. It would cost nothing; the Dards, uncowed, would continue to defend their independence as fiercely as ever, and would naturally favour whichever power was most willing to respect it; their country, undisturbed by road and bridge builders, would remain as impenetrable as ever; and together these two factors would make of the region a far more effective barrier against the Russians than the most ambitious network of outposts and supply lines. Grombtchevski had confided to Younghusband that he had seen enough of Hunza and Safdar Ali not to risk his neck there again; the Dards could be trusted to see off any subsequent agents and, if the Pamirs could be made a neutral zone thus doubling the line of defence, so much the better.

By the 1890s Leitner was no longer alone; Younghusband, for one, also had his reservations, though of a more moderate nature. The Russian menace was as real for him as for anyone and he accepted that Dardistan must be more effectively controlled. But he doubted whether force need be used; instead of Algy Durand's policy of inviting confrontation, more effort should be made to work with the Dards. He was a great believer in having a man on the spot; it was no good exchanging letters and trading ultimata for insults. What was needed was a good political officer in Hunza and another in Chitral; and if this policy had been pursued from the start the co-operation of the Dards could have been won without a shot being fired.

Support for such views was also growing in official circles. Lord Lansdowne and Morty Durand faced increasingly stiff opposition both within the Government of India and at Westminster. Apart from the rights and wrongs of the policy, there was the little matter of expense. Lockhart's scheme for the reopening of the Gilgit Agency had been greeted with horror because it entailed the services of nineteen British officers and a sizeable nucleus of British Indian troops. Algy Durand, in 1888, had been sent to draw up an economy version of the same scheme that would cost half as much. Four British officers, he concluded, would be enough, plus a small bodyguard of British Indian troops; the rest of the necessary troops, as well as finance for an elaborate system of roads and telegraph lines, was to be provided by the Kashmir government. This looked fine on paper but it soon proved the thin end of an extremely thick wedge. Two years after its re-opening there were eighteen British officers attached to the Agency, two hundred British Indian troops and a mountain battery. By 1892 the number of officers had risen to twenty-three, and still Durand cried out for more. And in 1895 Chitral alone claimed the attention of close on fifteen thousand troops. Not surprisingly people wondered if it was all worthwhile. Questions were asked in Parliament and a long debate on the whole future of Chitral and Gilgit resulted.

Durand and his men in Biddulph's now much extended and handsomely furnished bungalow had no time for such criticisms. If Younghusband ever dared voice his doubts there, no-one paid much attention; a good fighting man, thought Algy, but 'not overburdened with brains'. As for Leitner he was 'a liar and a traitor to boot'. There were just so many imperatives for extending British control to all the Dard states that the methods employed were almost irrelevant and criticisms hardly worth answering. But if pushed, the one stock answer, which even those unacquainted with the day-to-day exigencies of frontier relations must acknowledge, was the Russian threat.

Algy Durand honestly believed that as matters stood in 1889 'there was absolutely nothing to stop a Russian officer with a thousand Cossacks from reaching Astor in ten days after crossing the passes of the Hindu Kush, and from watering his horses in the Wular Lake [in the Kashmir Valley] four days later'. Imagine, he went on, the repercussions. Out of Kashmir in a wild stampede would come tumbling the British Resident, the Maharaja and a gaggle of holidaying *memsahibs*; the Indian Army, straining its eyes in search of Russian columns advancing across the Afghan deserts, would find its flank already turned and its lines of communication across the Punjab exposed. Regardless of expense such a calamity must be forestalled; 'the Gilgit Game was well worth the candle'.

Durand had joined the Intelligence Branch of the Q.M.G.'s department just after MacGregor's departure, but 'old Mac' would surely have approved of this lurid deduction. His disciple knew every inch of the Gilgit road and spoke with the greatest authority. So alarming was his prognosis that had it been leaked, like *The Defence of India*, it would have caused a furore. Perhaps for that reason it was never examined as closely as it might have been. For Durand, letting the cat out of the bag many years later, failed to note that such a manœuvre by the Russians would only have been possible during four months of the year and then always assuming that the weather had been favourable. Furthermore the Dards would have had to show unprecedented forbearance if a small army was to be allowed to pass unscathed through their valleys, whilst the Dogra troops, incompetent as they were, could hardly have failed to take such an elementary precaution as withdrawing their Indus ferry. But assuming favourable conditions and assuming that, for reasons inconceivable, both Dard and Dogra welcomed the Russians, they would have first had to get across the Pamirs undetected and intact; Durand had no experience of this part of their route. Nor had he of the glaciers and gorges into which the Hindu Kush passes immediately debouched; but every traveller who had, from Biddulph onwards, had declared them totally unfit for the passage of troops. Finally, on the Gilgit-Kashmir section of the route, his experience indeed illustrated the possibility of moving large bodies of troops. Conveniently, though, he seems to have forgotten the appalling headaches and losses this occasioned, and that success was only achieved after two years of road building.

However interesting it would have been to put these points to the new Gilgit Agent, it would scarcely have altered the course of history. Durand would simply have changed his ground; how to stop the Hunza raids and counter Chinese claims? Or how to guard against a conflagration throughout Dardistan as a result of a disputed succession in Chitral? Or perhaps he would have held to the still more questionable view of maintaining that the Dards were the aggressors; that he was somehow forced into invading not only Hunza but states like Nagar and Chilas who had long since thrown in their lot with Kashmir. Doubtful, indeed, is it that he would have confessed the obvious, that given the role envisaged for the new Gilgit Agency, given its constitution and given the men sent to staff it, Dardistan was doomed and war of some sort inevitable.

The new scheme had been approved as if it was merely the re-establishment of Biddulph's Agency in the light of changing circumstances. In fact it was nothing of the sort; Durand's position was radically different. For one thing he had companions, only four to start with but all his closest friends, and soon many more. Secondly and far more important, though he had only a small bodyguard of British Indian troops, he was in command of the entire Dogra force in Dardistan. The change had been achieved as a result of the creation of the Imperial Service Corps in 1888. One can only assume that Dufferin and Morty Durand had Gilgit much in mind when they launched this scheme whereby troops employed by the native states of India were to be trained by British officers and were to serve alongside troops of the regular Indian army. It was projected as a useful way of augmenting the standing army and also of restoring some dignity to those feudal battalions of martial Sikhs, Rajputs and Dogras who previously had no obvious role other than as playthings of their Maharajas. In effect it neatly solved the whole problem of entrusting the defence of Dardistan to the dispirited Kashmir forces. It maintained the fiction of Kashmir's role without all its drawbacks, and it obviated the need for British Indian troops by providing a force that would soon, under British tutelage, be just as effective.

Durand held not only the military reins at Gilgit but also the political reins. Unlike Biddulph he was entrusted with sole responsibility for all dealings with the Dards. Kashmiri officials continued to exercise powers of internal administration but even here his precedence in matters of supply and communications gave him a commanding say. Like his predecessor he would still find the Kashmiris highly obstructive, but at least his efforts were not habitually sabotaged; and he was never the object of an assassination plot. Subsidies, like that dangled before Safdar Ali in return for abandoning his raids, were now to be offered not on behalf of Kashmir but of British India. One of his first assignments was to tour Nagar, Hunza and Chitral and explain just how different the new Agency was; the chiefs were to be convinced that a new era in Anglo–Dard relations was beginning.

Immediately, all this authority was to be deployed in curbing the independence of Hunza. Safdar Ali had precipitated the re-establishment of the Agency and he was to be the first to receive its attentions. In mid-August 1889, just as Younghusband was settting out from Ladakh, Durand, accompanied by his trusty comrade, Surgeon-Major George Robertson, had edged his way up the Hunza gorge. Already anticipating the day when they would have to fight their way through it, they sketched the main defensive positions and pondered the engineering problems of making the track fit for supply trains.

At Chalt they diverged from the route followed by Biddulph and Lockhart and crossed the river on the long swaying bridge of plaited brushwood to the Nagar side. Durand claimed they were the first Europeans to set foot in Nagar; he conveniently forgot that, by his predecessors, Chalt and Chaprot had both been regarded as part of the state. The chief was an octogenarian, 'wise and amiable' according to Leitner, 'a patriarch with a large family and preserving the keenness of youth in his old age'. Durand found him just 'a paralytic debauchee' with a persecution mania. His audience chamber was reached through a trapdoor in the floor to which the only access from below was by a single long tree trunk. As the Gilgit Agent heaved himself through the hole, spiked helmet first, then frock coat, dangling sword, high boots and spurs, he noted that this arrangement must be the Dard equivalent of a portcullis and moat. He was not surprised that the Dard chiefs had a reputation for longevity. Nor, in this case, did he regret it. The chief was remarkably co-operative, 'Raja Jafr Khan and his son Uzr Khan are undoubtedly desirous of being on friendly terms with the British government', he reported.

He might profitably have recalled the difficulties Biddulph had had in reconciling his early friendships with later developments; he would soon regret ever having said a good word about the ruling family of Nagar. Before he had met him he had pigeon-holed Uzr Khan, the heir apparent, as a 'rascal of the first water'; much later he would become 'the Nagar cur'. But now he found him simply 'boorish'. The photographs suggest a rather fine figure, a trifle jowly but bewildered rather than mischievous. They correspond better with the man's history than Durand's erratic judgements; it was he whom Lockhart, three years before, had dispossessed of Chalt and it was he who, two years hence, would be made the pretext for armed intervention.

Durand and Robertson were more exercised by their reception from Safdar Ali of Hunza. On another perilously frayed rope bridge they crossed the chasm, three hundred feet deep and about the same across, that divides the two states, and climbed through the neatly terraced fields. The reception was on a more lavish scale than at Nagar; amidst the Bukhara carpets and the silks of the courtiers Durand felt less conspicuous. But the chief was a sad looking figure, twenty-two years old and delicate, 'with shifty Mongolian eyes' and a foxy little red beard. When some of the Agent's bodyguard were prevented from crowding into the audience chamber, Durand found him 'showing a tendency to insolence'. And when he 'funked' taking a dose prescribed for him by Robertson it was clear that he was also a coward; 'this sounded bad for a rank coward is a dangerous man to deal with'.

So it proved. Safdar Ali, true to Hunza tradition, was out to extract the maximum benefit from his visitors. In return for promises of no caravan raids and of entertaining no Russians, he was being offered a subsidy of 20,000 rupees. He would make no bones about the promises—he had no intention of keeping them anyway—but he would insist on a larger subsidy. Durand refused, whereupon the Mir flew into a rage. The British presentation—a breech-loader or two (but very little ammunition) plus the usual collection of knicknacks—was hurled about the room. Back in camp Durand ordered his escort to arms and broke open the cartridge boxes. As night fell pickets of Hunza sharpshooters were seen to command the camp on all sides; to the two Englishmen it seemed like 'the beginning of the end'.

It was, of course, no such thing. Safdar Ali was just piling on the pressure—successfully too, for he did eventually get the extra 5,000 rupees he sought. At the time, though, Durand stood firm; before day broke, the pickets had vanished and the mission was free to scuttle back along the cliffs towards Gilgit. As they dropped with a sigh of relief from the Hunza ledge into the gloomy gorge, they heard a farewell salute booming away from the country's only cannon. Soon after, the Mir's chief minister panted up with his master's best wishes and a few anxious questions about when the subsidy might be expected. 'After Younghusband is safely in Gilgit,' replied Durand. He himself intended to continue straight on to Chitral but he made a mental note to be back in time to march to Younghusband's aid if required.

Durand was now convinced that there must needs be a day of reckoning with 'young Saffy'. Younghusband's visit would not, however, be made the occasion for it. 'That intrepid and never to be denied traveller has arrived [in Gilgit] safely,' reported the Indian Foreign Department in December 1889. He had not only arrived safely but he was the first British officer to pass through without even being threatened. He may have been 'too soft' by Durand's standards but at least he made some attempt to understand Safdar Ali's predicament. One wonders whether they are writing of the same man. Far from being shifty and Mongolian, Younghusband's Safdar Ali was 'almost European in appearance and could have passed for a Greek or an Italian'. He had a good sense of humour and, though rebuked for his importunate behaviour, bore no ill will. When the shortage of cultivable land was given as the reason for the caravan raids, Younghusband was all sympathy for the desperate straits to which the providers of Hunza were reduced; the raids were just a repetition of the survival tactics of highlanders throughout the world. Safdar Ali was more to be pitied than anything. Immured in his mountain fastness, his intransigence was simply the product of ignorance. When asked if he had ever been to India he replied that great kings like himself and Alexander the Great, from whom he claimed descent, never left their kingdoms. The traditional nature of

Hunza's external relations was that of extracting blackmail from their richer but more vulnerable neighbours. He honestly believed that the British and Russians feared him as much as did the Kirghiz and Dogras; and when they sent representatives to treat for his friendship he treated them accordingly.

Younghusband's more sympathetic report did less to win Safdar Ali a reprieve than the fact that Durand was not yet ready for hostilities; having seen the Hunza road he now knew better than to attempt it with no more than 'a corporal's guard'. The new policy of buying Hunza's co-operation thus got a trial, albeit a short one. Six months later Algy wrote to brother Morty, 'all my savages have been going wrong', and cited in particular the news that Safdar Ali had again been after the Sinkiang caravans; it was on this raid that Hunza men relieved Younghusband's Kirghiz friends of their defence fund. The raiders also killed one of Grombtchevski's servants, but Durand was giving no credit for this. The prospect of 'a row with Hunza and Nagar' was again in the forefront of his mind and feverish attempts were made to build new barracks at Gilgit, to improve the supply line back to Kashmir and to construct the first stage of a mule road to Hunza.

All should have been ready for pursuing a more active policy by the end of the year; more troops arrived from Kashmir as did the Agency doctor and a team of engineering contractors. Durand however had retired on leave to India and thence to England. By the time he got back to Gilgit it was November and his new troops were still a long way from being battle ready. As usual, nothing like enough grain had been brought over the Great Himalaya during the short season of open passes and, though the engineers had arrived, their workforce was stranded on the Kashmir side of the passes. Safdar Ali had won another reprieve.

Younghusband's complaint was that for all this time, in fact for two years after his own visit, no British officer went near Hunza or Nagar. In view of the otherwise adventurous character of British policy at the time, one can only assume that this was deliberate. As will be seen, Younghusband himself spent most of the period prowling about the Pamirs and badgering the Chinese authorities in Sinkiang. With an equally fine disregard for possible consequences, Surgeon-Major Robertson was sent by Durand to the other side of Dardistan to re-open dealings with the Kafirs. He paid them a brief visit in late 1889 and the following September returned to spend over a year in the country, assessing 'the exact value of Kafiristan as a factor in the general problem of how best to secure the safety of the North West frontier of India'. Often sick and invariably in danger, he somehow survived this grim exile amongst the most primitive people in Asia and, in the process, achieved the distinction of being one of the first field-workers in social anthropology. It would, however, be naïve to explain his long stay on the grounds of scientific curiosity. 'It seems to me a great pity', he wrote in 1889, 'that a fine vigorous race such as the Kafirs should ever come under the yoke of the Afghans.' Instead he searched diligently for a pretext, strategic or political, to bring them within the sphere of Gilgit's authority. This quest proved self-defeating. The Kafirs showed themselves too disunited ever to be a political asset, whilst his own activity amongst them was actually intensifying Afghan jealousy. In the end, all he could hope to achieve was a holding operation. To stave off the evil day of an Afghan invasion he let it be thought that the British were still interested in the country, first by staying on as long as possible, then by leading a deputation of Kafirs back to India.

All this was to have disastrous consequences for the Kafirs; but the solicitude shown them at the time was in marked contrast to the cold shoulder turned on Hunza. While Robertson was in Kafiristan, Durand's other political assistant was kept firmly at Gilgit. Even when a man had to be sent up to the Pamirs he was routed via Yasin rather than Hunza. As early as 1889 Durand had been committed to the idea of a Hunza campaign; he did nothing to make the subsidy arrangement work and merely awaited the completion of his preparations and a pretext to attack.

This might have come in May 1891. A report reached the Agent that Uzr Khan of Nagar had murdered one of his brothers and was about to attack the Dogra troops at Chalt. There is no doubt about the murder. The brother appears to have been Durand's rival candidate for the succession; he had been living at Gilgit and, whatever the reason for his return to Nagar, the moment he set foot outside Kashmir territory he was asking for trouble. Fratricide, to a Dard prince, was the must normal behaviour and Durand had no right to be so indignant about it. Whether Uzr Khan also decided that this was the moment to reassert his claim to Chalt is less certain. But Durand needed an excuse to strengthen the Chalt garrison and to push his mule road forward another stage. The opportunity afforded by the rumour of Nagar's supposed mobilisation was too good to miss; he was in Chalt with four hundred men and a mountain battery, and had cut the 'rope' bridge across the river, before Uzr Khan had made a move. Taken in conjunction with two other minor incidents, the kidnapping of a Kashmiri and the disruption of mail passing through Hunza to Younghusband on the Pamirs, this affair also strengthened his case for more troops and bore out his predictions of imminent hostilities. As a down payment he received the services of another two British officers and in the autumn he set off for Simla to bargain for more officers and more troops.

According to one of those who served on the Gilgit staff at this period there were three reasons for a man being posted to the Hindu Kush. The first was debt, the second the Intelligence Branch and the third 'the chance of a scrap'. He should have added a fourth, the right connection. Algy Durand would never have been given the Agent's job if he hadn't been Morty's brother—the eldest brother, as Resident in Nepal, had not been forgotten either—and few of those who followed him to Gilgit would have done so if they hadn't been Algy's friends. It is no coincidence that those not straight from the Intelligence Branch were largely from his old regiment, the Central India Horse.

In spite of the notion of banishment to the outposts of the Empire, Gilgit was a much sought-after posting. The men who in 1891 received telegrams—'Colonel Durand applies urgently for the services of . . .'—were overjoyed. It was the big break, the reward for years of regimental slogging and patient lobbying. A scrap must be in prospect; if not, in Gilgit of all places surely, one could be engineered. The heading on the Agency's notepaper read '*Telegrams*: Gilgit via Srinagar, *Railway Station*: Rawal Pindi'. None of the new recruits imagined they could climb into a cab at Pindi station and be whisked off to the Gilgit Agency for dinner. But with the Indus, the Great Himalaya and a few hundred miles between Gilgit and the nearest telegraph office or railhead, and with the encircling mountains reputedly teeming with promenading Russians and brigand chiefs, what better chance could be hoped for; C.B., C.S.I., C.I.E., a campaign medal at least, must be in the offing and always there was an outside chance of the real thing, a V.C.. Promotion too; everyone in Gilgit, including Durand, who in eighteen months had risen from Captain to Lieutenant-Colonel, seemed to hold an acting rank above that to which they were entitled. Nor was this just wishful thinking. Over the next four years six British officers would win the V.C. in Dardistan and many more be recommended for it. Durand succeeded in mentioning in despatches so many of his fellow officers that he would be singled out in Parliament as having brought the whole system into disrepute.

Arrived in the hard dry air of the Hindu Kush the young officers soon caught the sweet scent of distinction; it made them keen to the point of incitement, brave to the point of folly. One or two had served in the Sudan under Wolseley and Kitchener; with Egypt peaceful, they had transferred to India and now chased appointments to wherever there was the best chance of action. Their lack of interest in the Dards as people or the mountains as scenery was shared by most of their colleagues. It was a measure of their professionalism. The fact that many of them were also deeply in debt in no way contradicts this; Durand's cronies just happened to be a trifle racy and high-spirited. From time to time Algy himself had found it necessary to reassure Morty that he was living within his means. Lieutenants 'Charlie' Townshend and 'Curly' Stewart, the two men who joined him after the Chalt business, were outspoken devotees of riotous living and were more at home backstage with the ladies of the Alhambra; while Algy grimly chronicled his manic forebodings to brother Morty, Townshend and Stewart would rattle off love letters to their favourite actresses. Another type was exemplified by the meticulous Manners Smith and the languid Bruce, both of whom were athletes so reckless they might have qualified as stunt men. One looks in vain for the introvert or the man of even average sensitivity.

Only Younghusband was an obvious misfit; he must have felt it just as he had amongst his hard-drinking fellow subalterns in the King's Dragoon Guards; and no doubt it heightened his sense of somehow being set apart. But if Durand's pals ridiculed this odd little officer with the wide credulous blue eyes and heavy conversation, they paid a grudging respect to his achievements. They also had cause to be grateful for them; for it was Younghusband, of all people, who eventually precipitated the first campaign.

* * *

On September 29, 1891 a cable reached *The Times* from their Bombay correspondent. 'In spite of repeated contradictions it is persistently rumoured here that Captain Younghusband has been killed by the Russians in the Pamir country'; an officer from Gilgit had recently been sent up to the Pamirs and no confirmation or denial could be expected until his return. Not surprisingly this was too much for the victim's father who promptly got the Foreign Office to wire the Indian government. Young Frank, it transpired, was alive all right, but the incident which had given rise to the rumours, though still obscure, was of such an explosive character that nothing more could as yet be revealed.

The Prime Minister had in fact just sent a letter of protest to the Russian Foreign Minister; its tone was such that the latter thought war was about to be declared. So did another *Times* correspondent who happened to be in Kashmir at the time; he regarded the incident itself as equivalent to a declaration of war. General Roberts, Commander-in-Chief in India, agreed; he promptly mobilised a whole division with the idea of grabbing Afghanistan before the Russians got under way. Weeks later when Younghusband got back to India, Roberts was still of this opinion and, with a friendly squeeze of the arm, assured the explorer that 'Now's the time to go for the Russians'. Younghusband, for his part, needed reassurance. He was so shaken by the whole affair that he told his father he would resign unless full satisfaction were exacted from the Russians. Anything less and he must assume that he no longer enjoyed that full support of the government which meant so much to him.

What had actually happened was that, at last, the genteel jockeying for control of the Pamirs had become a muscle-testing brawl. In June 1890, less than six months after his return from Hunza, Younghusband had been sent back to the Pamirs to continue the work of Ney Elias; the latter's report had finally won recognition as the most constructive contribution on meeting the threat of Russian territorial advancement to the Hindu Kush. Younghusband was to take up the question of where the Afghan and Chinese boundaries should be made to meet. Contrary to Elias' recommendations though, he was to champion the Chinese cause and, having made his award, he was to press on the Sinkiang authorities the need to make their occupation effective right up to the new frontier. Elias had found the Afghans infinitely more co-operative, and militarily more formidable, than the Chinese. Now, however, it was rightly felt that for political reasons the Russians were more likely to respect Peking's sovereignty than they were Kabul's.

In his published account of the journey, Younghusband, like every other visitor to the Pamirs, found precious little to comment on. It was a mountain wilderness certainly, but the grandeur and the glory of the Karakorams were sadly lacking, nothing here to rouse a man's spirit, no 'essence of sublimity'. The perils were not the sudden sweep of an avalanche or the treacherous grin of a crevasse but something more abstract and insinuating, a relentless physical deterioration occasioned by the ceaseless wind, sustained cold and excessive altitude. At a spot called Somatash, well west of Elias' proposed Sino-Afghan boundary, he found a sheltered rock inscribed in Chinese to record some forgotten foray; it provided a useful salient round which to construct his new boundary. He also visited the great Lake Karakul in the extreme north of the region which was the one Hayward had hoped to establish as the source of the Oxus. Younghusband was now a gold medallist of the R.G.S.; it was not inappropriate that he was the first Englishman actually to see it. A fine stretch of water, wind-tossed beneath scudding snow clouds, the barrenness of its black beaches was set off by the snow clad slopes of the Alai, But as Elias had learned, precious little water flowed into it and none at all out of it.

With the temperature inside his tent falling to below zero Fahrenheit, Younghusband adjourned to Kashgar, the Sinkiang capital, for the winter. One may ridicule Elias presenting a carefully shaven cheek to the cruellest wind known to man, but Younghusband had taken his spartan habits one further. He continued to indulge his passion for an early morning dip. It became less of an indulgence, he records, when the water, thawed for the purpose and poured steaming into his rubber tub, had acquired a coating of ice before he had had time to undress.

Six months of patient negotiations with the Chinese authorities in Kashgar and he felt that he had made his point about the new frontier. A Chinese general was on his way to Somatash to establish an outpost. The gap had been closed and the Russians could now only advance towards the Hindu Kush by 'committing an act of very open aggression'. Unfortunately Petrovski, the Russian consul in Kashgar, and Grombtchevski, now governor of the Russian frontier post at Marghilan, thought otherwise. The former with his 'trumpery kind of cleverness' ran rings round the straight-forward Younghusband and was able to report every move of the negotiations back to Russia. Grombtchevski duly despatched a force of close on two hundred to stake out a prior claim, and when the Chinese general finally came up against them at Somatash he opted for discretion. What should have been the occasion for establishing 'an act of very open aggression' turned into a harmonious Sino-Russian rendezvous; the Chinese general, according to his superiors, had made the excursion simply to offer felicitations.

Younghusband knew nothing of this about-face, but just before his recall to India he got wind of the Russian manœuvre. To investigate it he decided to return home via the Pamirs. He took with him a companion, a young lieutenant called Davison who, fired by his own example, had recently set out to scale the Mus-tagh pass; unable even to find it, he had fetched up without pass-port, money, baggage or friends in Sinkiang. As they climbed west into the mountains the scent grew strong. There appeared to be two Russian detachments in the field and their object was nothing less than to annex the whole of the Pamirs. One was at Somatash whither Davison was promptly despatched. Like a character straight out of G. A. Henty, the spirited young subaltern cantered off to witness the expected Sino-Russian clash. Only he was disappointed; there was no clash and instead of becoming the hero of the hour he was promptly arrested by the Russians and marched off to Marghilan.

Meanwhile Younghusband went after the other party that had made straight for the Hindu Kush. He found their base camp on the Little Pamir beside a crumbling tomb known as Bozai Gombaz in what was thought to be Afghan territory. There he awaited them. On August 13, six Russian officers with thirty Cossacks, and the Russian flag carried before, them rode into camp. Younghusband

21   Uzr Khan of Nagar with attendants

22 The defenders of Chitral outside the fort: Lieut.
Gurdon, Surgeon-Capt. Whitchurch, Major Townshend,
Surgeon-Major Robertson, Lieut. Harley and Major Campbell

23 Col. James Kelly and officers of the 32nd Punjab
Pioneers inside the fort of Chitral

offered tea and demanded the facts. Was it true that they were annexing the Pamirs? It was. Marked in green on their map the whole of the Pamirs, excluding the inhabited parts of Wakhan, were now Russian territory; they had a frontage on the Hindu Kush fifty miles long and direct access to nearly all the passes into Yasin and Hunza. Indeed, that was where the Cossacks had just been. They had crossed, not without difficulty, into the Ishkoman valley of Yasin and thence, hugging the watershed, had crossed the Darkot and Baroghil passes back to Wakhan and the Little Pamir. Younghusband must have been starting out of his camp-chair. Whatever the status of the Pamirs, this latter foray was unquestionably a provocative infringement of British territorial sovereignty.

On the other hand, there was nothing he could immediately do about it; on the present expedition he didn't even have a Gurkha escort. The Russians were pleasant enough and Colonel Ianov, their commander, wore the coveted Cross of St. George, equivalent to a V.C. An invitation to dine was therefore accepted and that night, to Ianov's proposing the health of Queen Victoria, Younghusband dutifully replied with the health of the Tsar, Alexander III.

Next morning the Russians departed north. Younghusband stayed put, waiting for Davison and waiting to make sure that the Russian exit was not a feint. At 11 p.m. on the night of the third day as he lay in bed, there came again the clattering of hooves on the stony ground and the jingle of swords and spurs. Peeping out. he saw in the moonlit wastes the Cossacks returning with the flag in their midst. Hastily pulling on a greatcoat, he again greeted Ianov and invited him in for a meal. The Russian was grim faced. He had come, he explained, on an unpleasant mission; Younghusband was trespassing and he had now received orders to escort him from Russian territory back to Chinese; he must leave in the morning or face arrest.

Ianov was as courteous and apologetic as the situation permitted. Next day he presented Younghusband with a haunch of Marco Polo sheep and volunteered to trust him to make his own way back without the embarrassment of an escort. But the insult remained and it was the indignity of the whole affair that rankled most of all. British prestige had suffered a body blow. A British officer on Afghan soil and within sight of his own frontier had been hauled out of bed in the dead of night by a Russian patrol and told to scram. The political implications of the annexation of the Pamirs and the trespassing across the Hindu Kush were horrifying, but this picture of the solitary Englishman shivering in his pyjamas while some officious Russian colonel gave him his marching orders was somehow worse. It was no wonder that the victim demanded satisfaction nor that, within the incredibly short time of two weeks, the strongest possible protest had been lodged in St. Petersburg. Nor was it surprising that a projected adventure in the Hindu Kush that promised to restore British prestige suddenly found unexpected favour; Younghusband had made the Hunza–Nagar expedition an urgent necessity.

First, though, a summary of subsequent events on the Pamirs. Faced with such a storm of protest the Russian foreign office backed down. Younghusband had been threatened with arrest, it was claimed, not because he was trespassing at Bozai Gombaz but because he had trespassed on Russian territory near Lake Karakul. This he did not dispute. As for Bozai Gombaz it was not and never had been, according to the Russians, part of Afghan Wakhan. The Indian government first contested this, then conceded it, while Younghusband tried to argue that if it wasn't Afghan then it must be Chinese; what else could it be in view of his having established that the two frontiers met further north at Somatash?

He had actually done rather more than join the two frontiers, he had made them overlap. To award Somatash to the Chinese he had had to get the Afghans to withdraw. Inevitably the Amir took exception to his troops being thus shunted around. He protested to an embarrassed Indian government which duly apologised and retracted. As a result, when the Chinese after Ianov's departure deigned to take up their option on the place, they found it again in foreign hands. Quarrels broke out between the two garrisons and more protests, this time from both Peking and Kabul, rained down on the Indian government. Eventually the Chinese decided they had had enough of trying to co-operate with British schemes on the Pamirs and, withdrawing completely, urged the Leitnerian idea of neutralisation.

The Russian foreign office also disowned Ianov's action in declaring the Pamirs to be Russian territory. This did not mean that they disclaimed all rights to the region, merely that they felt annexation was premature and that their objects might be better gained by negotiation. With this the Russian military command and, in particular the military governor of Turkestan, did not agree; better to move in first and talk about it afterwards. In May 1892 the military party won the ear of the Tsar and Ianov was despatched on a repeat performance. This time the unfortunate Afghans took the brunt of it. In a bloody little affray at Somatash all but one of their garrison was killed. The Russians then removed the inscribed stone by which Younghusband had set such store and, for good measure, continued south destroying a Chinese fort and again scaling the Hindu Kush. Before returning they installed a permanent garrison on the Murghab where for the first time Europeans got a taste of living on the Pamirs. It was not a success; their hens perished, the only crop to thrive was a woody radish and their greatest excitement was when a passing British sportsman taught them the secrets of ludo.

More serious were the consequences of the Russo-Afghan clash at Somatash. Like the Chinese, the Amir was now having serious doubts about defending such an unremunerative chunk of tundra. As he threatened to withdraw towards the Oxus, the gap which Elias and Younghusband had endeavoured to plug yawned a hundred miles wide. The Indian government recoiled from the idea of trying to match Ianov's promenades and now pinned all their hopes on reaching an agreement on a frontier delimitation direct with the Russians. The diplomatic negotiations that followed were long and complex. The Chinese would take no part in them. The Amir vacillated between wanting as much territory as he could get and wanting none at all. The Viceroy and his council were also uncertain about their priorities and caused the Foreign Office in London almost as much heartache as did the equally contradictory Russians. The ebb of concessions and the flow of revived apprehensions continued to have an influence on the course of policy in Dardistan but by 1893 the Tsar was listening to more moderate councils and all sides were committed to delimitation. The British priority of a strip of Afghan territory between the Hindu Kush frontier and the Russian was accepted in principle; in return the Russians got most of the Pamirs; the Amir, who stood to lose by this arrangement, was mollified by British concessions elsewhere on their joint frontier (most notably, as will be seen, in Kafiristan). Thus was created that anomalous strip of Afghan territory known as the Wakhan corridor. In 1895 a joint Anglo-Russian boundary commission marked out its eastern extremities and, separating Pakistan from the Tadjik S.S.R., it survives virtually untouched to this day.

12. Precipice Warfare

News of Younghusband's expulsion from Bozai Gombaz reached India in early September, 1891. For Algy Durand, just arrived in Simla, it could not have been better timed. He had expected a tough wrangle to get the authorisation and troops necessary for a strike up the Hunza gorge; now his path was made smooth. Another fifteen British officers, two hundred Gurkhas of the regular Indian army, two more mountain batteries and a much cherished Gatling gun were placed at his disposal. He was also given carte blanche to handle the affair as he thought fit. If anyone still had doubts about the need for a campaign it was explained that all these precautions were purely defensive; with the passes about to close for the winter it was the only way of ensuring that Durand would be able to forestall another Dard attack such as that supposedly intended against Chalt in the previous May.

But if these same preparations, and the terms Durand was empowered to offer Hunza and Nagar, were not also intended to goad the Dards into defiance one wonders what would. In May the fort at Chalt had been reinforced, its garrison augmented, an old fortification that commanded it demolished, and the road thither from Gilgit had been improved. Now it was intended to go further. The road which, battered by landslips, had a way of reverting to its previous condition, was to be again taken in hand. The fort, the strategic importance of which Ghazan Khan had likened to that of his wives' pyjama strings, was to be demolished altogether, and new military roads were to be driven into the heart of Nagar and right through Hunza. Sadly Ghazan Khan was no longer around to give his metaphor the obvious twist; but this was the rape of Dardistan with a vengeance. With the new roads was to go the right to move troops to any part of Nagar and Hunza; it meant the end of their isolation and so of their independence.

Durand's terms allowed of no compromise. Had Safdar Ali's flagrant disregard of those accepted in 1889 been made the pretext for interference he might have wriggled off the hook; certainly

Nagar would have been in the clear. As it was, no mention was to be made of past misconduct. The two chiefs were to be told that the roads were vital for the defence of India against Russia. If they objected they were to understand that the roads would be built regardless, but that troops would first clear the way. Should they wish to retain their freedom they must therefore fight; it was as simple, and as brutal, as that.

The British case was based on the premise that neither state had much to lose since they were already tributary to Kashmir. In the case of Hunza this was a distortion of the facts. Like many other Dard states, the Mir had reciprocal tributary arrangements with all his neighbours. The subsidies received were regarded as protection money; the token tributes paid out were simply pledges of good conduct. As Elias had pointed out, there was no difference between Hunza's tributary arrangements with Sinkiang and those with Kashmir. Younghusband agreed and was even now urging that the Chinese must at least be consulted.

Nagar's position was different to the extent that her tributary arrangement appears to have been exclusively with the Kashmiris at Gilgit. The reason was geographical; Nagar's only feasible outlet lay over the Chalt bridge and down the road to Gilgit. The place, in other words, was a dead end. But, by the same token, one wonders how its subjugation could be justified in strategic terms. None of the Hindu Kush passes debouched into the state and, to judge by their maps, the Russians were not even aware of its existence. Aside from the vexed question of Chalt, the only reason Nagar was being drawn into the conflict was because Durand had decided that much the easiest way to invade Hunza was to move up the Nagar side of the river. Ever since Biddulph's day the Nagaris had been regarded as less militarily formidable than their Hunza neighbours. Furthermore, with Nagar conquered, the flank of Hunza, in the elementary strategic language of the day, would have been turned. In winter there should be no difficulty in fording the Hunza river at any number of places and the whole country would thus be exposed.

Durand, marshalling his troops and arranging extra rations and clothing for them with the overstrained Kashmir commissariat, left his departure for Gilgit to the last moment. He arrived there on the very day that the final detachment of his precious Gurkhas was overwhelmed by the first blizzard of winter on the Great Himalaya. Significantly the casualties almost equalled those that would be sustained during the whole of the forthcoming campaign; a hundred men were frostbitten, many lost hands and feet, and twenty died. The weather and, above all, the mountains could be as formidable as the firepower of the Dards.

As the passes were slammed shut behind him Durand, like a breathless traveller who has hurled himself aboard a moving train, settled down to the counting and disposition of his possessions. The greatest worry concerned supplies and transport. One of his officers reckoned that to keep a single regiment supplied for a week required nine hundred and twenty porter loads. At Gilgit there were two Kashmir Imperial Service Regiments—not to mention the Gurkhas, Agency bodyguard, engineers, etc.—and they were about to be marooned for six months. Gilgit produced barely enough for its own inhabitants, so that everything had to be brought in from Kashmir. Wending over the Great Himalaya passes to Astor, down the Hattu Pir descent to the Shaitan Nare, then across the Indus in a flimsy ferry boat and on to Gilgit, there had plied all summer a never-ending stream of Balti porters and mules. To be pressed into service on the Gilgit road, according to one observer, was the equivalent of being sent to a Siberian salt mine. Men and mules died like flies and the track became a grizzly two-hundred-mile-long knackers' yard. The guideless traveller followed the bones; a blind man could have followed his nose.

The situation by the end of October was that most of the supplies had crossed the high passes but were stuck at Astor. To bring them on down the worst stretch of the whole road from Astor to the Indus required the services of every man and beast available. But these thousands of extra mouths could not possibly be fed through the winter. Somehow they had to shift the supplies during the next three or four weeks and then be got out of Dardistan to Kashmir or Baltistan. This massive operation was still in progress when the guns finally opened fire up the Hunza gorge. A combination of superhuman effort and a favourable turn in the weather saw its successful conclusion, but those who described the war as 'one of the most brilliant little campaigns in military history' were thinking as much of the logistical achievement as of the heroics at the front.

Matters were made somewhat easier thanks to teams of Pathan road-builders and Kashmiri boat-builders. Captain Aylmer, Durand's only military engineer and a key figure in the campaign, threw a new bridge across the Astor river and, with the help of a roll of telegraph wire awaiting erection at Bunji, constructed a rope ferry across the Indus. In the previous year Robertson, en route for Kafiristan, had lost all his baggage and most of his followers when the current had swept away one of the ferries. Now, with new boats and with Aylmer's wires to attach them to, the crossing was both quicker and safer. The improvement of the Kashmir–Gilgit road had been entrusted to private contractors who were working round the clock. With road-building envisaged as the rationale for the whole campaign, these contractors were now needed at the front. The Pathan navvies, to their huge delight, were formed into a paramilitary force and issued with guns. So were their English overseers, who were enrolled as officers in the Volunteer Reserve. A couple of globe-trotting sportsmen who had got caught up in the mêlée were similarly pressed into service as was Mr.E. F. Knight, special correspondent of *The Times*; he found himself commanding a platoon of Pathan navvies.

Including a few local levies this gave Durand a total force of about two thousand men. Half of these, however, had to be kept in reserve to organise and guard the supply line. The possibility of the Chitralis exploiting the situation or of the Chilasis descending on Bunji was as real to Durand as it had been to Biddulph. In fact, in the case of the Chilasis, Durand rather hoped that they would rise; already he was thinking ahead and looking for a pretext to occupy Chilas and open direct communications from there to the Punjab.

It was thus with just on a thousand men that in late November the Hunza Nagar Field Force moved up to Chalt. On the 29th the ultimata about extending the road to Nagar and Hunza were sent off. The replies were a mere formality; Durand had already jumped the gun to the extent of building a new bridge across the Hunza river. Uzr Khan of Nagar deprived the envoy of his horse and sent him packing. Safdar Ali was so abusive that his actual words were deemed too unpleasant for publication. 'We will cut off your head, Colonel Durand, and then report you to the

Government of India' had been one of his more recent threats. On December 1 the British force duly crossed the river and entered Nagar territory. By nightfall they occupied the first ridge and were within sight of the fortress of Nilt. No opposition had been encountered but it was known that Nilt was held in strength.

Just what the enemy's strength amounted to was an open question. Estimates at the time put the combined forces of Hunza and Nagar at five thousand men. But given the total population of thirteen thousand this is certainly too high. Four thousand might be nearer the mark but of these half were stationed on the Hunza bank and appear to have taken little part in the action. In the main their arms were matchlocks, long cumbersome weapons that had to be loaded by ramming the charge down the barrel and ignited with a smouldering fuse. A few, indeed, had breech-loaders left by the likes of Lockhart and Grombtchevski, and much was made of this fact by those anxious to prove that it was a fair fight. It seems unlikely, however, that there can have been more than a hundred modern weapons and the ammunition for them was almost exclusively home-made. The British force, on the other hand, was equipped throughout with breech-loaders and also had the Gatling—a machine gun—and two seven-pounder mountain guns.

These last were expected to make short work of the Nilt fortifications. On December 2 they came into action at the unprecedentedly short range of two hundred and fifty yards and had no effect. The Dards, howling their derision and firing from the narrowest of peepholes, plugged away at anyone foolish enough to provide a target. Casualties mounted, while the defenders went practically unscathed. 'It was a terrible task to set any man', but the only way Durand could see of gaining the advantage was to send Aylmer with fifty Gurkhas to blow up the main gate. As the latter scurried forward to lay their charge, Durand, giving a display of heroics out of keeping with his position, stood in full view and a comfortable hundred and eighty yards range of the enemy; he was promptly bowled over. The bullet, a homemade one consisting of a garnet encased in lead, had hit him in the most delicate part of the body variously described as the upper leg, the pelvis and the groin.

Meanwhile Aylmer had reached the main gate and was laying his gunpowder. According to the man from *The Times*, who seems to have deserted his post in order to get a good view of the action, this was 'one of the most gallant things recorded in Indian warfare'. The sappers were being fired into at such short range that when Aylmer was hit in the leg his uniform was scorched by the gunpowder and his skin singed. At the first attempt the fuse went out. Again he had to brave what looked to Mr. Knight like certain death. A rock, hurled from the wall, crushed his hand but, at the third go, he struck a match and re-ignited the fuse. 'This time a terrific explosion followed'. Before the debris had settled three British officers and six Gurkhas, their revolvers blazing and *kukris* flashing, tore into the breech. In a desperate scuffle in which all but one was wounded they held the position and prayed for reinforcements. Unfortunately though, in their frantic pursuit of glory, they had forgotten to sound the advance or to tell the rest of the storming party what had happened. The breech was enveloped in dust and smoke, and to all but the nine sappers it looked as if the explosion had come from a powder magazine inside the fort. The storming party therefore stayed put, the guns continued to pound the walls and the sharpshooters to fire at the peepholes. Not till Lieutenant Boisragon, the only one of the nine still unwounded, retraced his steps through the fire of his own side to look for reinforcements, was it realised what had happened. The news was greeted with lusty cheers that echoed across the valley. Within minutes a steady stream of men was pouring into the fort whilst on the far side the Dards poured out into the ravine of the Nilt tributary. 'The boys had behaved like heroes', thought Durand, and for Aylmer and Boisragon V.C.s were waiting.

'And now', according to Durand who wrote a fraught letter on the engagement to brother Morty, 'came the mistake of the day.' Instead of pursuing the Dards down into the Nilt ravine as he had ordered, the whole force entered the fort and stayed there, 'collecting flags' and generally ransacking the place. This gave the Dards time to occupy a network of prepared defences on the far side of the precipitous ravine; by morning they were in a defensive position stronger than that provided by the walls of Nilt. Captain Bradshaw, the luckless individual on whom command devolved when Durand was hit, maintained that the Kashmiri regiment had let success go to their heads and were out of control. No such excuse was made by their commanding officer, the flamboyant

Townshend. He seems to have been in complete ignorance of Durand's masterplan.

However this may be, by next morning Durand's fears had been justified. As the Pathan navvies moved forward to repair the zigzag track down the ravine they were met by a devastating fusillade from the other side. Three men were killed and five wounded, including the British officer in charge of artillery. This was half as many casualties as during the whole of the previous day's action, and it brought the number of British officers seriously wounded up to four. Bradshaw hastily withdrew and Knight was in no doubt that the skirmish must count as a victory to the Dards. Worse though was to follow. For there was no way round the enemy's new position; the guns made no impression on their stone breastworks and reconnaissances along the bed of the Hunza river and across to the other side of the valley revealed no chinks in the defensive position. The advance was halted, the officers scratched their heads at what seemed to be a position more formidable than any dreamt of in the military text books; and for nearly three weeks the affair hung in the balance.

Durand, tossing on his sick bed, was frantic. What the devil had Bradshaw been doing? 'The game was in our hands . . . or rather we had won all but the last trick and my partner threw that away and the rubber.' He was in despair and for the first time the cracks began to show in his deadpan, devil-may-care outlook. The failure of the expedition and the incompetence of Bradshaw became obsessions. 'There was nothing to stop us, nothing that evening, and if I had been on my legs we should have had another fort by nightfall.' He was tempted, he later admitted, to blow his brains out. His nerves were so shattered that, instead, he ordered himself back to Gilgit, 'for here I cannot worry'. But worry he did and most of all for the blow to his reputation and for the effect this reverse would have on the future of the Agency. Lansdowne and Morty would stand by him but 'the fools at home may funk'.

'I am wonderfully well, no pain in the day and only discomfort at night and bad rest,' he wrote on December 11. Had the bullet been fired from a rifle he would have been dead. As it was, half-spent, it had 'threaded half a dozen important passages without injuring one'; as a curiosity the lead-encased garnet would have been better in a museum than in his groin, but he would now present it to his sister as a keepsake; Morty was to get the cane he was carrying at the fatal moment.

This levity soon faded when it was discovered that an abscess had developed inside the wound. The scar had to be reopened and it was months before he was on his feet, and a year before he could walk without a stick. As an explanation for his wildly erratic state of mind throughout 1892 the constant pain and frustration go a long way. Durand was nothing if not a man of action. Fortuitous though his appointment to Gilgit may have been, he had soon acquired a taste for the mountains and longed to come to terms with them. A little surprisingly it was he who wrote most convincingly of the lure of mountain travel.

It was the existence of the nomad, the charm of which, once tasted, works like madness in the blood and suddenly fills the sufferer, when mewed up within the four walls of a house, with a wild longing to be away, wandering it matters not where.

For the next three months he would have his fill of being mewed up within four walls and the experience did not please him. Gilgit became hateful, the steep drab slopes seemed to imprison him and the distant snow-capped peaks to mock him. He must live vicariously, through the heroics of his boys and above all through the exploits of his closest friend, George Robertson. If there is another explanation for his state of mind it is the comings and goings of the Surgeon-Major. Robertson was two years his senior but looked more. He was tall, bald and stern faced, a man 'whose determination was matched only by his tact'. The less stable Durand didn't just trust his judgement implicitly; he hung on his strength and maturity; Robertson was reassurance. When he was about, everything was possible but when he left the world fell apart; there was no-one to talk to, no-one to encourage him.

All had been worry and uncertainty before the departure of the Hunza Nagar Field Force. Then in the nick of time Robertson had arrived back from his long exile in Kafiristan; it was almost as if the expedition had been delayed specially for him. Along with the Kafir chiefs he was piloting back to India, he had been redirected up the Hunza road to serve as Durand's assistant for the duration of the campaign. It was knowing that Robertson was still there at

the Nilt ravine that kept Algy sane during the anxious days after
his disablement. In spite of Bradshaw, George would pull something out of the bag.

George, acting as Agent in Durand's absence, was doing his
best; but the news was not good. 'Still at Nilt,' he cabled on
December 3; 'desultory firing; weather fine; troops in good
health', on the 4th; 'force remains at Nilt, everything satisfactory',
did for the 6th. But by the 8th something more by way of an
explanation was obviously called for; 'the position to be taken is
practically a precipice unturnable at both ends. The seven-pounder
gun has no effect on rebel's defence.' On the 9th the troops were
still healthy and in good spirits and everything satisfactory, but
by the 15th there was again no progress to report; 'all our reconnaissances have failed to find a way of forcing rebels' position so
far. It is of immense strength while they multiply their sangars
[breastworks] daily. There is nothing for it but patience.'

This was all very well, but the spectacle of the first British
offensive in Dardistan being brought to a standstill was not doing
much for imperial prestige; the wonder was that all the other
Dard tribes had not already risen. There was also a very real
threat that if the stalemate lasted through the winter Safdar Ali
would have either Chinese or Russian allies by the spring. By now,
too, news of the expedition had broken in the London press.
The traditional way of disarming Westminster's chariness about
such escapades was to announce that the action was already over,
the frontier readjusted, British arms triumphant and the natives
garlanding those who had delivered them from oppression. This
time there was only the storming of Nilt to report. All the evidence
suggested that the enemy was offering staunch and united support.
By Robertson they might be labelled as rebels, but to the few who
had ever heard of Hunza it was not at all clear that the state lay
within India's traditional frontiers nor that any good would come
of its conquest. On the 13th a Reuters' correspondent, in search
of background, filed a long report from the Oriental University
Institute, Woking, in which Leitner castigated the whole Gilgit
policy. 'I cannot conceive anything more wanton or suicidal than
the present advance'. The doctor had just had a letter from Jafr
Khan of Nagar and was confident that, if only the government of
India had asked him, he could personally have settled the whole

business without a shot being fired. Next day he addressed a public meeting in the Westminster Town Hall and again went over the same ground. The metaphors might get mixed and the grammar muddled—the government was 'troubling waters in order to fish in them', and Hunza-Nagar had been 'mismanaged owing to the incompetent manner in which my information has been misused' —but the meaning was clear enough. The Gilgit Agency must be withdrawn, the Dards left alone and, in particular, the policy of opening up the place with military roads—which could only assist any Russian advance—must be abandoned.

By now the unfortunate Bradshaw might have been tempted to agree. He was doing his best—full scale attacks were mounted on the 8th and 12th—but the Dards were better entrenched than they had been two weeks ago. The position looked hopeless and, with the cold at night becoming intolerable, he was all for blowing up Nilt and withdrawing to Chalt. Supplies were also running short and first the Pathan navvies were ordered to the rear and then Bradshaw himself was recalled by Durand. It looked as if the game was over.

The Dards, inferior in every department save a doubtful numerical advantage, had played their one trump and it was unbeatable. What every traveller in the region had noted about the incredible strength of some of the natural defensive positions was being dramatically demonstrated. The largest and best equipped force that could reasonably operate in such terrain had been halted less by men than by mountains. How instructive it would have been to have watched the action from the glistening terraces of Rakaposhi immediately above. And how sobering. Tearing one's gaze from the majesty of rocky summits sailing above a sea of billowing snow, one would dutifully peer down the spine of some lolling glacier to the dark ledge where the Dards sat huddled round their cooking fires. From a pile of stones on the extremity of the ledge would come a puff of smoke; the thin report would arrive minutes later. Across the chasm that divided this ledge from the next the reply would be a loud sharp crack or the thump of a seven-pounder. A reconnaissance party crawling down the cliffs to the bed of the Hunza river would appear as absurd and unworthy of the setting as Mr. Knight out practising with his golf clubs, or the Gurkhas chasing a football. There is something not just ridiculous but profane about organised war-mongering in such wild and mighty surroundings.

Come December 20 the watcher on Rakaposhi might have noticed that the firing was brisker and that, today, in the very bottom of the chasm, there was a small force of a hundred or so British and Gurkhas; they had crept down there during the night. Now, with ropes and pickaxes, they started to climb the two thousand feet of sheer precipice directly below four of the Dard breastworks. The defenders craned over their *sangars* to see what was happening and were greeted by a hail of bullets from across the chasm. The climbers continued to inch their way upwards; an avalanche of boulders toppled down by the Dards narrowly missed them. By mid morning they were near their destination. A flash of bayonets and a few fleeing figures were all that could be seen of the first encounter. But as the attackers issued from the captured breastworks and worked their way to the next and the next, a pattern emerged, the sudden rush, the flurry, the bolting figures, the dynamiting of the *sangar*. As the defenders fled they provided an easy target for the guns across the ravine; 'it was like potting rabbits'. The answering fire faltered, Dards no longer waited to be attacked, and a mass exodus gathered momentum. Not only from the Nilt ravine but from all the forts further up the Nagar ledge and from their equivalents on the Hunza side, the men streamed out, discarding their guns, heading home.

Insignificant as it would have looked from Rakaposhi, it meant a lot to the men who had spent three weeks on the Nilt ridge. Imperial and regimental honour had been satisfied, another legend added to the many, a handful of reputations made, another V.C. won. The 'unassailable position' had been turned, 'the rebels' routed, and the British Indian frontier established, at last, on the Hindu Kush. If one looks at the Nilt ravine today and one ponders the problem as it then presented itself, one cannot but marvel at the bravery and ingenuity that led to its capture. The trouble is that as one looks on the setting as a whole, from the dark and terrible river gorge to the stacked grandeur of precipice and peak, the thin strata to which human endeavour is limited is almost lost to sight.

'Brilliant achievement on the 20th', began Robertson's telegram. 'Shall be in Nagar tonight. Jafr Khan has made complete submission. Uzr Khan fled.' On the 22nd an advance party crossed the

Hunza river and occupied the Mir's palace. Safdar Ali had also fled and resistance was at an end. 'If you only knew how happy and relieved I am,' wrote Durand from Gilgit. 'I was heartbroken at the thing failing that should have been a success and now luckily owing to George Robertson and Colin Mackenzie [who had succeeded Bradshaw as military commander] it is again a brilliant success. Morty is not landed in a hole and my reputation is saved.'

Safdar Ali was pursued up towards the Killik pass but he escaped to Sinkiang with his wives. Uzr Khan, having no such bolt hole, was eventually captured and deported. The Hunza palace was ransacked and its contents, including what Leitner called the archives of the Hunza state, were auctioned in Gilgit. As military governor of Hunza, Durand appointed Charlie Townshend—'I didn't know how to thank him'—and his pal, Curly Stewart, as political officer. The Mir's zenana was soon decorated with pin-ups of the Alhambra starlets; and as Stewart, gazing forlornly across the moonlit valley at Rakaposhi, bemoaned the absence of 'mashing' in the Hindu Kush, Townshend shattered the serenity of the loveliest view in the whole world with a rousing chorus to the accompaniment of his beloved banjo.

A proclamation was issued declaring that Hunza 'now belongs to the British government and so long as the inhabitants obey the British officer at Hunza all will go well with them'. It was clearly Townshend's impression, and Durand's intention, that annexation and the post of military governor would be permanent. This was a far cry from earlier protestations that the demands of imperial defence need not interfere with the independence of the state, or that the British quarrel was not with the people of Hunza but with their ruler. Durand himself was still suspicious of the Dards and would continue to regard the smallest incident as evidence of treachery. But fortunately wiser counsels prevailed. Townshend was quickly withdrawn and his post abolished. Stewart soldiered on as political officer until the summer when Younghusband came up from Kashmir to relieve him. By then a half-brother of Safdar Ali had been installed as Mir and the Chinese were laboriously moving towards an acceptance of the loss of their 'outlying dependency'. Younghusband's position was further helped by the presence of a small garrison of Kashmir Imperial Service Troops. But he still found evidence that his earlier diagnosis had been

24 The upper Oxus (Panja) valley and the Pamirs from
the crest of the Baroghil

25 Kafir effigies of the dead

26   In the Chitral valley with Tirich Mir as backdrop

27   On the road from Nastuj to Chitral

correct; that the war had been unnecessary and that the right sort of officers could have won the co-operation of the people without a shot being fired. Far from resenting their conquerors, the men of Hunza showed a ready loyalty and rather proved Younghusband's point when in 1892 and again in 1895 they voluntarily furnished a force of irregulars to serve under Gilgit's orders in Chitral.

But an even more damning indictment of the 1891 war was revealed by the map-making activity that followed. The Russian Foreign Minister of the day is supposed to have said, on hearing news of Hunza's defeat, 'ils ont fermé la porte au nez'. In fact the door had been closed for a very long time. When the Killik, Mintaka, Shimshal and all the other passes that led down into Hunza had been mapped and assessed, the officer in charge of the survey reported that 'we have no reason to fear a Russian advance through the passes'. This was borne out by the officers of the Pamir Boundary Commission in 1893. An invasion force half the size of that feared by Algernon Durand could never have reached Hunza, let alone Kashmir.

13. A Stroll Down the Indus

'One down and two to go' would have been an apposite toast for the Gilgit officers as they ushered in the new year of 1892. Durand himself was feeling a new man. The wound seemed better, the papers were hailing the Hunza expedition as 'brilliant' and his precious reputation was restored. He had just written to Morty apologising for recent gloom, and he was putting a brave face on the imminent departure to India of George Robertson. It was to be business as usual. The success of the Hunza–Nagar affair vindicated his hard-line approach to the Dard problem; he was emboldened to proceed further. Of the two other centres of Dard intransigence, Chitral might have to wait; Aman-ul-Mulk still clutched the reins of power and no pretext for direct intervention could be expected till he died. But Chilas, which it would anyway be preferable to secure first, was a different story. The Chilasis had held back during the Nagar fighting but now they were showing more spirit; in January they ejected a man who was said to be the Kashmiri agent in the place. 'I am of course going to make something out of this', Algy wrote to Morty. A few weeks later he had worked out a scheme; 'I think it could be done without fighting, or with hardly any, this winter if we manage it properly.'

Chilas, lying south of Gilgit in the sweltering canyon of the Indus, was a long way from the Hindu Kush watershed and had no obvious relevance to the Russian threat. Since Leitner had brought its existence to notice quarter of a century before, it had been neglected and probably no European had ever entered the town itself; the people had a reputation for fanaticism and were best left alone. True, they could in theory cut Gilgit's vital supply line by falling on Bunji whenever they felt like it. But, since defeat at the hands of the Dogras forty years before, they had been a peaceable if not punctilious feudatory of Kashmir; the recent expulsion of one Kashmiri was no reason to suppose that all this had changed.

What had changed, though, was the relative importance of the place. For, far from the Indus valley being a dead end of impenetrable gorges and savage tribes, Durand now believed that through Chilas and south from there over a pass called the Babusar lay the most direct route between Gilgit and British India. He might make a lot of the vulnerability of his supply line at Bunji but the fact of the matter was that Chilas was less a threat than a temptation. If he could open the Babusar route he might in time be freed from his dependence on Kashmir. No more pleading with devious Kashmir officials and no more heartache over the inefficiencies of the Srinagar commissariat. When reinforcements were needed, instead of waiting for months for another ill-equipped batch of half-trained Dogras, he could whistle up a battalion of regular Sikhs straight from their barracks in the Punjab. Except for the Babusar pass, 14,000 feet, the route was comparatively low lying and supposedly in use for nine months of the year; it cut the distance from Gilgit to the railhead at Rawal Pindi by almost a third. Once opened, the government would soon realise the absurdity not just of trying to service Gilgit via Kashmir but of trying to control Dardistan through the Maharaja. The agent would soon be reporting, not as at present to the Resident in Kashmir, but to the Lieutenant-Governor of the Punjab. And once that was established as more logical and expeditious, Kashmir must soon be relieved of all responsibilities in Gilgit and Dardistan.

That was Algy Durand's dream—it had been Lockhart's too—and one that Morty probably shared. It was not, however, the policy of the Government of India. 'Rumours as to the prevalence of excitement amongst the Chilasi tribes', which was all they would concede to Algy's repeated warnings of trouble, were not to be·used as a pretext for a move down the Indus. No action was to be taken 'that might lead to a collision with the Chilasi tribes', and there was no intention of opening the new road. All this was made as plain as could be during the summer of 1892. At the time Algy was unable to heed it, later he was simply unwilling to.

The flash of new year sunshine which had bathed all his schemes in a bright and possible light had been followed by black despondency. Gilgit, a far from beautiful place at the best of times, is dreary beyond credence in winter. The riot of pasture and blossom that in summer marks out the little oasis from river sand and mountain rock is gone; the town is indistinguishable from the scarred sterility of its surroundings. The dust turns to mud, the snow is more often slush, and firewood is at a premium. The noblest of Dards looks less than picturesque as, pinched and snivelling, he coughs away the hours in some dripping, smoke-filled *chai* shop.

By February Durand still couldn't walk and remained confined to the Agency. The absence of Robertson began to tell. Manners Smith, his other political assistant and the man who had won the V.C. at Nilt, ·was no comfort; he presumed to have serious misgivings about the Chilas scheme. Stewart was in Hunza and the irrepressible Townshend had been sent to Baltistan; in Gilgit his Kashmir regiment could not be fed through the winter. With the exception of Mackenzie, 'the only man I can talk to', his heroes were getting on his nerves. Once again, brooding gave way to an unreasoned sense of danger; disaster, imminent and disgraceful, stalked his day-dreams and filled the long wakeful nights. He must have more officers, more troops, more encouragement.

As February gave way to a long and dismal March, his letters to Morty plumbed the depths of a despair that was now close to manic depression.

I can see nothing but defeat unless we are reinforced and you cannot do that before June. It is a nightmare to me that we should be beaten here, and it will in the end ruin my head and my heart. I have had three years of anxieties and worries which no-one who has not been here can conceive—folly, ignorance and lies in Kashmir have driven me to the utmost limits of my endurance over and over again. We have no roads, no bridges, no food, consequently not enough troops. I can see nothing but disaster every night and try to think things are brighter in the morning, but this is no condition for a man to be in. My wound is not yet healed up and I am weak and useless. It is not right to leave me here for the country's sake. I had rather die in obscurity than fail and bring defeat on the first force to meet the Russians. . . . How can one do any good with such depression? If you can get me away from this place with honour by April 1, for God's sake do so.

And a few days later.

I must get away and trust you have sent for me. I cannot stand this place much longer. .... I am beginning to hate the whole thing and to loathe the sight of my table. .... I feel that if you do not send for me at once on duty, I must leave or resign my appointment.

There was no need to read between the lines; Algy was cracking up and the sooner he was out of Gilgit the better. Morty sent Robertson to take over as Acting Agent and Algy was recalled to India. He was to take six months' home leave. But as soon as the pressure was off, he regained his equilibrium. He spent three months in Simla showing no anxiety to see England; then, when occasion offered, he gave up the whole idea of rest and dashed back to Gilgit. Morty, who alone had the evidence of his erratic state of mind, should have stopped him. He didn't and by October Algy was back in the Agency bungalow, still badly crippled, still far from stable and about to face the worst crisis in his career.

The occasion that had offered itself was certainly tempting. On August 20 Aman-ul-Mulk of Chitral at last died; the long foreseen struggle for the Mehtarship began immediately. Afzul-ul-Mulk, Lockhart's manly favourite and Durand's too, chanced to be in the vicinity of Chitral fort and promptly seized power. From a British point of view it was most satisfactory. There was therefore no great outcry when he proceeded to liquidate every conceivable rival; only Nizam-ul-Mulk, Lockhart's *bête noir*, and a half brother, Amir-ul-Mulk, managed to escape. Nizam sought asylum in Gilgit, which was something of an embarrassment; better that, though, thought Durand, than that he should turn to the Russians. The half-brother, who survived the holocaust because he was thought mentally defective, fled south to his uncle, an agressive Pathan prince called Umra Khan who was observing the situation in Chitral with as much interest as Robertson. The latter swiftly congratulated Afzul on his succession and waited on the Government's permission to visit Chitral, there to dictate terms for recognition of the new Mehtar and for the continuation of the subsidy paid to his father.

It was just as well that for once Gilgit did wait. For, in November, almost simultaneously with the go-ahead from Simla, there came news that Afzul was dead. He had been murdered, and succeeded,

by an uncle with the confusingly similar name of Sher Afzul.*
This was truly a bolt from the blue. It was known that Umra Khan
had been intriguing with both Nizam and Amir-ul Mulk, but this
Sher Afzul was a complete outsider. He had in fact been lurking
in Badakshan for most of his brother's thirty-five year reign. A
pensioner of the Amir of Kabul, he was presumably the Afghan
candidate—which was distinctly bad news for Gilgit. Anglo–
Afghan relations were going through another uncomfortable
phase; and with Ianov showing scant respect for Afghan territory
on the Pamirs, Chitral too could soon be the venue for Cossack
manœuvres. Suddenly the presence of young Nizam in Gilgit
took on a new significance. From being the liability of Lockhart's
day and the embarrassment of Afzul's short reign, he emerged as
the great white hope. Was he not, argued Robertson and Durand,
the rightful successor? And for all his faults was he not uncharacteristically humane, well disposed towards the British and, above
all, totally dependant upon them?

Lord Lansdowne was not so sure; he was all for waiting to see
how Sher Afzul behaved. But Algy Durand could not let the opportunity pass. Dispensing, this time, with the obligation of referring
his plan of action to India, he simply launched the new candidate
from the top of the Shandur pass into the choppy waters of Chitral.
Officially he pleaded that the idea was Nizam's, that he had no
right to detain him in Gilgit, and that if Nizam succeeded it could
only be in the best of British interests. In fact, he almost certainly
instigated the move; he definitely encouraged it and he took every
possible precaution against its failure. This included massing
troops and artillery in Nizam's rear and sending the local levies,
that is the Hunza volunteers proudly sent by Younghusband, to
march with him. If the boat was somewhat frail it had been launched
with enough push to send it clean across the pond.

While Durand, having limped to the confines of Chitral, gazed
approvingly on Nizam's progress, Robertson, showing even less
respect for Dard feelings, was burning down Chilas. Durand
would soon concede that it was a big mistake to tackle Chilas at the

---

*The Dards were not the only ones with a confusing similarity of
names. Amongst less than fifty British officers who would serve in Gilgit
between 1890 and 1895 there were two Stewarts, two Bruces, a Dr.
Roberts as well as a Dr. Robertson, and a Gorton, a Gordon and a Gurdon.

same time as Chitral. It would strain his staff, his troops and his transport, not to mention his peace of mind, beyond breaking point. But, on the other hand, why not strike while the occasion offered? Arriving back in Gilgit in October he had found the place so well stocked with grain and supplies that he could afford to keep all his troops in Dardistan throughout the winter. Chilas had furnished further provocation; another Kashmir agent had just been ejected, this time with a bullet in his back. And finally, for this winter, he had the services of Robertson. He had just wangled another six British officers out of the Viceroy bringing his total to twenty-four, but George was worth more than the whole lot together. Moreover George shared his dream about the Chilas–Babusar route. If he himself had been impressed by the official warnings against interference in the Indus valley, Robertson had soon chafed away his anxieties. The thing had to be done and, if Algy was a trifle chary, the Surgeon-Major was quite happy to shoulder the responsibility. At the beginning of November, just as the Chitral crisis was exploding, he had marshalled a small force and set off for Bunji and a stroll down the Indus valley.

Unlike the Hunza–Nagar expedition, or the later siege of Chitral, the Chilas affair would be ignored by contemporary chroniclers of British bravado. It scarcely made the newspapers, let alone stiff covers. No V.C.s were awarded and no congratulations telegraphed. Inglorious, even a little shaming, it was hushed up and then speedily forgotten. 'It had no pretentions to being war,' explained one of those involved; 'it was just a thoroughly important and sporting move which included fighting'. For Lieutenant C. G. Bruce, the man who wrote this, it was quite true. He shot the Indus rapids with a couple of convicted assassins and, in the absence of supplies, provided for his troops by stalking partridges; the troops covered him while he did so. It all looked very casual and if things didn't go according to plan it could be maintained that there wasn't a plan and that the various actions were just impromptu skirmishes. A plan there was, however, as witnessed by Durand's letters of the previous winter. He regarded it as the boldest stroke of all and characterised the whole business as 'l'audace, toujours l'audace'. The two principal engagements were serious and hotly contested battles in which casualties were heavy. And if the paraphernalia of full scale war was missing, if there was no ultimatum or declaration, if the troops involved were comparatively few, and if supply and communications arrangements were negligible, this was not because they were thought unnecessary; rather because there was no opportunity to arrange them. It was a rough and ready affair which clearly revealed the Agency's tactics towards the Dards as the stark combination of recklessness and provocation that Leitner had always suspected.

Robertson's proclaimed destination was Gor, the small semi-independent settlement above the Indus between Bunji and Chilas. According to Durand's published account the move had been sanctioned by the government and was made in response to a request from the local people for closer ties with Gilgit. The first part of this was quite untrue. The government knew nothing of the move, would have stopped it if they had, and had anyway forbidden interference in this direction. The pretext, too, sounds unconvincing. The people of Gor proved less than enthusiastic about their visitors. Moreover, had they really sought closer ties, it should not have been necessary to send two senior officers—Robertson had with him a Major Twigg—to such a remote cluster of villages. Nor, if it was meant to be a peaceful mission, should they have needed three hundred troops.

Durand's account is also very insistent that no advance beyond Gor was originally envisaged; for what followed he laid the credit —or as others saw it, the blame—on Robertson. Perhaps this time he was being honest, though Bruce didn't think so; he baldly states that it was Durand who 'found it necessary to move into Chilas with troops'. Certainly Durand can't have overlooked the unsettling effect of sending such a force into a hitherto untouched area. The possibility of a hostile reaction from Chilas was something he probably counted on; as he told Morty, it certainly was not cause for alarm. 'All promises to go without a hitch,' he wrote, 'we shall make a good business of it in time.' His only real anxiety was that the government might get alarmed.

In Gor, Robertson left instructions with Twigg to push forward more troops and supplies as soon as carriage could be arranged and then, with as many men as he could feed, promptly 'disappeared into space'. This colloquialism of Bruce's is a fair description of the Indus valley; there is something distinctly other-worldly about its horrifying emptiness. Save for the dramatic changes in temperature, the seasons pass unnoticed; rainfall is negligible, vegetation non-existent. The scenery, if one can call it that, is a testimony less to the gentle forces of nature than to sudden primordial upheavals. Seismic rumbles set the crags oscillating; cataclysms scour out the defiles. When earlier in the century, a chunk of Nanga Parbat fell across the river, it dammed it to a depth of a hundred fathoms and the lake tailed back almost to Gilgit; when it broke, a Sikh army camped two hundred miles away in the Punjab had been wiped out.

Undeterred by this 'abomination of desolation', Robertson led his little force along precipitous tracks on the right bank of the river from Gor to a village called Thalpen. It was the only defensible place within his reach, he explained; it was also well beyond Gor territory and immediately opposite the town of Chilas on the left bank. The attack, for fear of which he had sought shelter, now obligingly materialised. Twigg was ambushed in Gor, relief detachments from Bunji had to fight their way through and, before Thalpen, the enraged Dards surrounded the invader in their hundreds. In a move that would soon be repeated in Chitral, Robertson tried to cross to Chilas and seize that first. The enemy anticipated him, his rafts were fired on and for a time the situation looked extremely grave. Because of the troops concentrated on the Chitral frontier in support of Nizam, there were insufficient at Gilgit to provide a relief force. It was too late in the year to call for reinforcements from Kashmir and the most that could be done was to try and keep open the communications line down the river.

But ultimately it was the patent weakness of Robertson's position that saved him. Instead of starving him out, the Dards decided to rush in for the kill. Outnumbered by ten to one Robertson still had the important advantages of superior arms and a well entrenched position. The attack spent itself and, as the enemy turned, out rushed the defenders. In the rout that followed, the Kashmiri soldiers pulled off their trousers the better to give chase; the Dard losses were considerable. Robertson immediately crossed the river, burned Chilas and began construction of a fortified position just above it. No doubt the Chilasis would be back, but for the time being the place was in his hands. Predictably Durand decided to retain it and throughout the winter of 1892–93 all efforts were directed to improving communications back to Bunji.

As in the previous year, Christmas again brought plenty to celebrate. Sher Afzul had fled back to Afghanistan and Nizam was safely installed in Chitral; true to his promises, he was now requesting the visit of a British mission to confer recognition of his title and the establishment of a permanent British agent in Chitral. Durand, again without waiting for government approval, acceded to the first request and Robertson was withdrawn from Chilas to head the new mission. 'He is everything to me,' Algy told his sister-in-law; 'no one has any brains to compare with his or knows anything of the management of natives.' As for Chilas, 'I knew I was right and that though the game was bold it was the only one worth playing.' If Robertson could now 'keep his head for a week in Chitral', the Gilgit Game would be won.

By the new year Algy's optimism had risen to a wild euphoria. 'It's a lovely game we have on this frontier', and if any of 'those dogs in [the Viceroy's] council' presumed to question his recent moves, 'God smite their souls to the depths of Hell'. Would that Morty could come up and look over 'this place that I have made'; how good he would find it. With the whole of Dardistan about to fall into his lap he was planning for the future—a political agent in each of the Dard states and, of course, more troops to provide a garrison for each of the passes. Robertson should get at least a C.B. and he himself should be made a full colonel and an A.D.C. to the Queen. 'Then I do not despair of being Commander-in-Chief some day, but I must get on *now*.' Brother Edward had just been knighted and Morty had been Sir Mortimer for some time; surely it was now his turn.

Morty should have taken the hint, not about the knighthood but about his brother's frame of mind. Algy was again embarking on that vicious psychological see-saw; the higher the high the lower the low. By February he was betraying a sense of unease. A hundred miles away Robertson, finding Nizam both unpopular and unnerved, was getting dangerously embroiled in Chitrali politics. Worse still, seventy miles in the opposite direction, the Chilasis, with their warlike neighbours from further down the Indus valley, were reportedly massing for a counter-attack. With troops already committed to Yasin in support of Nizam and others needed to keep an eye on Nagar and Hunza, Durand had few men to spare and no idea which way to send them.

In the event it was Chilas which exploded first. The Indus Valley Rising, which had been anticipated for three months, nevertheless took the garrison in their makeshift fort above Chilas completely by surprise. The town was re-occupied under cover of darkness. When an attempt was made to clear it, a third of the garrison was either killed or wounded and all but one of the officers, including Major Daniell in command, fell. It was probably the most disastrous battle yet fought in Dardistan; had the Chilasis continued to press their attack nothing could have saved the rest of the garrison. But when Robertson had burned the town in November he had also burned the year's grain supply. 'Nice move that', thought Charlie Townshend who was now on his way back to Gilgit. Without food the attackers dispersed to their villages after twenty-four hours.

News of the disaster reached Durand while he was playing polo on the Gilgit *maidan*—the leg was at last better. He immediately sent a small detachment to relieve the Chilas garrison and, calculating that the Chilasis would allow a forty days mourning period for the slain, set early May as the deadline for reinforcements. Then came news from Robertson in Chitral; from a man who was normally impervious to panic it was serious indeed. 'We seem to be on a volcano here,' he announced. The Pathan, Umra Khan, had already grabbed a corner of the state and was threatening to chase Nizam all the way back to Gilgit. He was also threatening to attack the Kafirs. Supposedly to frustrate any such move but more probably to grab Kafiristan first, the Afghan Commander-in-Chief with three thousand troops was poised at Asmar just south of Chitral territory. From Dir in the east a fanatical mullah with a wide following was sending hired assassins against the infidel British emissaries; and, in Chitral itself, popular contempt for Nizam and his revelling was rapidly curdling into an active resentment of his foreign backers. So accustomed was the mission to threats of imminent extinction that when one of their few supporters was shot during the night on their threshold, Robertson scarcely woke to register the news. Nevertheless he was alarmed and urgently requested Durand for more troops and for the Agent himself to come to his rescue.

'It is too much,' cried Algy. 'I have had some anxious times in my life but "upon me God", as Curly Stewart says, this about takes the lead.' He had just paid a visit to Chilas, and the vulnerability of his Indus valley conquests had suddenly dawned on him. Chilas itself was being properly fortified but, should the next wave of attackers decide to mask Chilas and concentrate on its supply line, there was no way he could see of keeping communications open. There was still no news of reinforcements from Kashmir and he had barely two hundred men left to play with. If every one of them was moved into the Indus valley, it was unlikely that the outposts dotted down that now simmering gorge could be protected. 'I am anxious about Chilas but Chitral is *what I am afraid of*.' Not only were there no more troops to send to Robertson but the Shandur pass was closed; snowblindness and frostbite had got the last consignment. For the next month at least Robertson would be cut off.

All this was written on April 16. Exactly a week later he again wrote to Morty. Now mysteriously, his reserve force numbered three hundred and he was keeping them for Chitral regardless, apparently, of the state of the Shandur. As for Chilas, that was now acknowledged as a hideous mistake; the Indus valley was a death trap and troops should never have been allowed to stay there. In fact the whole game had gone sour at the last throw. His contradictory judgements were symptomatic of a deep disillusionment. Had even Morty deserted him? Not a word, not a line about the desperately needed reinforcements.

I have wished myself dead over this business. . . . If I can live through this fortnight or month I must come down to India and go home. I cannot stand this sort of thing any longer and I will never return to Gilgit again . . . but I don't think I shall get out of it and I see nothing but smash and despair before me, though I try to look at the best light but it is black. . . . Oh how I wish I had never come to this place.

On each frantically scrawled sheet of paper he was mocked by that fatuous direction, *Railway Station: Rawal Pindi*. Would he ever see civilisation again? He thought not and ended with the ominous news that he had just drawn up his will.

Whatever the wild imaginings of his tortured mind, it is pretty clear that the danger was less of defeat than of despair. Gilgit itself was in no immediate peril and his own position was less vulnerable than that of any of his predecessors. The letter was not the composition of one going forth to die for his country but of one in a state of mental collapse. It was a suicide note and probably he was only saved by the arrival of instructions recalling him to India. This time they were not issued on compassionate grounds. Within the Viceroy's Council the outcry over his unauthorised attack on Chilas and support for Nizam had become irresistible. Robertson was again to take over as Agent and Durand would never more sit at the table he so loathed nor walk through the orchard where Hayward lay buried—and where he had so nearly joined him.

14. Finis Dardarum

In the event, none of Algy Durand's gloomy forebodings of April
1893 materialised. The Chilasis did not renew the attack and the
Indus Valley remained peaceful; Robertson extricated himself
from Chitral; and Nizam-ul-Mulk, though still menaced by
Umra Khan, managed to dig in as Mehtar. Furthermore, in
November 1893, Mortimer Durand negotiated an agreement with
the Amir which, while clearing the air as a prerequisite to the
solution of the Pamirs' problem, included the question of Kafiristan.
In effect the Kafirs were partitioned; the southern valleys, which
Robertson and Lockhart had scarcely travelled, went to Afghanistan,
but the northern ones, notably the Bashgal river and its tributaries,
were declared outside the Amir's sphere of influence. If the stabil-
ity of Dardistan could not as yet be guaranteed, the threat of
Russian or Afghan intervention was visibly receding and, under
the steadier hand of George Robertson, the Gilgit Agency could
afford to open its doors a little. In 1893 a stream of privileged
sportsmen passed through on their way to stalk on the Pamirs
and the first mountaineering expeditions began to explore the
glaciers and reconnoitre the peaks of the Karakorams.

Hard on their heels came the first politician 'to see for himself', a
Tory who was then Member for Southport. Globe-trotting M.P.s
were a standing joke in British India and the butt of many a
Kipling tale; but the one who descended on Gilgit in the autumn
of 1894 was no ordinary student of the East. He was, in fact, 'that
most superior person', George Nathaniel Curzon. With a typical
mixture of determination, scholarship and arrogance he was doing
his homework for the position he most coveted, and would so
young achieve, that of Viceroy of India.

Travelling from Kashmir along the new road constructed during
the hectic days of 1891, he marvelled as much at the telegraph
line that now ran all the way to Gilgit as at the scenery—'more
impressive than beautiful, more sullen than joyous, more rugged
than picturesque'. On a lintel at Bunji he carved his initials beside
those of all the other sportsmen and soldiers who had ventured

beyond the Indus, and then crossed 'that Tartarean trough' on the suspension bridge just completed by Captain Aylmer, V.C. Robertson was on leave at the time but the Agency afforded a warm welcome; he was particularly impressed by Biddulph's bungalow. In addition to a tennis court there was now a golf links where the wise player took a gun as well as clubs, the object being not self-defence but snipe. The whole place seemed to be booming. Besides the still numerous complement of political and military officers there was also, at last, a regiment of British Indian infantry; Algy Durand, though censured, had managed to make his point about more troops. A less acceptable sign of the times was the presence of the first British woman in Gilgit. The wife of 'some fellow in the transport corps', she was not exactly a *pukka memsahib* and it was an occasion for shudders of horror when lines of 'dubious looking lingerie' were spied in an orchard.

From Gilgit Curzon strode and rode up the new Hunza road to the Pamirs. Rakaposhi inspired a purple passage—'In that remote empyrean we visualise an age beyond the boundaries of human thought, a silence as from the dawn of time', etc.—the ruins of Nilt furnished an excuse for a rerun of the events of December 1891, and the Hunza road, still 'one of the worst tracks in the world', accounted for 'the personal physical accretions of an entire London season'. Thence over the Killik pass to the Pamirs. Like a conscientious sightseer, he quickly bagged his Marco Polo sheep and set about the sources of the Oxus. The famous paper on the subject which he later delivered to the R.G.S. lists eight Pamirs, of which he visited three, and four contending streams. Built upon the reports of every traveller and geographer who had ever hazarded a guess on the subject, buttressed with a wealth of classical allusions, and crowned with his own magisterial pronouncement, this monograph on the Oxus is a truly monumental work. But with the draft of the Anglo-Russian Pamirs agreement in its final stages, the important point was that political significance no longer attached to the subject. Elias had shown that the Panja tributary was the main feeder, Curzon decided that the Sarhad was the main feeder of the Panja, and the Wakh-jir of the Sarhad; thus the Wakh-jir glacier was the source of the Oxus. With no-one having a vested interest in disputing the matter, his verdict still stands.

Returning by way of Wakhan and Chitral, the M.P. was welcomed back to British territory at the foot of the Baroghil with a
glass of cold beer and a vigorous handshake from Frank Younghusband. Younghusband, five years older and a good deal more
reserved than in the days of his Karakoram travels, was now the
British representative in Chitral. He had gone there with Robertson
in the early days of 1893 and had stayed on when the latter was
recalled to take over from Durand at Gilgit. The position should
have suited him well. In Nizam-ul-Mulk, as in Safdar Ali, he was
able to see the good as well as the bad; he made a real attempt both
to understand and enlighten the Chitralis and he relished the
responsibility of being the sole political officer in the country. He
had always believed that personal contact was the best way of
handling the Dards; during his stay, Nizam had strengthened his
position and the country had remained at peace. His only reserv-
ation was that he wasn't actually in Chitral. He was based at Mastuj,
three days' hard travelling from the capital.

The swing of the political pendulum accounted for this. In
London the Liberals were back in power (which was why Curzon
was at a loose end), in India Lord Lansdowne had been succeeded
by Lord Elgin and on the frontier 'forward' policies were again out
of favour. While Younghusband, supported by Robertson, urged
that he must be permanently established in Chitral town, the most
the government would concede was that he might remain temporarily at Mastuj. The Afghans had agreed to keep Sher Afzul out
of the country and, if Umra Khan could also be coaxed into leaving,
then Younghusband was to be withdrawn altogether as soon as the
Anglo-Russian Pamir agreement was signed. The object, in other
words, was not to establish an influence in Chitral—just to make
sure no-one else did.

Younghusband had taken the rejection of his plans much to
heart. 'Government gave the impression that they could get on
perfectly well without me', and they showed it by promoting
officers of half his experience over his head; it seemed that examin-
ations counted for everything, his missions for nothing. As soon as
his term in Chitral was over he would therefore resign from the
service. But the man with whom Curzon rode down to Chitral
was not exactly bitter. For one thing he had now finally decided
'to make religion the first interest of my life'. During the lonely

months spent amidst the magnificent mountain scenery of upper Chitral 'the exploring spirit' had again come upon him. Reading and meditating, he longed to be free of government service and to devote his life to 'showing men the way across the spiritual unknown'. His mission was still vague, his belief in Providence still naïve and his motivation somewhat arrogant. But, over the years that led up to his founding of the World Congress of Faiths in 1936, he would become the first to recognise these faults.

Another consoling influence was Curzon himself. Cerebral, incisive, polished, frigid, the guest was everything the host was not. Discussing frontier policy Curzon seemed totally to discount his companion's experience and to enjoy ridiculing his opinions. Yet this was just the parliamentary habit; for to judge by his later reports in *The Times* he was lapping up every word Younghusband let fall. Unable to compete, but recognising in one another something each respected, they became the staunchest of friends. Moreover, they found common ground in a deep sense of England's imperial destiny and an equally deep mistrust of Russia. The sort of frontier bullying typified by Algernon Durand they both rejected; but their ideas were no less 'forward' and provocative for that. It was to Younghusband that Curzon, as Viceroy, would turn ten years later; and it was while doing Curzon's work as political officer to the Lhasa expedition, that Younghusband would become the scapegoat for a national sense of outrage over the handling of the Tibetans which far exceeded any doubts that were ever voiced over British policy in Dardistan.

Finding all well with Chitral and its Mehtar, Curzon returned to Gilgit over the Shandur pass. At Gupis, the first fort of any importance on the Gilgit side of the pass, Charlie Townshend, his 'somewhat unusual host', posed a rich contrast to Younghusband's austerities. His house was decorated with 'daring coloured illustrations from Parisian journals of the lighter type; and he regaled us through the evening with French songs to the accompaniment of a banjo'. A few miles upstream his 'mucker', Curly Stewart, was the political officer in Yasin and together they were again lending a distinctive style to frontier life through itching for another 'scrap'. Gupis fort was 'The Garrick' and Stewart's new house 'The Adelphi'. Of an evening they foregathered to plan their next assault on the West End. Cheap cigarettes and whisky were a poor substitute for cigars and brandy, but there was no denying a certain innocent pleasure in writing to the ladies about the privations and dangers of frontier life.

'I don't see how we shall get through this winter without a pantomime rally of sorts up here,' confided Townshend to one of his girlfriends at the beginning of November. But Curzon passed on, primed with first-hand impressions; then came Younghusband, muttering a farewell to the mountains but with the inner light burning bright. And still all was quiet in Chitral. At the end of the month Robertson, just back from leave, arrived on an inspection tour of his domain; he brought with him Captain Campbell, his senior military officer and Lieutenant Gurdon who was to resume Younghusband's duties at Mastuj. These four men, Townshend, Campbell, Gurdon and Robertson, would soon be seeing more of one another than was conducive to mutual respect. During the siege of Chitral, Robertson would blame Townshend for never having taught his Dogras to shoot straight. At the time, though, Townshend has him approvingly exclaiming 'Those are the men for us.'

December passed without incident, but on January 4, 1895, the Gupis 'Garrick' exploded into activity. According to news frantically relayed to Gilgit by Townshend, Nizam-ul-Mulk had just been shot in the back by the half-witted Amir-ul-Mulk. The murderer had assumed the Mehtarship, and Gurdon, who had gone to pay his respects to Nizam, was still in Chitral town and, with an escort of only eight men, surely in the gravest peril. Townshend immediately moved troops up to the Shandur and waited for Robertson's authorisation to speed to the rescue.

For the Agent, as for Townshend, this was the long-awaited pretext. At last it was to be Chitral's turn. But if they were spoiling for a fight, it is also true that events played into their hands in such a way that the whole manœuvre appeared unavoidable. Gurdon wrote that he was in no immediate danger and that though Amir-ul-Mulk was the candidate of Umra Khan, he was now seeking British support. Here was justification for a political mission. On the other hand Gurdon felt that if he attempted to withdraw he might well be attacked—obviously cause for a hefty military escort. Accordingly Robertson, with Campbell, Townshend and three other officers plus some five hundred troops, embarked on the fatal mission of 1895. In intense cold they crossed the Shandur pass and reached Mastuj on January 25. If it was just a question of observing developments and standing by to rescue Gurdon, here they should have stopped. But again events played into their hands. News now came that Umra Khan had crossed the Lowarai pass and invaded Chitral proper. Gurdon was in imminent danger again and the whole mission must press on to Chitral town. It was altogether too much like a repeat of the Chilas affair. Robertson still believed in the bold dash; communications, supplies, artillery would take care of themselves so long as one retained the initiative. The essence of dealing with the Dards was to dodge through the mountains before they could stop you, dig in and then invite attack.

On January 31 the mission reached Chitral and Robertson immediately began angling to get his force installed in the Mehtar's fortress. The situation now developed with alarming speed and unforeseeable complexity. Umra Khan's forces advanced on the important base of Drosh. Amir-ul-Mulk, who had supposedly called in the Pathans, now opposed them and begged Robertson to send his troops to stiffen the Chitrali resistance. Robertson was highly suspicious of any move that would divide his force and refused. On February 10 came news that Drosh had been betrayed. Robertson used this as grounds for taking over the fort and, once safely installed behind its twenty-five foot walls, agreed to send a token force to help against Umra Khan.

The fort was unquestionably the largest and most defensible building in the country, if not in Dardistan as a whole. Each of the four walls was about eighty yards long and the four corner towers rose to sixty feet. If there was to be fighting, its occupation was essential. On the other hand, no single move contributed more to the inevitability of conflict. For this was not just a fort; it was the *Noghor*, the ancestral home of the Mehtars of Chitral, their armoury, their treasury, their palace and, to a Mohammedan most important of all, the zenana of their womenfolk. No man had been acknowledged as Mehtar unless he held the *Noghor*, and to Chitralis of every class it represented the independence of the kingdom. Amir-ul-Mulk, for perhaps the only time in his unhappy reign, spoke for the whole of his people when he declared to Robertson that no such shame had ever come to Chitral before.

Eighty years later, it is this move that the Chitralis still regard as the most shameful and provocative of the whole siege.

Robertson realised this. 'Not one argument, plausible or ridiculous, was left unuttered to stop us making this move.' Chitralis who genuinely favoured British intervention were as incensed as the rest, and all considered it 'tantamount to annexation'. Not a single man could be pressed into moving the mission's baggage and, had not all the Chitrali troops been engaged in the hostilities with Umra Khan, there would certainly have been armed opposition. After such an outrage Robertson's belated offer to assist in the defence of the country was politically worthless.

As it was, some Chitralis were already fighting not against Umra Khan but for him; the supposed explanation was that they had no faith in Amir-ul-Mulk. Desertions now increased and, about February 20, reached landslide proportions. For it was then that Sher Afzul, the Afghan candidate, again taking everyone by surprise, reappeared on the scene. Robertson was flabbergasted. The man was supposed to be in Afghan custody four hundred miles away. Yet here he was, still the most popular claimant to the Mehtarship and now apparently inclined to side with Umra Khan. Robertson tried to negotiate and was even prepared to accept Sher Afzul as Mehtar. The government had specifically ordered him not to recognise anyone till it had been consulted; but the Agent was now down to his last card. When Sher Afzul refused to co-operate unless the *Noghor* was evacuated, Robertson promptly turned again to Amir-ul-Mulk. In a last bid to secure the loyalty of at least a few Chitralis, he recognised Amir as Mehtar. The combined forces of Umra Khan and Sher Afzul then advanced up the valley, and the British and Dogras withdrew into the fort. The order of battle was all but established—except that at the eleventh hour Robertson dramatically changed his mind about Amir-ul-Mulk. A brother of Amir, a boy of twelve whose extreme youth had alone saved him from liquidation, was suddenly preferred. After only three days as the British candidate, Amir was ceremoniously deposed in full durbar and, leading young Shuja-ul-Mulk to the biggest armchair in the fort, Robertson proclaimed him the Mehtar of Chitral.

Thus was installed the fifth Mehtar in three years. The odd thing is that throughout this period of instability there is absolutely no evidence of Russian intrigue. Fear of it had provided the rationale for the policies that Robertson was now following to their logical conclusion. Yet the Russians were apparently not interested. As in the days of Lytton and Biddulph, the real complication was provided by the Afghans. There could be little doubt that Kabul had connived at Sher Afzul's escape from custody: it was later established that some Afghans were actually fighting at his side. Robertson himself was firmly convinced that there was some massive plot uniting all the various opposition forces and it was for this reason that he had finally turned to the youthful Shuja. Just how formal the plot was he could only conjecture; but he could see how all four parties stood to gain by it. In return for providing the fighting muscle Umra Khan would get territorial concessions; by virtue of his being the Afghan candidate, and in return for later acknowledging Afghan suzerainty, Sher Afzul would get the Mehtarship; Amir-ul-Mulk, as a reward for his co-operation, would be recognised as Sher Afzul's successor; and Abdurrahman, Amir of Kabul, who alone was capable of masterminding such an abstruse intrigue, would have thwarted British designs on Chitral.

Looking at the thing from the outside, the Government of India reached much the same conclusion. As the plight of the besieged Chitral mission slowly dawned on British India, the foreign department concentrated its diplomatic offensive on neutralising the Afghans. Up to a point it succeeded; the large Afghan force still lurking around Asmar on the confines of Chitral stayed on the sidelines, the Amir was mollified and Umra Khan's jealousy of the Afghans was re-aroused. But the price for all this was high—no less, in fact, than the surrender of the remaining half of Kafiristan.

It was not exactly a betrayal. To the bureaucrats in Simla, Kafiristan appeared a dead loss; they were not even certain that under the terms of the 1893 Durand treaty, the Bashgal river, the northern part of the country, was rightfully theirs. No-one had yet made out a good case on strategic grounds for a British interest, the Kafirs were too disorganised even to treat with, and, by all accounts, Afghan influence in the shape of Islamic proselytising was already eroding their independence. To meet the Russian threat British policy had long favoured a strong and united Afghanistan; and it had always been accepted that the modern weapons so readily supplied to Kabul might be used for subjugating any pockets of internal resistance.

But the irony of the whole business was that the Kafirs were being sacrificed to save the one man who might successfully have pleaded their cause. For George Robertson, the surrender of Kafiristan *was* a betrayal. Long ago he had observed that the equilibrium which had permitted the Kafirs to survive into the nineteenth century had been irreversibly upset by the arming of the Afghans; against modern breech-loaders the mountains and defiles of Kafiristan no longer compensated the Kafir archers; unless protected and patiently nursed to political maturity, the Kafirs were doomed. More than any man he had studied their way of life. He had experienced some rough handling and he had voiced some stern condemnations. Yet he had found much to admire—their blind courage, their feral grace of movement, their stamina and agility, their gaiety and, above all, their uniqueness as an ethnic curiosity. His first book, which would surely have aroused enough interest in the Kafirs to bring their imminent plight to public attention, was, in 1895, already in manuscript. But by the time it appeared, and by the time the dust settled over Chitral, it was all over; precious few independent pagan Kafirs still defied the Afghan troops; and they, like their brothers, would soon be sold down the Bashgal river—literally, if the Anti-Slavery League was to be believed.

*   *   *

Nothing military captures the imagination of the man in the street like a long and desperate siege. 'What is Gilgit?' was apparently not an unusual reaction in the early 1890s; but by the summer of 1895 most people knew about Gilgit and everyone about Chitral. In the press, from small beginnings as a telegram, the story blossomed into whole page reports and spilt over into the leader and correspondence columns; every traveller with experience of Dardistan or the frontier rushed into print. More stirring news came from the main relief expedition as it fought its way relentlessly into the mountains. But would it reach Chitral in time? The plight of Robertson and his men lifted the whole thing above the level of an ordinary frontier affair. For seven weeks not a word was heard from the beleagured *Noghor*. If they were still holding out, what was it like in there; had they enough food and water and ammunition; and if they were forced to capitulate what would be the fate of Robertson and the rest? Mrs. Robertson, a bride of only a few months, was on the high seas en route to join her husband; what news would await her in Bombay? And what price now a love-letter from Charlie Townshend?

The story of the siege has been told often enough, though never so well as by Robertson himself. It lasted for forty-eight days and included three serious engagements. The first, on March 3, the day after Shuja-ul-Mulk's installation, resulted in the defeat of a major reconnaissance effort by the garrison. One British officer, two Kashmiri officers and twenty-three other ranks were killed while the thirty men seriously wounded included Campbell, the military commander. The Kashmiri forces were reduced to a state of demoralisation from which they never really recovered, whilst the enemy were given just the encouragement necessary to press the siege with vigour.

The next potentially disastrous situation arose a month later in the early hours of April 7. A major assault on one side of the fort was used as a cover for setting fire to the other. One of the main towers went up in flames and, during frenzied attempts to extinguish it, Robertson himself fell a casualty, badly wounded in the arm. But the fort was nearest to falling on April 16. That night the sound of digging was heard in the bowels of the building. Connected with a lot of recent activity round a summer house just outside the walls, it could only mean that the place was about to be mined and that the shaft had already reached its destination. Next day the cream of the garrison's troops stormed the summer house, found the mouth of the mine, bayonetted thirty-five men who were work-ing in it and blew the whole thing open. It was not a moment too soon; the Chitralis evidently intended to fire the mine that night and, had they been able to do so, it would not only have breached the wall but have brought most of the fort down on top of its defenders.

Fortunately the Chitralis and Pathans, though well-off for breech-loaders, were entirely without artillery; hence the attempts to mine and fire the place. The other, very real, possibility was that the garrison might have to capitulate. Arrangements were successfully made for bringing water along a covered way from the river, but food was short; by the end all were reduced to quarter rations and the officers had eaten their way through their horses. Small deprivations caused disproportionate distress; the cigarettes ran out, tea was rationed to a quarter of an ounce per man every day and, for want of a grinding stone, the only flour was dangerously impregnated with grit. Worst of all, though, was the stench. Four hundred troops, plus another hundred and fifty servants and 'loyal' Chitralis, were cooped up for seven weeks in a space not much bigger than a football pitch. The old stables were designated as the latrines, but there was a limit to the number of trenches that could be dug and refilled; because of incessant rain in the middle of March this limit was speedily reached. The men sloshed through the mud in search of relief and came out retching. The sick list grew till nearly a quarter were out of action. Even the exuberant Townshend, who, with Campbell incapacitated, was in military command, grew to hate the life and, in spite of the prospect of glory, to wish himself elsewhere.

Between him and Robertson there arose something more than the inevitable friction occasioned by anxiety and close living. Robertson preferred to think less in terms of being relieved than of being reinforced. The last letter smuggled out of Chitral asked for more troops to be rushed down from Mastuj. From the top of one of the towers Robertson would daily scan the hills. There was no question of peering up a long open valley; two miles upstream a wall of rock made one wonder where the river came from. Behind and above it ridge upon ridge of mountains paled away till the eye rested on that other world of cloud and snow that was Tirich Mir. Compared to the scarps on either side, it was at least a view, though not one to inspire hope. Robertson knew the *paris* and *gols*, the cliff faces and chasms, of the Mastuj road and he knew how difficult it would be to force a way through them. But he didn't despair easily. This was how it had been at Chilas. The important thing was to be ready so that, when reinforcements did show, they could immediately assume the offensive.

Townshend, on the other hand, was more realistic. After the disastrous engagement of March 3 he refused to countenance the idea of any more forays and prepared for a long siege. He had no great hopes of seeing anything of the small detachments that were supposed to be marching from Mastuj, and he agreed with

Algy Durand's criticism that Robertson was 'inclined to bluff about troops and get away with less than necessary'. In short, unconcerned about the questions that must one day be asked of the Agent—like what was he doing in Chitral in the first place, and how come he had assumed the role of the country's kingmaker— Townshend accepted the situation as a purely military problem and reached the obvious answer; their only chance was to sit tight. Twenty years later he would use exactly the same tactics when besieged in the fortress of Kut during the Mesopotamian campaign of the Great War; only then it would be for one hundred and fifty days. Imperturbable, patient and, so long as he had the banjo, end-lessly exuberant, he was discovering in long sieges his vocation.

The last note to come out of Chitral was dated March 1 and warned that future communications might be interrupted. Ten days therefore slipped by before the horror of the situation began to dawn on the government. When it did, frantic calculations were called for. It was estimated that the besieged could not hold out beyond the end of April. But could a relief force large enough to cope with the expected resistance also make good speed over the snows of the high passes when they were just beginning to soften and when the weather was at its most unpredictable; spring is the worst possible season for mountain travel. A force sent via Kashmir—or even via the Babusar pass and Chilas—had little chance of reaching Gilgit in time, let alone Chitral. Yet the only other way into the place was the route through Dir pioneered by MacNair in 1883. MacNair was still the only European ever to have tried it. Meantime the xenophobia and fanaticism of the Pathan tribes who lived along it had not diminished. Umra Khan was one of their leaders; as the main objective of any advance, he would see to it that every inch of the route was bitterly contested.

If there were a few in the councils of state who, at first, resisted the general panic and were more concerned about how on earth Robertson, the shrewdest of Agents, had managed to get himself into such a mess, they too changed their tune about the middle of March. For it then became clear that Mastuj, too, was under siege and the whole of Chitral therefore disaffected. Worse still was the soon-confirmed rumour that both the detachments of reinforcements sent from Mastuj to Robertson's aid had been ambushed on the way; the Agent was wasting his time scanning the foothills of Tirich Mir. Half of the first batch of sixty men had been killed and the rest taken prisoner including their two British officers; in addition to such eminently ransomable material, the enemy had also acquired the forty thousand rounds of ammunition they were convoying. The second batch, also about sixty strong, was virtually annihilated. Only ten men straggled back into Mastuj having left their commanding officer, Captain Ross, and the rest of their comrades-in-arms strewn among the rocks of a treacherous defile and bobbing thence down the river towards Chitral. No doubt, at the time, none of the officers concerned fully appreciated the gravity of the situation. But equally they took not the most elementary precautions. Ross, in particular, scorned the idea of reconnaissance and accused anyone who suggested it of cowardice. Ever contemptuous of the Dards, and tortured by the possibility that they might miss out on the anticipated heroics before the walls of Chitral, they paid the price of the Gilgit conceit.

'An undertaking of great magnitude', was how the Viceroy described the relief force that was now clearly imperative. He was not exaggerating. A whole division, fourteen thousand strong, under Major-General Sir R. C. Low, was assembled at Nowshera; it included both British and British Indian troops amongst which were such prestigious regiments as the Gordon Highlanders, the Buffs and the Bengal Lancers. To Umra Khan was sent a formal ultimatum telling him to get out of Chitral, whilst to all the intervening tribes a proclamation was issued in the hopes of winning their acquiescence. Both were ignored. On March 14 the Division was formally mobilised and two weeks later the first troops crossed the frontier and headed for the hills; assured of fighting most of the way, they would not be disappointed. 'We have before us a single issue', declared the Viceroy, 'the claim of brave men, British and Indian, who have not flinched in the performance of their duty, to the support of their countrymen in their hour of need.' According to the Commander-in-Chief, this lent a degree of sanctity to the expedition. It was unnecessary for either to draw the obvious parallel; the memory of Khartoum, the spectre of Gordon hacked to death on the steps of the beleaguered palace, and the tragedy of the relief force arriving only a couple of days later, were engraved on every heart.

Meanwhile, two hundred miles away in Gilgit, the situation was regarded with less solemnity though plenty of fervour. Curly Stewart, acting as British Agent in Robertson's absence, had summoned all his available troops and was looking forward to leading them to poor Charlie Townshend's aid. So, far away in Calcutta, was Algy Durand, now military secretary to the new Viceroy. (He had just married the Viceroy's niece.) Durand had lost confidence in Curly Stewart; he was good for nothing but sending the 'most infernal stupid telegrams'; in fact the whole Agency seemed to have become terribly casual. Should he not personally return to sort out the Northern Marches? And was this his 'chance of getting level with those devils, the Dards'?

It wasn't. The government turned to neither Durand nor Stewart for the very good reason that they had just discovered a fully fledged lieutenant-colonel lurking in the Indus canyon near Chilas. A small, fragile-looking Irishman, now in the evening of an undistinguished career, Colonel James Kelly was ordered to take over command of the Gilgit troops and make whatever arrangements he could to co-operate with the main relief force. For Kelly, belatedly—he was nearing sixty and sported a beard that had been out of fashion since the Mutiny—the trumpet of destiny had sounded; Kelly's March has been well acclaimed 'one of the most remarkable in history'.

Frankly the government didn't give much for his chances; 'relief from that side [i.e. Gilgit] was felt impossible' according to Lord Elgin. It was made still more so by the fact that Kelly could have no reinforcements and that he was ordered, at all costs, to avoid taking risks; there had been too much in the way of disastrous heroics already. In this respect Kelly looked a safe bet; he was simply to do his best with whatever troops the already depleted garrison of Gilgit could spare. Foremost amongst these were the men of his own regiment, the only British Indian one in Gilgit, the 32nd Punjab Pioneers. The pioneer regiments were a peculiarly Indian phenomenon. Recruited from the lowest castes and Untouchables, their speciality was digging. They could perform other tasks, carpentry and the like, but essentially they were the army's road-builders. A pickaxe was as vital a piece of each man's kit as a rifle. When the alarm sounded in Chitral they had been hacking a track round the base of Nanga Parbat. They were not strangers to action and they enjoyed a reputation for stubborn bravery; but they were probably not the one regiment the authorities would have selected for the stirring challenge ahead.

Kelly duly made his arrangements. Four hundred of the Pioneers and four of their officers would be the core of his expedition. Then there were a hundred Hunza–Nagar irregulars, invaluable for reconnaissance and precipice work, plus Lieutenant Beynon of Intelligence, the only man around who had actually been to Chitral, and Lieutenant Cosmo Stewart with a Kashmir mountain battery. This last choice was either a stroke of genius or a colossal blunder. If just one or two guns could somehow be lugged into Chitral it would have as salutary an effect as a thousand troops. Yet the Chitralis were confident that it was quite impossible and so too, presumably, was the Indian government; it would be hard enough to get men across the Shandur pass in April, never mind artillery. Kelly, however, thought it worth a try; and in Cosmo Stewart, another Irishman, 'the most bloodthirsty man I have ever met' according to Beynon, and one who loved his guns as if they were his children, he had found just the man to pull it off.

The force marched out of Gilgit on March 23. It crossed the snowline at Ghizr, twenty-five miles short of the Shandur and ran into difficulties soon after. Porters absconded and the mules carrying the guns ground to a standstill in snow that reached to their girths. Reluctantly Kelly turned back to Ghizr. Next day the blizzard, which had been blowing for five days prior to their arrival, returned. An advance guard which had been pushed to one march short of the pass was marooned. Neither they nor anyone else had tents and, since they depended on the country for both supplies and carriage, the plight of the expedition looked desperate.

Cosmo Stewart thought otherwise and spent the day experimenting. As a preliminary, the Kashmir troops who were based at Ghizr were told to commandeer what spades they could and dig a track for the guns over the pass. This was clearly a long term solution; even a snow plough would have taken weeks to do the job. Meanwhile he considered yaks. There were not enough to carry the guns but he thought that by driving them in front a usable track might result. Unfortunately he knew nothing about the dainty footwork of the yak. Each beast trod exactly in the footsteps of the leader; the result was a neat but useless line of holes. As a final throw, someone suggested sledges. This, surely, was the answer. Using tree trunks for runners and with eighteen men pulling, the prototype carried nearly a ton. A few trial runs round the camp were successful and the regimental carpenters were soon busy knocking up a whole fleet.

Next day, April 3, the snow stopped. At dawn the guns were sent forward to join the advance guard. On mules they were lugged up to the earlier point of return and then transferred to the sledges. Disaster. The track beaten by the advance guard was too narrow for the runners while the frozen crust of the virgin snow was not strong enough for the weight. There was nothing for it; they must be abandoned. But by now the whole force had become infected with Stewart's determination. The guns were everything, a talisman, a symbol of the expedition's corporate esprit, and a challenge as great as the relief of Chitral itself. Simultaneously an officer of the Pioneers and an N.C.O of the Kashmir gunners stepped forward to volunteer to carry the precious pieces. The rest soon followed suit. Each box of ammunition weighed over a hundredweight, the barrels and carriages more like a quarter of a ton. Strung from poles, and with four men to each pole, fifty yards could be gained before the men collapsed and another team took over. It was not just the weight. In places the snow was shoulder deep; when a man lost his balance and slipped from the narrow track he disappeared. There were also the problems of altitude exhaustion—they were now approaching 12,000 feet—intense snow glare and a wind so cold that no thermometer went low enough to record it. That night they struggled on till long after dark making scarcely five hundred yards an hour. Then they slept in the snow, every six men huddled together beneath their pooled blankets and sheepskins. At dawn they started again. So it went on for three days, till on the night of April 5 they were cheered into camp on the far side of the pass.

Nothing, [recorded Beynon] can be said too highly in praise of this splendid achievement. Here were some 250 men, Hindus and Mussulmans, who, working shoulder to shoulder, had brought two mountain guns, with their carriages and supply of ammunition, across some twenty miles of deep soft snow, across a pass 12,320 feet high, at the beginning of April, the worst time of the year. These men were also carrying their own rifles, greatcoats and 80 rounds of ammunition and wearing heavy sheepskin coats; they had slept for two nights in the snow and struggled from dawn to dark, sinking at every step to their waists. . . . Their officers took turns with the men in carrying the guns and gave their snow glasses to sepoys who were suffering from the glare.

In the wake of such an achievement the rest of the expedition crossed with confidence. Amongst the troops there were a few bad cases of frostbite; the officers found their faces shredded by the wind till the blood ran and some suffered slightly from altitude sickness; the only one totally immune seemed to be the bearded Kelly who, belying his years, 'trudged along without a halt all day'. But, really, it was the gunners and their companions who assured the march of immortality. As they started off down the valley towards Mastuj, Stewart and his men had to be led by the hand; their heads swathed in bandages, they were still blinded from the snow glare. Yet they had achieved the impossible and Kelly, with the immense advantages of surprise and of possessing the only artillery in Chitral, was in with a real chance of becoming the saviour of Chitral.

First, though, there was Mastuj. The siege there had never really been pressed. The fort, with three British officers and a small garrison, was well placed for defence and the enemy had been happy to isolate it. The Pathans, who constituted the most formidable opposition, seem never to have penetrated much north of Chitral town and the whole of the upper part of the valley was held by Chitralis under the command of Sher Afzul's foster brother. Had they anticipated an attack from Gilgit the logical place to have stopped it would have been between the pass and Mastuj. Short of supplies, short of carriage and with only the snows to turn back to, Kelly could have been in real trouble. And indeed there was opposition. At one point the way ahead was blocked by a well planned net of breastworks. But they were manned by only an estimated four hundred. Stewart got the longed for chance of showing off his seven-pounders and the Chitralis duly panicked after the first few shells. There were no fatalities amongst the Pioneers and by April 9 they were in Mastuj.

Seventy miles to go and by now the prospect of beating a path to glory ahead of Low's so-called 'Chitral Relief Expedition' was in the back of every mind. Beynon's 'first man in Chitral gets a C. B.' was funny because it was exactly what they were all thinking. They didn't know it but Low had almost exactly the same distance to go. After a stiff fight up the Malakand pass he had crossed the Swat river and Aylmer, of Nilt fame, was throwing a bridge across the Panjkora. Militarily they were repeatedly getting the better of the tribesmen, but between them and Chitral there still loomed the Lowarai pass; and as Kelly could vouch, the physical difficulties were likely to be every bit as formidable as the human.

Besides playing David to Low's Goliath, the Gilgit column sought the added satisfaction of demonstrating that the Agency could look after its own. Given a choice, Robertson would surely prefer to be relieved by his own men; it would go some way towards vindicating his handling of the Chitralis and, in the last analysis, would show that the idea of controlling Chitral from Gilgit was not impracticable. However, the game wasn't over. The enemy were reported gathering in strength at a notorious black spot a couple of miles below Mastuj. On April 10 and 11 Kelly cast about for supplies and porters, on the the 12th he sent out a reconnaissance and on the 13th he moved out to the attack.

The place to be attacked was known as the Nisa Gol. By the Chitralis it was believed impregnable and with a force of fifteen hundred, over double that of Kelly's, plus the immense advantage of prepared positions, they had good reason for confidence. In configuration it was a bit like the Nilt ravine. A sloping ledge, shut in by the mountain wall on one side and the river on the other, was sliced in two by a cleft three hundred feet deep. The sides of this ravine were perpendicular and the enemy's position consisted of a line of bunkers and breastworks along the far side. High up in the mountains more men were stationed with the object of panicking the exposed attackers with landslides, while across the river, from a staircase of breastworks that reached well above the snowline, sharpshooters commanded the whole ledge across which the advance would have to be made.

The Chitrali breastworks were concentrated at the one spot where it was feasible to get down into the ravine and up the other side. Kelly's only chance was to find another crossing place, and with this in mind he had made some elaborate preparations. But first the Hunza irregulars were told off to scale the mountains and work round towards the landslide men. Meanwhile Stewart's guns got to work silencing the *sangar* that controlled the longest reach of unscaleable ravine. Under cover of this heavy fire Beynon crept up to the lip of the chasm, selected a spot and gave the signal. On trotted the secret weapon, a troupe of men brandishing ladders and ropes. It must have been a bit like the Royal Tournament. Over the edge in a flurry of belays went the storming party, the guns were limbered up to fire on the main concentration of breastworks, and as the first heads started to appear out of the cleft on the far side, down from the heights with bloodcurdling screams came the Hunza levies; the position was turned. The Chitralis started to bolt and the main force advanced in good order by way of the proper track. Bar the fact that the guns were not then slung across the ravine on pulleys, it was a show worthy of a command performance. Six of Kelly's men had been killed for nearly sixty of the enemy and the prestige of British arms had been restored in Chitral. It was too cheap, too quick a victory to rate as a classic; but it was a very creditable example of how careful reconnaissance, intelligent thinking and complete co-ordination could take care of the most impossible terrain.

Much the same could be said of the whole of Kelly's March. One looks in vain for brilliant strategy or personal heroics. His moves were always deliberate, his innovations simple and his successes corporate. In the heat of battle he himself, unlike Durand or Robertson, stayed well under cover and out of the limelight. Instead of inflaming the enthusiasms of his young officers he threw cold water on them. In Mastuj he wouldn't be panicked into a dash for Chitral but spent three days reorganising. And in the earlier action he had had occasion to remonstrate with Stewart for coming into action at too close a range and thus causing unnecessary bloodshed; after neither engagement was any attempt made at pursuit or a punitive demonstration. Nor were there any acts of conspicuous bravery or any obvious candidates for a V.C. This was not the Gilgit way and it won Kelly neither the adulation of his subordinates nor the unqualified approval of his superiors; he was duly recommended for both a knighthood and a generalship but got neither. On the other hand it resulted in the most successful and most humane campaign ever fought in Dardistan.

It was also the last. The Nisa Gol battle would in fact be the last set engagement between the Gilgit forces and the Dards. Steadily, keeping his men together, refusing to countenance a flying column and moving all at the speed of the cumbersome guns, Kelly closed on Chitral. By the night of the 17th he was within three marches of the town. Low was still on the wrong side of the Lowarai and, though there was still the prospect of the Chitralis making a final stand, the prize was surely his. And so it proved, though not quite in the classic style most would have wished.

There was as yet no news from Robertson and, beyond the fact that the *Noghor* was still holding out, Kelly had no idea what to expect. His officers looked forward to a grand fight beneath the walls but, as they did so, the whole business was being decided in that summer house by the shaft of the mine. The besiegers seemed to have staked everything on this last ploy and when, on the 16th, it was foiled, the game was up. Umra Khan's Pathans had already drifted south to oppose Low's remorseless advance and, alone, Sher Afzul now recognised that he had no chance of taking the *Noghor*.

Leitner quotes an apt Chitrali aphorism of the day; 'a sparrow who tried to kick a mountain himself toppled over'. Deserted by his allies and demoralised by Kelly's eruption and the disaster of Nisa Gol, Sher Afzul threw in the sponge. On the 18th the garrison awoke to find the besiegers gone and on the same day, instead of another line of *sangars*, Kelly was greeted by a messenger from the fort with the news that the siege was over.

On the 20th, dressed in their best, with the buglers to the fore and the guns still in their midst, Kelly's men crossed the Chitral river and approached the battle-scarred fort. From one of the towers a home-made Union Jack fluttered in the spring breeze; the whole place was strangely quiet. Outside the main gate five wan officers were assembled in line. Kelly, from the back of his diminutive Chitrali pony, gave a wave of his walking stick, the officers replied with a salute, hands were shaken. Robertson had his arm in a sling and his expression was as stern as ever; later, though, he admitted that he had been near to tears. A skirl of

GG—S

the pipes from Low's Highlanders would have made for a more
romantic conclusion and there were many, particularly Stewart,
who were bitterly disappointed that the Chitralis hadn't made a
final stand. But if there was a sense of anti-climax it was not so
much because of the let down as from utter exhaustion.

A week after Kelly's arrival a harbinger of Low's brigade
galloped up in the shape of Frank Younghusband. As special
correspondent of *The Times* he had accompanied Low's troops
from Nowshera and had now dashed ahead to be the first man from
the south into Chitral. After awarding full credit to Townshend,
though not to Robertson for whom he had never had much time,
he selected Kelly and his men as the heroes of the hour. 'This
famous march', he cabled, 'will ever be remembered as a unique
exploit of the Indian Army.' The Commander-in-Chief agreed,
citing in particular the crossing of the Shandur, and from the
Queen herself came 'gracious approbation of this remarkable
exploit'. Robertson too was deeply impressed; but what struck
him most was the unusual reserve and mutual solicitude shown by
this bunch of heroes. 'They were the most singularly generous
and modest men I have ever met'; it just wasn't in the Gilgit
tradition.

Hard on Younghusband's heels came the Buffs, the first of
Low's battalions. It wasn't easy for true British troops to doff their
hats to the low-bred Pioneers; but as soon as the serious business
of ceremonial manœuvres got under way, first Kelly's men, then
Robertson's, were given a sort of benefit parade and each man
was awarded an extra six months' pay.

As the celebrations wore on, the garrison must have begun to
wonder whether they were still under siege; Townshend, in
particular, was hankering to get back to civilisation and the promotion of his now promising career. Robertson just felt weary. The
siege had been more of a strain than he had realised; and now that
it was all over he was still the senior political officer and there were
still a lot of questions to be answered. But deliverance was on its
way; last on the scene came 'my long time friend and former
chief, Colonel Algernon Durand'. Durand had watched the whole
siege with mounting horror, he had postponed a visit to England
and pestered Lord Elgin to let him return to the aid of the man
'who once pulled me out of my mess'. With the crisis over, the

Viceroy relented and Durand was allowed to make one last visit to Dardistan. There was talk of writing a report on the siege and of delivering some Viceregal paean, but really he had come to conduct Robertson back to Simla. In an ending worthy of the wide screen, they galloped off over the Lowarai pass together; significantly they forwent the Shandur and a sentimental visit to Gilgit.

* * *

'I should be less than human if I did not break a last lance for the tribes that befriended me,' began Dr. Leitner in July 1895. The siege of Chitral had occasioned the sort of public discussion, including a parliamentary debate, for which he had always canvassed. The point at issue was whether Chitral should be retained and garrisoned as part of India's frontier; this involved discussion of the whole Gilgit policy in relation to the Dards. Ranged against the extension of British territory into such a hostile wilderness there were now many big guns; and with the Afghan and Russian frontiers in the area finally defined, they had a convincing case. But none was so strident and indiscriminate in his rhetoric as the now ageing doctor.

For thirty years he had been pleading for the independence of the Dards and the preservation of their way of life. He had watched the peace-loving Nagaris and Chilasis being gunned down with Gatlings, he had noted the desecration of Hunza—'that cradle of human thought as expressed in language', and now it was the turn of the affectionate and submissive Chitralis. 'I have no hesitation in stating that one and all of the complications with these places have solely arisen from the personal ambition of our officers under the influence of the K.C.S.I. or K.G.B. mania.' Excluding Biddulph, not one man, not even Robertson ('that ambitious medico'), who had lived amongst the Kafirs, had bothered to learn one of the local languages. Yet 'long before journalistic knights met three empires in all safety [Knight, the *Times* man, wrote of the Hunza campaign in *Where Three Empires Meet*], or travelling MPs rediscovered the friendship of an old ally [Curzon and Nizam-ul-Mulk]', Leitner had elicited the linguistic secrets of the Dard peoples and made them readily available to all. Having uncovered this unique ethnological treasure-chest he had consistently raged against its exploitation. Yet, in Hunza and Nagar the Dard tongues were already being corrupted, the prophetesses were silent, etc.; in Kafiristan the Afghans, using breech-loaders supplied by the British government and as a result of an agreement with the same government, were forcibly converting and dispersing the wild and wonderful Kafirs. Chitral was all that was left of Dardistan as he knew it and Chitral must, and could, be saved.

For once it looked as if he might just get his way. Convinced that there was no longer a strategic imperative for a British interest in Chitral, the Liberal government opted for a complete withdrawal. In June 1895 they declared that the Nowshera–Chitral road would not be kept open and that, as planned in 1893, there would be no permanent political agent in the valley. The debate, however, raged on and, a matter of days after reaching this decision, the Liberal government fell. By the end of the month Lord Salisbury's Tories were back in power and by August they had reversed the decision. Chitral was to have not only its own agent but a bigger garrison than Gilgit; the Nowshera road was to be kept open and another garrison was to be posted on the Malakand pass to police it. In effect Chitral was to be more closely integrated into British India than Gilgit itself.

By 1896 Leitner was forced to concede defeat. In a letter to *The Times* prompted by the publication of George, now Sir George, Robertson's second book on the Kafirs, he started with the usual recitation of his past dealings with the Dards. But then, instead of some explosive indictment, there came a quiet, diffident and rather sad surrender.

All in vain. No one perhaps has struggled more on behalf of the Dards and Kafirs than myself during thirty years, but the cause is lost and now their only chance of survival is a complete and loyal acquiescence in the new order of things.

The new order of things eventually led to the detachment of Chitral from its Dard neighbours in the Gilgit Agency and its incorporation in the North-West Frontier Province of British India, and now Pakistan. Greatly outnumbered in this predominantly Pathan province the Chitralis have nevertheless retained something of their identity. Political unrest is still a feature of the valley and the Afghans, as part of their policy to support self-determination for all the peoples of Pakistan's frontier province, continue to take an interest in the place; the tribal frontier agreed in 1893 and now known as the Durand Line is totally repudiated. Yet, if Leitner would not be entirely disappointed by Chitral today, it is more thanks to geographical facts than political ones. The Lowarai pass is still closed by snow and avalanches for months on end; whole busloads of travellers get robbed and ransomed in Swat and Dir, and no vehicle larger than a jeep can negotiate the rocky bluffs of the valley itself. Gun-runners and miscreants still dodge undetected across the Dora pass and the tourists who are flown into Chitral's miniscule airport have less of an impact on the country as a whole than the far-ranging sportsman-administrators of the British Raj.

The same might be said for the rest of the old Gilgit Agency. Until 1947 it continued as an anomalous and much sought after posting in British India. Retired Indian officers often maintained that the Great Game was still being played in the 1930s, but in Gilgit, with the Pamirs frontier finally settled and with Chitral no longer its responsibility, anxieties over the proximity of Russia were purely theoretical if not imaginary. Compared to the excitements of the 1890s all was peace and quiet in this remote look-out post of the declining Empire. Individual officers were free to concentrate their energies on an all out assault on the markhor and ibex or a further study of the tribes.

With Independence and the partition of the subcontinent in 1947, the Maharaja of Kashmir, after much vacillation, elected to incorporate his state in the Indian Union; he was after all a Dogra Hindu. His Mohammedan subjects resented this; the peaceable people of the Kashmir valley pinned their hopes of altering his decision on a plebiscite to be held under United Nations auspices; the Dards simply took up arms. The successors of those Hunza and Gilgit levies who had fought with Robertson and Kelly in 1895 were known as the Gilgit Scouts, a crack mountain unit which had been armed, trained and uniformed under British officers. With the help of Pathan co-religionists they bundled the Maharaja's representatives out of Gilgit and pushed the Dogras back to Astor and up the Indus to beyond Baltistan. Leitner would surely have applauded this evidence of the unbroken spirit of the Dards; and by a curious coincidence the Kashmir ceasefire line of today is not very different from what he and Hayward believed the Kashmir frontier always should have been.

Bibliography

I CHAPTER NOTES

Chapters 1 and 2

Dr. G. W. Leitner's principal works are *The Results of a Tour in Dardistan*, Lahore 1877, *The Languages and Races of Dardistan*, Lahore 1877, *The Hunza-Nagyr Handbook*, Lahore 1889 (second edition, Woking 1893) and *Dardistan in 1866, 1886 and 1893*, Woking 1893. These include most of his pamphlets up till 1893; after that his views can be traced in *The Asiatic Quarterly Review* published sporadically from Woking. A review of the *Life and Labours of Dr. G. W. Leitner* by J. H. Stocqueler, Brighton 1872, provides some biographical detail but with the subject still in his early thirties and the author one of his staunchest admirers, it is neither exhaustive nor balanced. His reputation in Lahore can be surmised from *Thirty-five Years in the Punjab* by G. R. Elsmie, Edinburgh 1908, and his standing as a traveller and savant from the *Journal of the Royal Geographical Society* (*J.R.G.S.*) (vol. XLIII, 1873, contains some of the many scattered references to him). His brush with the Government of India can be followed in the India Office Records (Political and Secret Home Correspondence, vol. 128, and Political and Secret Letters from India, vol. 65). His work with the Oriental University Institute is described in *Victorian Woking* by J. R. and S. E. Whitemen, Guildford, 1970. His obituary is in *The Times* for March 25, 1899.

The view from the cliffs above Gor was first seen by Col. H. C. B. Tanner and Major J. Biddulph and is described in *Proceedings of the Royal Geographical Society* (*P.R.G.S.*), vol XIII, New Series, 1891.

Chapters 3 and 4

George Hayward wrote no books and there are no books about him. The only published work seems to be the article by Dr. G. J. Alder in the *Journal of the Royal Central Asian Society* for January 1965. To Dr. Alder and, for biographical information, to Brigadier R. A. Gardiner of the R.G.S. I am deeply indebted. Hayward's career as an explorer is best followed through the Journals and Proceedings of the R.G.S. (*J.R.G.S.*, vols XL and XLI, and *P.R.G.S.*, vols. XIII, XIV and XV) and in unpublished material in the R.G.S. archives. The Society's publications also include a full account of the murder but reference should also be made to extensive reports on the affair in the India Office Records (India Foreign and Political Proceedings, 766; Secret Home Correspondence, 71, Political and Secret Letters from India, 14, and the Argyll Papers on microfilm, reel 312). Further accounts of the murder occur in F. Drew's *The Jummoo and Kashmir Territories*, London 1875; J. Duke's *Kashmir and Jammu, A Guide for Visitors*, second edition, 1910; A. Wilson's *Abode of Snow*, Edinburgh 1875; W. S. A. Lockhart and R. G. Woodthorpe's *The Gilgit Mission*, London 1889; and the *Edinburgh Review*, January 1892.

Chapters 5 and 6
The Tribes of the Hindoo Koosh by John Biddulph, Calcutta, 1890, gives no indication of the author's work in Gilgit. Fot this one must go to unpublished sources. I am indebted to Dr. Alder, again, for putting me on the track of Biddulph's journals, and to the Hereford County Record Office and the Hon. Edward Biddulph for letting me see them. They do not, however, afford a short cut as against a scrutiny of the official records in the India Office. (Political and Secret Letters from India, vols. 14, 18, 21, 23, 25 and 26; Political and Secret Memo, A18 1878 and 1881; the Lytton Papers and the Northbrook Papers, 1878-80). *The Journal of the Asiatic Society of Bengal* has an interesting description of a trip to the Gilgit valley by Captain H. C. Marsh in vol. LXV, 1876. For the Forsyth missions to Sinkiang see the bibliography in my *When Men and Mountains Meet*, London 1977.

Chapter 7
The starting point for a study of Kafiristan should be Dr. Schuyler Jones' two-part *Bibliography of Nuristan (Kafiristan) and the Kalash Kafirs of Chitral*, Copenhagen, 1969. It is far more than a mere record of sources and I am deeply indebted to Dr. Jones, in spite of failing to consult his work until this book was almost finished.

MacNair's paper on his *Visit to Kafiristan* is in *P.R.G.S.*, vol. VI, New Series, 1884, and is reproduced in the interesting pamphlet, *Memoir of William Watts MacNair*, by J. E. Howard, published in India but undated. Political and Secret Letters from India, vol. 39, gives the official attitude towards the journey and MacNair's detailed report is entitled *Confidential Report on the Explorations in part of Eastern Afghanistan and in Kafiristan during 1883*, Dehra Dun 1885.

MacGregor is far better documented and I have used only published sources. His personality and the whole system of advancement come over strongly in *The Life and Opinions of Sir C. M. MacGregor*, edited by Lady MacGregor, London 1888. He is noticed in a number of contemporary memoirs and biographies, including A. V. Lyall's *Life of the Marquis of Dufferin and Ava*, London 1905, and P. M. Sykes' *The Right Hon. Sir Mortimer Durand*, London 1905. The fatal report, *The Defence of India*, was published in Simla, 1884. For a recent appraisal of MacGregor's work I have also consulted the article by Adrian Preston in the *Historical Journal*, vol. XII, 1969.

Chapters 8 and 9

The published account of the Lockhart Mission is a book to cherish. Entitled *The Gilgit Mission 1885-6* by W. S. A. Lockhart and R. G. Woodthorpe, 1889 it is extremely hard to come by, immensely long, thoroughly entertaining and illustrated with delightful photographs. I am indebted to the India Office Library for processing a photocopying order that far exceeded their regulations. Lockhart himself is referred to in many standard biographies of the period and has an entry in the *Dictionary of National Biography* and the *Dictionary of Indian Biography*, ed. C. E. Buckland 1906. His obituary is in the *Geographical Journal* (*G.J.*), vol. XV, 1900. Where MacNair and Lockhart left off in Kafiristan Sir George S. Robertson took over. For more information on some of the customs referred to by Lockhart I have used his *The Kafirs of the Hindu Kush*, 1896, also R. C. F. Schomberg's *Kafirs and Glaciers*, 1938.

The Elias biography referred to at the beginning of Chapter 9 is *Ney Elias, Explorer and Envoy Extraordinary in High Asia* by Gerald Morgan, London 1971. This is based on the voluminous Elias papers in the R. G. S. Archives. I have referred to these only for the journal of the Pamir journey 1885-6 and letter drafts, etc., of that period. Colonel Morgan has kindly made available the fruits of subsequent research including references to Elias in the Dufferin Papers. He has also provided a copy of Elias' *Official Report of a Mission to Chinese Turkestan and Badakshan in 1885-6* and the note by Sir S. Bayley *On the Pamir Question and the North East Frontier of Afghanistan*, London 1891.

Chapters 10, 11 and 12

There is a wealth of sources on the last years of the Gilgit Game. Recorded here are only those I have found particularly useful.

Sir Francis Younghusband badly needs a new biography; the existing one by George Seaver, 1952, scarcely does him justice. Nor do Younghusband's own works on the period, *The Heart of a Continent*, 1896, *The Light of Experience*, 1927, and *Wonders of the Himalaya*, 1924; the last was written for the young reader but the same popular and rather patronising style characterises all of them. The best appreciation of the man is probably that by Peter Fleming in *Bayonets to Lhasa*, 1961. One volume of his journal for the 1889 journey is in the R.G.S. archives but the others are missing. Instead there are his letters in Demi-Official Correspondence, vol. 3, in the India Office Records, his *Reports of a Mission to the Northern Frontier of Kashmir in 1889*, Calcutta 1890, and a report in *P.R.G.S.*,vol. XII, N.S. 1890. For the Pamirs journeys of 1890–91 there is an interesting letter to his father, dated August 20, 1891, amongst the papers in the possession of Dame Eileen Younghusband to whom I am most grateful. Reference has also been made to *P.R.G.S.*, vol. XIV, N.S., 1892 *G.J.*, vol. II, 1893, and the note by Sir S. Bayley referred to above; also to *Macartney in Kashgar* by C. P. Skrine and P. Nightingale, 1973. Useful sidelights on his travels of this period are shed by R. P. Cobbold in *Innermost Asia*, 1900, C. S. Cumberland in *Sport on the Pamirs and Turkestan Steppes*, London 1895, the Earl of Dunmore in *The Pamirs*, London 1893, and R. C. F. Schomberg in *Unknown Karakoram*, London 1936. The photograph of the Younghusband–Grombtchevski meeting was traced to the *Eastern and Western Review* of 1895. Leitner's *Asiatic Quarterly Review* is a good source for Grombtchevski's travels, especially vols. 2 and 3, N. S. His journey of 1889–90 was translated from the Russian by E. F. H. MacSwiney, Simla 1892. There are scattered references to his movements in *P.R.G.S.*, vol. IX, 1887, vol. XII, 1890, and vol. XIII, 1891, N. S., and in *G.J.*, vol. III, 1894. *High Road to Hunza* by B. Mons, 1958, sheds some light on his negotiations with Safdar Ali.

The thinking behind the re-establishment of the Gilgit Agency can be followed in Political and Secret Letters from India, vols. 57, 58 and 59. The account of the Hunza–Nagar campaign has been put together from five contemporary sources: *Where Three Empires Meet by* E. F. Knight, London 1894, *The Making of a Frontier* by A. Durand, London 1899 (and the comprehensive introduction to same by Dr. G. J. Alder in the recent Graz reprint), *Townshend of Kut and Chitral*, by E. Sherson, London 1928. Parliamentary Papers, Command No. 6621, *Correspondence relating to Operations in Hunza–Nagar* and last, but by no means least, the very personal letters of A. Durand amongst the papers of Sir H. M. Durand in the archives of the School of Oriental and African Studies, London. Dr. Alder directed my attention to them and again I am in his debt.

Chapters 13 and 14
In addition to the sources listed above for A. Durand, C. G. Bruce's *Twenty Years in the Himalayas*, London 1910, has been creamed for details of the poorly documented Chilas campaign. Chitral, bibliographically, is a very different matter. The fullest and most readable account of the siege is Robertson's own, *Chitral, the Story of a Minor Siege*, by Sir G. S. Robertson, 1898. Sherson's *Townshend of Kut and Chitral* as above, includes long extracts from the papers and letters of Townshend, while *With Kelly to Chitral* by W. G. L. Beynon, London 1896, was compiled from the letters of the author written to his mother at the time. There is also an account by Cosmo Stewart of the artillery's part in Kelly's March; it first appeared in *Blackwood's Magazine*, Nov. 1926, and has recently been included in *Tales of the Mountain Gunners* by C. H. T. MacFetridge and J. P. Warren. Edinburgh 1974. Both of the two Younghusbands who collaborated for *The Relief of Chitral*, London 1895, accompanied Low's division but it was Frank, who knew the Shandur route as well as anyone, who wrote the chapters on Kelly's March. Another contemporary account is H. C. Thomson's *The Chitral Campaign*, London 1895. More recently the story has been retold briefly by P. G. Fredericks in *The Sepoy and the Cossack*, London 1971, and with great spirit in *Much Sounding of Bugles* by John Harris, London 1975. Brigadier F. R. L. Goadby has kindly lent me a *Regimental History of 32nd Sikh Pioneers*, Calcutta, n.d.

For facts and figures I have relied on the *Official Account of the Chitral Expedition* by W. R. Robertson (no relation), Calcutta, 1898, and for official correspondence on that reproduced in Parliamentary Papers, Command no. 7864, relating to *Chitral, 1895*, and Command no. 8037, relating to the occupation of Chitral, 1896.

The last also includes correspondence relating to Afghan proceedings in Kafiristan. *The Pamirs and the Source of the Oxus*, 1896, was Curzon's great work but for the story of his travels in Dardistan it is necessary to turn the *Leaves from a Viceroy's Notebook and Other Papers*, 1926. An article by G. H. Bretherton in the *Contemporary Review*, vol. 74, 1898, gives an interesting picture of Gilgit towards the end of the century. Sources for Younghusband and Leitner are as given above, with the addition of Leitner's letter to *The Times* of Dec. 26, 1896.

II GENERAL BIBLIOGRAPHY

The bible for anyone interested in the Western Himalayas in the second half of the nineteenth century must be G. J. Alder's *British India's Northern Frontier 1865–95*, London 1963. Without it, this book could scarcely have been written. Dr. Alder's forty page bibliography renders any further attempt at a comprehensive list of sources redundant. The works listed below are merely those of general or peripheral interest which have not been mentioned in the Chapter Notes but which have provided facts or ideas.

BARKER, A. J. *Townshend of Kut*, London 1967.

BELLEW, H. W. *Kashmir and Kashgar*, London 1875.

BLACK, C. E. D. *Memoir of the Indian Surveys 1875–90*, London 1891.

BONVALOT, G. *Through the Heart of Asia*, London 1889.

CONWAY, W. M. *Climbing in the Karakoram Himalayas*, London 1894.

CURZON, G. N. *Russia in Central Asia*, London 1889.

DANIELLI, G. *La Esplorazione della Regione fra L' Himalaja Occidentale e il Caracorum*, Bologna 1934.

EDWARDES, M. *Playing the Great Game*, London 1975.

FAIRLEY, J. *The Lion River, The Indus*, London 1975.

GILLARD, D. *The Struggle for Asia 1828–1914*, London 1977.

GORDON, T. E. *The Roof of the World*, Edinburgh 1876.

HEDIN, S. *Southern Tibet*, Stockholm 1922.

HOLDICH, T. H. *The Indian Borderland 1880–1900*, London 1901.

—— *Gates of India*, London 1910.

KIPLING, R. *Kim*, London 1901.

—— *Departmental Ditties*, 18th edition, London 1904.

LANSDELL, H. *Chinese Central Asia*, London 1893.

MARAINI, F. *Where Four Worlds Meet*, London 1964.

MARVIN, C. *Russia's Advance towards India*, London 1882.

MASON, K. *Abode of Snow*, London 1955.

MASON, P. *A Matter of Honour*, London 1974.

SEVERIN, T. *The Oriental Adventure; Explorers of the East*, London 1976.

SHAW, R. *Visits to High Tartary, Yarkand and Kashgar*, London 1871.

STONE, S. J. *In and Beyond the Himalayas*, London 1896.

WOOD, J. *Journey to the Source of the Oxus*, Second Edition, London 1872.

Index

Abdurrahman, Amir of Kabul, 247
Afghanistan, British India and, 2, 42,
  44, 45, 99–100, 125, 127, 208;
  Second Afghan War (1879), 105,
  107–8; Afghan Boundary Com-
  mission, (1884–6), 125, 127, 151,
  156, 157, 159, 161, 162, 164, 167–9;
  Chitral and, 99, 106, 232, 237, 247,
  263; Kafiristan and, 99, 146, 205,
  237, 240, 247–8, 262; Kashmir and,
  104; Elias in, 156–7, 165–6, 167–8;
  Lockhart in, 161, 164–6, 167
Afzul-ul-Mulk of Chitral, 135–7, 138,
  231
Aga Khan, The, 153
Aksai Chin, 71
Aksu River (Bartang, Murghab), 87,
  158, 159, 213
Alai Mountains, 89, 105, 153, 173
Aman-ul-Mulk of Chitral, Hayward
  and, 60, 61, 67, 69, 70, 72, 73;
  Biddulph and, 100, 104, 106, 109–
  12; MacNair and, 117–18, 120, 153;
  Lockhart and, 128–9, 133–7, 142,
  166–7; Elias and, 168, 169; and
  British India, 99, 106, 128–9, 134,
  137, 169, 231; and Kashmir, 69, 72,
  100, 106, 135; and Yasin, 69, 99,
  107, 111–12, 135
Amir-ul-Mulk of Chitral, 135, 231–2,
  244–7
Amritsar, Treaty of, 5, 27, 28, 61
Asiatic Quarterly Review, 37, 113
Asmar, 237, 247
Astor, 13, 14, 29, 33, 35, 199, 217, 218,
  263
Aylmer, Captain, 218, 219–20, 241,
  257

Babusar Pass, 229
Badakshan, 67, 69, 72, 86, 99, 138;
  Lockhart in, 142, 165–6; Elias in,
  144, 146, 155–6, 168; see also
  Afghanistan
Baltistan, 11, 13, 25, 26, 27, 44, 68,
  183, 263
Baltit, 93–4
Baroghil Pass, 88, 89, 95, 131, 173,
  211, 242
Barrow, Captain, 130, 131, 133, 141
Bartang River, see Aksu

Bashgal River, 240, 247, 248
Bengal Asiatic Society, 24
Berlin, Congress of, 105
Beynon, Lieut. W., 254, 255, 257, 258
Biddulph, Col. J., 81–112 *passim*,
  130–1, 261
Boisragon, Lieut., 220
Bonvalot, G., 173
Bozai Gombaz, 210–11, 212
Bradshaw, Captain, 220, 221, 224
Bruce, Lieut. the Hon. C. G., 207,
  233–4
Budlas, 92
Bukhara, 29, 45, 87
Bunji, 14, 16, 17, 25, 29, 31, 33, 86,
  109, 130, 218, 233, 240
Burnes, Sir Alexander, 46
Burzil Pass, 111

Campbell, Captain, 244, 249
Campbell, Sir George, 24
Chalt, 91, 93, 162–3, 174, 201, 205–6,
  215, 218
Changchenmo, 71, 122
Chaprot, 91, 93, 108–9, 162–3, 174
Chilas, 4, 13, 88, 102, 109; Leitner
  and, 16, 25, 28, 35; Campaign
  (1892), 218, 228–9, 232–9, 240
China, 1, 2, 178, 182; Hunza and, 163,
  174, 216, 226; Pamirs and, 209–10,
  212–13; see also Sinkiang
Chitral, 3, 4, 32, 34, 102, 132;
  British India and, 126, 128–9, 135,
  137, 169, 198, 228, 231–2, 236–8,
  242, 261–2; Siege of, 244–52, 259;
  Relief of, 252–62; Afghanistan and,
  4, 86, 99, 106, 108, 232, 237;
  Kashmir and, 28, 72, 106, 107, 108,
  111, 112, 135; Hayward and, 46,
  47, 60, 61, 67, 68, 70, 72; Biddulph
  in, 82, 106–12; MacNair in, 115–21,
  128; Lockhart in, 128–9, 132–7,
  142, 168; Elias in, 168–9; Robertson
  in, 236–8, 240, 242–62; Younghusband in, 242–3
Conrad, Dr., 191
Cowie, H., 23, 24
Curzon, The Hon. G. N., 18, 37, 153,
  189, 240–4, 261

Dalgleish, A., 152

273